CONSTANTINE
AT THE BRIDGE

CONSTANTINE AT THE BRIDGE

HOW THE BATTLE OF THE MILVIAN BRIDGE CREATED CHRISTIAN ROME

STEPHEN DANDO-COLLINS

TURNER
PUBLISHING COMPANY

Turner Publishing Company
Nashville, Tennessee
www.turnerpublishing.com

Cover design: Rebecca Lown
Book design: Erin Seaward-Hiatt
Maps design: Grace Cavalier

Library of Congress Cataloging-in-Publication Data Upon Request

9781684426829   paperback
9781684426836   hardback
9781684426843   ebook

Printed in the United States of America
17 18 19 20 10 9 8 7 6 5 4 3 2 1

With thanks to my longtime New York literary agent and good friend Richard Curtis, my publisher Todd Bottorff, and editors Stephanie Beard and Ezra Fitz for their support and encouragement. And special thanks to my wife Louise, who has been crossing bridges with me, hand in hand, for forty years.

TABLE OF CONTENTS

ROMAN EMPIRE EARLY AD 312

BRITANNIA
GERMANIA
TRIER
GAUL
MILAN
ARLES
ROME
GREECE
SOFIA
BLACK SEA
BYZANTIUM
SPAIN
SARDINIA
THESSALONICA
NICOMEDIA
SICILY
CARTHAGE
CYPRUS
ANTIOCH
MAURETANIA
MEDITERRANEAN SEA
SYRIA
PERSIA
ALEXANDRIA
EGYPT
AFRICA
ARABIA

CONTROLLED BY
CONSTANTINE

CONTROLLED BY
MAXENTIUS

CONTROLLED BY
LICINIUS

CONTROLLED BY
MAXIMINUS DAIA

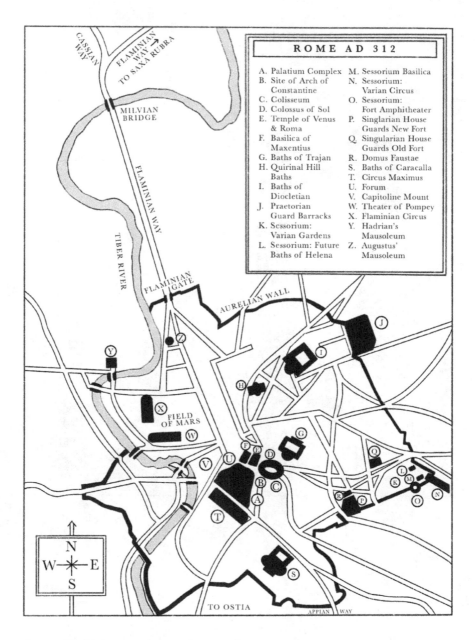

ROME AD 312

A. Palatium Complex
B. Site of Arch of Constantine
C. Colisseum
D. Colossus of Sol
E. Temple of Venus & Roma
F. Basilica of Maxentius
G. Baths of Trajan
H. Quirinal Hill Baths
I. Baths of Diocletian
J. Praetorian Guard Barracks
K. Sessorium: Varian Gardens
L. Sessorium: Future Baths of Helena
M. Sessorium Basilica
N. Sessorium: Varian Circus
O. Sessorium: Fort Amphitheater
P. Singlarian House Guards New Fort
Q. Singularian House Guards Old Fort
R. Domus Faustae
S. Baths of Caracalla
T. Circus Maximus
U. Forum
V. Capitoline Mount
W. Theater of Pompey
X. Flaminian Circus
Y. Hadrian's Mausoleum
Z. Augustus' Mausoleum

Roman World, AD 312, showing domains of Constantine, Maxentius, Licinius and Daia.

Bronze head of Constantine, discovered at Belgrade, believed to show him in later life. *Bridgeman Images.*

The young emperor Maxentius, Constantine's brother-in-law and opponent at the Battle of the Milvian Bridge, dressed in the regalia of the Pontifex Maximus. *Bridgeman Images.*

Surviving fragments from the Colossus of Constantine at Rome, including Constantine's ten-foot-high head. *Bridgeman Images.*

Arch of Constantine,
Rome, northern side.
Bridgeman Images.

Detail from Arch of Constantine, depicting Constantine being driven in a massive open
carriage from Verona, Italy, after conquering the city. *Bridgeman Images.*

AD 327 coin of
Constantine depicting,
on reverse, the Labarum
stabbed into a serpent,
issued to celebrate defeat of
Licinius.

I

THE EVE OF BATTLE

IN THE LAST WEEK OF OCTOBER IN THE YEAR A.D. 312, an army was marching on Rome from the north. On an autumn day, that army, of a little under 40,000 men, came down the Via Flaminia, the Flaminian Way, which linked Rome with the east coast Italian port city of Rimini and sliced through central Italy. Even though this was a Roman army, it was invading Italy, bent on conquering Rome.[1]

Of the 8,000 cavalrymen in this force, not one was Italian. Some were Alemanni Germans, rough and ready Swabian mercenaries from east of the Rhine whose only allegiances were to profit and their tribal confederacy. Others were Romanized Germans, Gauls, Belgae, and Britons. Filling the infantry ranks were detachments from legions and auxiliary units, including archers normally stationed in Britain and at bases on the Upper and Lower Rhine. By this time, legionaries were recruited in the provinces where they were stationed, with the sons of retired legionaries the first choice when it came to recruits. Apart from some centurions, who transferred from legion to legion as they were promoted, none of these troops were Italian.

Here, in Italy, these invaders were foreigners in a foreign land, and as they tramped confidently along in marching order with helmets slung around their necks, baggage poles over their right shoulders, and wooden shields on their left, they chatted and bantered in Latin accented by their native dialects.

"Look, Prima Porta!" centurions of the advance guard would have called, as the arch of an elegant aqueduct running across the plain straddled the stone-paved highway in their path. That aqueduct served the old Villa of Livia, an imperial country house that sat on a hill beside the highway at Saxa Rubra, farther down the Via Flaminia. Centuries earlier, travelers had nicknamed this arch across the road Prima Porta, or First Door. For, to them, this was like the first door to Rome, which lay ten miles to the south.

Riding in a massive open carriage in the middle of the strung-out column of cavalrymen, foot soldiers, and a baggage train of thousands of heavily laden mules and carts was the army's thirty-five-year-old commander, Flavius Valerius Constantinus, a deputy emperor of Rome. We know him as Constantine. He was a tall, powerfully built man. Roman historian Zosimus, writing eighty years later, said that Constantine's nickname was Bull Neck as a consequence of that build, and surviving busts show his thick neck and powerful shoulders. Zosimus also wrote that Constantine was only of average height, but all other sources, including several men who knew him, agreed that he was tall, and often stood out in a crowd. Hook-nosed, with penetrating eyes and close-cropped but fussily tended hair, Constantine was clean-shaven, as was becoming the fashion among Roman men after beards had been de rigueur for two centuries. His prominent jaw was square and determined. [2]

Even though he was Roman, Constantine himself would have barely recognized Prima Porta, if it all. For, although he was destined to become sole Roman emperor, Constantine is never on record visiting Rome prior to this. He had been born in today's city of Nis in Serbia—the Roman Naissus, then located in the province of Moesia Superior—and spent his youth on the Danube, in the Roman East, and in Gaul. The one time that many historians suspect Constantine may have been in Rome was nine years before this, accompanying the Eemperor Diocletian as an officer of his bodyguard. In November 303, Diocletian went to Rome to celebrate the anniversary of his reign following a summer military campaign on the Danube.[3]

Diocletian and his entourage may have come down from the north to Rome on the Flaminian Way, but it is also possible they used the central Cassian Way, or the Aurelian Way military road that ran along Italy's west coast. We know that, certainly, after Diocletian and his entourage departed Rome on December 20, 303, they would have traveled up the Flaminian Way from Rome all the way over the Apennines to Rimini, before continuing a little way along the Adriatic coast to the onetime major Roman naval base and capital city of Ravenna, where Diocletian subsequently spent several weeks.

So, if Constantine was with Diocletian in 303, he would have encountered Prima Porta, possibly from the north, but certainly from the south on their departure. After that brief passage nine years earlier, this northern approach via Porta Prima, with the snaking Tiber River away to his left, would not have been familiar to Constantine, and he was reliant on officers with local knowledge and cavalry scouts for his picture of the lay of the land. But, having first encountered the Tiber on October 26, now, on the 27th, he knew that Rome was close.[4]

Constantine had set the location for his army's overnight camp at a crossroads four miles north of Prima Porta, which in turn would put it within easy reach of Rome. This would give the force an easy march of two to three hours the following morning to take it to the walls of Rome, terminating an advance of several months that had brought Constantine and his army from Gaul via the Cottian Alps and northern Italy, and had involved several overwhelming victories against opposition Roman forces in a series of battles and sieges.

Sitting over the Via Flaminia at the Prima Porta crossroads in later times would be a house erected in the fourth century as a massive four-way quadrifrons arch, with those arches later filled in to create a residence. If a stamp in a brick of the vault of one of those four arches is to be a guide, the archway had been erected here a decade or two earlier by Diocletian. Either that, or material from an earlier construction by Diocletian was used to erect this monument after Constantine passed this way.

The name of the arch in Constantine's time is unknown, but in the fifteenth century, the landmark would gain the name the Arch of Malborghetto, taking the name of Malborghetto, the medieval village that arose in this vicinity. The Italian word Malborghetto can mean both Evil-Ville and Pain-Ville. Just one day would pass before this location would prove to have painful connotations for many thousands of Romans, as the jumping-off point for a bloody battle that would change history.

By the time that Constantine arrived at the crossroads campsite in the early afternoon, the *metatores*, the military surveyors, who marched with the army's vanguard, would have already staked out the camp, ready for the troops to erect tents for their officers and themselves once the outer fosse or ditch of the marching camp had been dug and earthen walls from the spoil had been thrown up around the site. Traditionally, Roman armies marched from early morning till noon, covering between eighteen and twenty-one miles per day. From midday, legionaries built their overnight camp while auxiliaries and cavalry mounted guard, with some troopers out foraging the district for food, fodder, and firewood, and others, serving as scouts, deployed to forewarn of enemy movements.[5]

According to legend, some little time after noon, as the camp was being constructed around him, Constantine was standing outside his newly erected tented pavilion with some of his officers. A dazzling cross-like vision now appeared immediately above the sun, a vision whose import the general could not quite understand. Writing after Constantine's death, Eusebius, Christian Bishop of Caesarea in Palestine, would say, "He saw with his own eyes the trophy of a cross of light in the heavens, above the sun, and bearing the inscription in Greek, 'By this conquer.'"[6]

That night, according to Eusebius, and also to Lucius Caecilius Firmianus Lactantius, Christian tutor to Constantine's eldest son at this time, while the general's army slept at its Prima Porta marching camp, Constantine had a dream. According to Eusebius, Constantine was a prolific and prophetic dreamer, and on this night of October 27–28, he is said to have dreamed that he was visited by a divinity who showed him a sign in the form of the same cruciform shape he had seen earlier, again accompanied by the words, in Greek, "By this conquer."[7]

When Constantine awoke the following morning before dawn, he sent for carpenters and goldsmiths among his army's ranks. Many legionaries of Rome came to the army with the skills and trades of prior careers, and the army made full use of them. Sitting with the craftsmen around him, the young general described a new personal standard that he wanted made for him at once. That standard, Eusebius was to write, took the form of "a long spear, overlaid with gold, [and] formed the figure of a cross by means of a transverse bar laid over it." Eusebius went on to describe a bejeweled cloth banner hanging from the transverse bar.[8]

This cross-shaped standard was nothing new. For hundreds of years, going back well before the time of Christ, the personal standards of Roman army commanders had taken the form of a cross, with a cloth banner suspended from a transverse pole which in turn was suspended from a wooden shaft. Called a vexillum, this form of standard was also routinely used by detachments from legions, which were called vexillations as a consequence. The standard's shaft had a pointed base that allowed it to be jammed into the ground. A fragment of the banner from a Roman military vexillum found in modern times in Egypt and thought to have belonged to a Praetorian Guard detachment was made of coarse linen dyed red. So, Constantine's standard would have taken the form of a cross prior to 312, but this was incidental and had nothing to do with Christianity.

Given that the army was already packing up around him in preparation for the last day of the march on Rome, which would commence shortly after sunrise, there was no time to fashion an entirely new standard for Constantine. He would have ordered his existing standard adapted to conform with his dream. We are told by Eusebius that the banner of his standard was "covered with a profuse embroidery of the most brilliant precious stones" and was "richly interlaced with gold." It is highly likely that this banner already existed, on Constantine's original standard, in which case the embroidery would probably have read CONST CAES, abbreviations for Constantine's name and official title, Caesar, or deputy emperor.[9]

Three large golden medallions, each roughly a hand-span in diameter, were suspended from the standard's cross-pole, bearing the images, we are told by Eusebius, of Constantine and his children. In A.D. 312, Constantine had at least two children—the teenaged Flavius Julius Crispus, only child from his first marriage, and his eldest daughter, the infant Flavia Julia Constantina, first progeny from his second marriage.

Such gold medallions as these, called *imagoes*, had long been a common feature of imperial Roman legion standards, bearing the portrait of the current emperor and sometimes also of his empress and children. There being no time to sculpt and cast new medallions in the hour or two available to the craftsmen assembled in Constantine's tent, this trio of medallions, like the banner on the new standard, almost certainly already existed, forming part of Constantine's original standard.

Quite apart from the established features just discussed, it was the *top* of Constantine's revamped personal standard that was to be new, and unique. On his orders, this was to take the form of the letter *P* superimposed over the letter *X*, forming what is known as the chi-rho. *X* and *P* were the first letters in the Greek word Christos, or Christ. However, *X* and *P* were also the first letters of the Greek word *chreston*, meaning "good," and use of the chi-rho symbol as a propaganda tool went back five hundred years to the Egyptian king Ptolemy III, who was of Greek extraction and reigned between 246 and 222 B.C.

Ptolemy had used the chi-rho on his coins to promote the "goodness" of his reign. Constantine would have been accustomed to the use of the chi-rho in that same sense as a result of his study of Greek, for students and readers of Greek had been inscribing the chi-rho symbol in the margins of books for centuries, to mark passages they considered to be good and worthy of note.

While the chi-rho was occasionally inscribed at Christian burial sites such as the catacombs of Rome, it is difficult to date them with accuracy. The symbol may have been used by Christians prior to Constantine, or it may have later been inspired by his use of it. Certainly, for a century prior to 312, the cross had been the symbol that Christians had been using to identify themselves, after initially using a fish symbol. Constantine was the first figure of authority in Roman history, inside or outside the church, to publicly adopt the chi-rho emblem.

According to Eusebius, the chi-rho added to Constantine's standard was set within a golden wreath, with the wreath in turn decorated with jewels. The golden victory wreath, a symbol of Victoria, goddess of victory, had long been common on Roman military standards, but we know that the gold wreath that Eusebius saw on Constantine's standard was not present in the standard's first incarnation here at Prima Porta. That initial version of the standard would be depicted on coins Constantine produced the year following this, without the wreath. Eusebius, who would not make Constantine's acquaintance for some years yet, obviously must have seen and described a later version of the standard, to which had apparently been added the jewel-encrusted golden victory wreath.

Lactantius the tutor would later claim that Constantine also ordered all his 40,000 men to paint the chi-rho on their shields this day, and the story would enter Christian legend as fact. However, few historians believe this occurred. For one thing, there would not have been the time for this mass painting exercise, let alone sufficient paint on hand. Eusebius, who tells us the most about Constantine's new standard, makes no mention of the troops painting the chi-rho on their shields on October 28. He did write that in later times Constantine's troops inscribed the chi-rho on their shields, and even then he made no claims that it was painted on, was widespread, or replaced existing unit symbols on shields.

Half a century after this, the Roman official Vegetius, writing a military manual for the Emperor Justinian II, noted that since ancient times Rome's legionaries had scratched their name and the identity of their legion and cohort on the inside of their shields. It is possible that the few Christians in the ranks later scratched the chi-rho on the inside or exterior of their shields.[10]

As Christianity spread during this fourth century, it was slow to penetrate the military, as the shield emblems of the Roman army attest. Even by the end of the century, by which time Christianity had been the official state religion for two decades, no unit of the Roman army bore a Christian symbol such as the chi-rho or an identifiably Christian cross on its shields. Just two units of the emperor's bodyguard of circa A.D. 400 may have borne Christian shield emblems—a pair of angels—although these figures may have been twin images of Victoria, goddess of victory, emulating earlier images of pairs of Victorias frequently used by Constantine and his sons and successors.

The Roman army's unit emblems seventy-five years after Constantine's death still had links to the gods of old, with some retaining the legion symbols of the first century. A number of others used the Wheel of Fortune emblem, which represented the goddesses Fortuna and Bellona, and the rosette, another of war goddess Bellona's emblems.[11]

It is clear that Constantine, who was described as impulsive in his early career, on this day suddenly decided that he wanted a modified standard to distinguish himself from his opponent and give himself an edge. What is much less clear is whether Constantine intended the standard to project a Christian image. Certainly, it is unlikely that any of his rank and file would have associated the Greek chi-rho with Christ at that time. What they saw was a unique glittering standard that would set Constantine apart in the coming fight. From its earlier applications, and as later indicated by Constantine's writings, where "goodness" often featured, he is most likely to have adopted the chi-rho to represent what he saw as the goodness of his military cause, not his faith.

In battle, Constantine's standard would be carried and guarded by a detachment of 50 volunteers from the general's elite bodyguard unit. These were men who, says Eusebius, "were most distinguished for personal strength, valor and piety." Their sole duty "was to surround and vigilantly defend the standard, which they carried each in turn on their shoulders." All were expected to defend the standard with their lives.[12]

This new standard of Constantine's would in time acquire a name, the Labarum. To this day, no one knows precisely what that meant. The closest Latin word to Labarum, *labare,* means to waver or quiver. Certainly, in battle, and accompanied by relevant trumpet calls, Roman generals' standards would incline in the direction the troops were required to move by the commander—advance, withdraw, move left, move right. Perhaps Constantine would require his new standard to waver or quiver for added effect as it bowed this way or that. Or perhaps the sight of it was intended to shore up the courage of wavering soldiers in his ranks.

In Spain, the Basque word *labarva* means standard, but this is likely have originated later, and been derived from Constantine's Labarum, not vice versa. In commemoration and confirmation of the creation by Constantine of the Labarum at this place on this day, a later village below Prima Porta would take the name Labaro, and, as Rome expanded, would become today's Labaro zone in the northwest of the city.

While the craftsmen hurried to fashion the Labarum, Constantine's army was breaking camp. Unlike earlier Roman generals, Constantine was not known to share his plans with those close to him or convene councils of war to discuss strategies and tactics. At this point, he would have given the appearance that he was planning to reach Rome by mid-morning and then lay siege to the city. Reports reaching him in the weeks leading up to this day had indicated that his opponent was preparing to withstand a lengthy siege.

That opponent was Constantine's own brother-in-law, Marcus Aurelius Valerius Maxentius, brother of Constantine's second wife Fausta. Even though he was a couple of years younger than Constantine, Maxentius was technically Constantine's superior, as holder of the title of Augustus, or emperor, of the Western Roman Empire. But, unlike his brother-in-law, Maxentius had no experience leading an army in battle; previously he had let subordinates fight his battles for him.

From his spies and informants, Constantine would have known that Maxentius had 170,000 infantry and 18,000 cavalry marching for him, forming one of the largest Roman armies in history; as many as 100,000 of these men were at Rome with their emperor. Constantine was also aware that Maxentius had collected large stocks of food at Rome, as part of his preparations to withstand a lengthy sieges.

To hamper the progress of Constantine's army once it reached Rome, Maxentius's troops had removed the timber decking from all bridges across the Tiber outside Rome, including the second century B.C. stone bridge that took the Flaminian Way across the river north of the city—the Milvian Bridge. That bridge, much repaired and renovated since, and today known as the Ponte Milvio, still spans the Tiber. So, as Constantine and his army commenced the march south, they were expecting steady and hopefully unopposed progress, to the west bank of the Tiber within sight of Rome's outer Aurelian Walls, where Constantine would order a siege camp built.

The lead elements of his army had not long been on the march—and the baggage train was still at the campsite—when breathless mounted scouts would have reached Constantine to pass on the latest news, which was that Maxentius had decided on a sudden change of strategy. His troops had, on the previous day, thrown a temporary bridge of boats across the Tiber to the east of the sabotaged Milvian Bridge, and since before dawn a massive army of cavalry and infantry had poured out of the city and was filing over this floating crossing before marching north up the Flaminian Way to confront Constantine.

Constantine wasted no time ordering new arrangements for his army. His troops would divest themselves of all superfluous equipment, and the army's baggage train would remain at the overnight campsite. The infantry and cavalry would then proceed south in battle order to meet Maxentius's troops on the river plain. The decisive Battle of the Milvian Bridge, as it was to become known, was just hours away.

II

THE RISE OF FATHER
AND SON

To understand why Constantine was marching on Rome in October 312, it is necessary to go back several decades, to Gaul. From A.D. 286, the Roman Empire had been ruled by a unique double act, and Rome had ceased to be the seat of power. Two men jointly sat on the throne. The east of the Empire was ruled by the Augustus, or emperor, Gaius Aurelius Valerius Diocletianus—Diocletian, as we know him. Son of a former slave, Diocletian had risen to power as a cavalry commander, coming to the throne in 284 after defeating a son of the previous emperor, Carius, in battle.

Diocletian had made his capital not at Rome, but at the city of Nicomedia, today's Izmit in Turkey. Almost equidistant between the Danube and Euphrates rivers, Nicomedia sat handily at the junction of highways from east, west, north, and south, and on the Gulf of Izmit, the most easterly extent of the Propontis, today's Sea of Marmara, in the Roman province of Bithynia.

The west of the empire was ruled by another Augustus of equal rank, Marcus Aurelius Valerius Maximianus. Known to history as Maximian, he was a tough, poorly educated, shaggy-bearded soldier appointed to the post by his friend Diocletian. Maximian's Western capital was at Mediolanum, today's Milan in northern Italy. Milan had been an imperial capital since the A.D. 253–268 reign of the emperor Gallienus, after Gallienus sought to be closer to barbarian threats from beyond the Rhine and Danube. Maximian had implemented a major building program at Milan, with new city walls, imperial palaces for his family and himself, and a massive baths complex, the Baths of Hercules, named for Maximian's patron deity.

Back in A.D. 66, King Herod Agrippa II had told the Jews of Jerusalem, "All men have the Romans for their masters already, or are afraid they will."[13] Two hundred years later, the empire was under continual threat from ambitious rebels within and warlike nations without, none of whom possessed the desire to have Romans for their masters. Between them, Diocletian and Maximian successfully stabilized a rocky empire after decades of internal revolts and barbarian attacks in the wake of the A.D. 260 capture of the emperor Valerian by the Persians.

Between the years 284 and 286, while Diocletian was sole emperor, Gaul and Britain had faced both internal and external menaces. Frankish and Saxon pirates from Germany roved the English Channel and North Sea in hundreds of ships, ravaging Roman shipping. On land, massive marauding bands of Gallic bandits, collectively called the Bacaudae, made travel, trade, and tax collection impossible. While some of these Bacaudae were runaway slaves, many were Roman citizens, Gallic farmers who took up arms under the Gallic leaders Amandus and Aelianus, initially around today's Lyon.

Emperor Diocletian had sent his then deputy Maximian to deal with the Bacaudae, and in A.D. 286, Maximian, who had risen from farmer to general through military skill and determination, had eliminated the rebels. This success had sponsored his promotion to the role of co-emperor with Diocletian. As Maximian headed back to his capital Milan after dealing with the Bacaudae, he left one of his deputies to deal with the remaining problem, the sea pirates. This officer was Marcus Aurelius Mauseus Valerius Carausius, admiral of the *Classis Britannicus*, Rome's Britannic Fleet. Carausius was a native of the Menapi tribe, whose territory roughly encompassed today's Belgian coast as far as the Rhine. A seaman by profession, Carausius had served as a maritime pilot prior to joining the Roman civil service, and he knew the Belgian sea coast like the back of his hand.

To deal with the pirates, Carausius came up with a novel strategy that involved land-based troops. Instead of putting hundreds of warships to sea to try to anticipate where the pirate fleets might strike next, and intercept them, Carausius identified the ports being used by the pirates. Using commando-style raids, he would land legionaries to await the return from raids of pirate ships. Once the ships arrived in port, Carausius's troops would strike.

Carausius, a massive, bearded, bull-necked man, made careful preparations at the headquarters of the Britannic Fleet, Bononia, today's Boulogne-sur-Mer on the French coast. To subdue the pirates, Maximian left Carausius 10,000 to 15,000 troops from the army he'd used to eliminate the Bacaudae. Those troops included, from their stations on the Lower Rhine, cohorts detached from the 1st Minervia Legion and the 30th Ulpia Legion. From their Upper Rhine bases, he had detachments from the 8th Augusta Legion and 22nd Primigenia Legion. From bases on the Danube, there were cohorts of the 7th Claudia Legion, and the entire 4th Flavia Felix Legion. Plus, from Italy, Carausius was given troops detached from the 2nd Parthica Legion and four cohorts of the Praetorian Guard.

For centuries past, the Praetorian Guard had served as the imperial bodyguard, accompanying the emperor everywhere. But Diocletian did not trust the Italians of the Praetorian Guard. Downgrading them to field troops, he had replaced the Praetorian Guard in the imperial bodyguard role with two new units of 6,000 men each, troops who had previously been based in Illyricum and made a name for themselves under Diocletian in numerous battles. Diocletian named his own new bodyguard unit the Jovians, after his patron deity Jove, or Jupiter, king of the gods, while the unit providing the bodyguard for Western emperor Maximian was called the Herculeans, after Hercules, Maximian's patron deity.

The shield emblem of the Jovians was the eagle, one of Jove's symbols. The Herculeans' emblem was Hercules with his wooden club, but within a century this unit would also be using the eagle emblem. According to Vegetius in *Military Institutions of the Romans,* the men of these two units were experts in the use of the *martiobarbuli,* or "little barbs of Mars"— small, lead-weighted, barbed javelins, or darts. The Jovians and Herculeans demonstrated "extraordinary dexterity and skill in the use of these weapons," says Vegetius, adding that "every soldier [of these two units] carries five of these in the hollow of his shield."

Maximian also created a mounted arm of his bodyguard, the Ala Herculea, or Herculean Wing, and Diocletian similarly created an Ala Jovia, the Jovian Wing, whose men were heavily armored cataphracts, relegating the longtime German household cavalry created by Trajan, the Singularian Horse Guard, to field army duties.[14]

To carry the troops allocated to him by Maximian, Carausius employed his Britannic Fleet, built more warships, and co-opted a number of Gallic cargo vessels into his navy. Within a matter of months, he was ready to wage war on the pirates. Very quickly, Carausius had his first successes, capturing pirate ships galore as they arrived back in port complete with the booty from their latest raids. But when word reached Maximian in Milan that Carausius was devastating the pirate fleets, he was also told that Carausius was keeping all the booty taken from the pirates and sharing it with his troops. Maximian's remedy, Admiral Carausius, had proven to be as bad as the problem, the pirates. Furious, Maximian ordered the arrest of Carausius.

When warning of the arrest order reached Carausius's ears, he simply embarked his troops and sailed for Britain. Over the winter of A.D. 286/287, Maximian arrived at Boulogne with an army, only to find that Carausius had escaped. Storms that lashed the Gallic coast then destroyed Maximian's plans to cross the English Channel to tackle Carausius. One account claimed that the storms actually destroyed the Maximian's fleet, but as Carausius controlled Roman shipping on the Channel, Maximian is unlikely to have had many ships at his disposal. With raiding Alemanni Germans now flooding across the Rhine into Roman territory, the Western emperor had to withdraw to deal with this latest threat, leaving Carausius for another day.

In the spring of the following year, Maximian and Diocletian jointly invaded Germany. While Maximian crossed the Rhine from the legion base at Mogantiacum, today's city of Mainz at the junction of the Rhine and Main rivers, Diocletian marched into Germany from the east via the province of Raetia, which covered much of today's Switzerland, Bavaria, and the Tyrol. For a time, the emperors' joint scorched-earth campaign cleared Rome's Rhine frontier of the Alemanni, a confederation of German tribes whose name meant "men united." Over time, the fearsome Alemanni warriors would have such an impact on the French that they would apply the name Allemagne to all of Germany. But Roman consolidation of the success on the Rhine achieved by Diocletian and Maximian was not possible because Diocletian was forced to return to the East to combat other threats, leaving Maximian to withdraw to Milan.

Carausius, meanwhile, bluffing his troops into believing that he'd been appointed deputy emperor in charge of Britain by Maximian, sailed his fleet around northern Britain and landed on the west coast of today's England. His landing seems to have taken place northwest of Eboracum, today's York. The capital of the province of Britannia Secunda, one of the four provinces into which Britain had been divided by Diocletian, York had commenced life as a riverside fifty-acre Roman legionary fort in A.D. 71.

Not only did Carausius's landing take the Roman authorities in Britain completely by surprise, it cleverly allowed Carausius to slip in between the Roman forces then based in Britain—to the north, the 2nd Augusta Legion, 20th Valeria Victrix Legion, and large numbers of auxiliary units based along Hadrian's Wall; and, to the south, the 6th Victrix Legion, based at York.

There is archaeological evidence of British towns in the region being burned at this time, as Carausius advanced southeast on York, with Carausius no doubt telling his men they were putting down an insurrection against Rome's authority as he allowed them to loot and burn. Outside York, Carausius was met by a force apparently based around the men of the 6th Victrix Legion. There is no report of a bloody battle ensuing, and it is likely the silver-tongued Carausius talked the outnumbered 6th Victrix troops into coming over to him without a fight. Before long, the two other legions based in Britain, the 2nd Augusta and 20th Valeria Victrix, were also bowing to Carausius's authority.

Carausius subsequently took to using the title imperator, literally meaning commander, which was usually given to Roman emperors by acclamation of their troops after a great victory. This suggests that Carausius gained wide popular support from all the military in Britain. That year, A.D. 287, when Carausius minted the pay of the troops now under his command, styling himself Augustus of Britain and putting his image on the coins, the three resident legions in Britain were included in the minting along with the units he had brought with him from Gaul.

Carausius hunkered down for a long stay, building forts at potential landing sites along the south coast of England, from where his troops could counter amphibious landings by Roman troops brought by the emperor Maximian to unseat him. One such fort was at Clausentum, today's Bitterne Manor, a suburb of Southampton. Carausius would continue to pay his Roman troops for another six years, producing their coins at mints in London and at another British location, possibly Clausentum. All through this time, Britain was no longer part of the Roman Empire, ceasing to contribute taxes or military recruits to Rome, and no longer taking orders from the emperor Maximian.

Emboldened by his success, "emperor" Carausius crossed the Channel and reoccupied Boulogne with part of his army. Then, to jointly control and exploit northern Gaul, he allied himself with the Franks, a confederation of aggressive German tribes originating between the Rhine and Weser rivers. Frankish warriors, who were easily identifiable by their short hair, mustaches, and tunics sporting broad horizontal stripes, fought without helmets or armor and used battleaxes to fearsome effect. As the Franks spread their influence south and increasingly settled in Gaul, they would eventually give their name to today's nation of France—from Francia, Latin for "land of the Franks." Carausius also made a deal whereby the Franks supplied him with mercenaries to bolster his army in Britain.

On March 1, 293, however, an appointment in Milan sealed Carausius's fate. That day, western emperor Maximian appointed a Caesar, or deputy emperor, of the West, to serve under him and counter the likes of Carausius. At the same time, at Nicomedia, eastern emperor Diocletian similarly appointed a Caesar for the East. The understanding was that, after Diocletian and Maximian had served twenty years as co-emperors, they would go into retirement and their Caesars would replace them on the Eastern and Western thrones. This four-man leadership team became known as the Tetrarchy.

The man appointed Caesar, or deputy emperor of the Western Empire was forty-three-year-old Flavius Valerius Constantius, known as Constantius Chlorus, or Constantius the Pale, apparently due to a pallid complexion. It is clear that Diocletian dictated Constantius's appointment, as Diocletian had previously been Constantius's commander when both served in the elite imperial bodyguard unit, the *Protectores Domestici*, or Household Guard, of an earlier emperor.

Constantius's eldest son was Constantine, the future Constantine the Great. By taking the dates of his coming of age and when he entered military service, which are discussed below, it can be calculated that Constantine was born in 275, and was therefore eighteen when his father was appointed Caesar to Maximian in 293. His mother Helena had been divorced by

Constantius four years before this to enable Constantius to marry the boss's daughter—Theodora, daughter of emperor Maximian. Constantius would have kept his eldest son and heir close, and it is likely that in the early years following his parents' divorce Constantine had resided with his father in Augusta Treverorum, today's Trier, on the Moselle River in western Germany, then capital of the Roman province of Belgica Prima and Constantius's center of operations.

Constantius, himself born into an undistinguished family in the Dardania region in the Balkans, had, in addition to his earlier Household Guard appointment, served diligently as an officer in the Roman army in the East. Prior to his appointment as Caesar of the West, he had been governor of the Balkan province of Dalmatia. From 288, he had served as Maximian's Praetorian prefect—which had by this time become the rank and title of each emperor's chief administrator.

Constantius was a severe, duty-driven man, ruggedly handsome, with prominent features, and, like his son, was clean-shaven in an age when the beard that Hadrian had made fashionable in the second century still predominated. We know from surviving busts that Constantius and Constantine shared the same physique and facial features. This was noted by Romans at the time.

"You have your father's appearance, Constantine," said an orator in 307. Similarly, four years later, a member of Constantine's staff told him, "A great likeness of appearance has passed from him to you," as if "imprinted on your features by Nature with a stamp." It was also noted that father and son shared "the same calmness in the gaze and in the voice," although Constantine was more prudish than his earthy father and was known to blush with embarrassment at times.[15]

Each deputy emperor was allocated part of the empire to personally administer. In Constantius's case, his areas of direct responsibility were Gaul and Britain. Spain would be added to the Western Caesar's domain some years later. Constantius would continue to be based in Trier, a cosmopolitan city then boasting a population of one hundred thousand made up of members of the Germanic Treveri and the Celtic Belgae tribes, as well as Gauls and Roman settlers. As Constantius returned to Trier from the ceremony in Milan that spring, the new deputy emperor arranged for his boy Constantine to move to the Eastern capital Nicomedia, to be close to Eastern emperor Diocletian and improve his education while Constantius went to war. Diocletian had made it clear he expected Constantius to do what Maximian had failed to do—deal with the rebel "emperor" Carausius and bring western Gaul and Britain back into the empire.

After parting from his father, young Constantine set off on a journey that spring to Nicomedia via Aquileia, a city in northwest Italy that sat at the head of the Adriatic Sea, between Italy and the Balkans. Aquileia was a favorite resort of Diocletian, who had built a palace in the city, and it was here that Constantine tarried for a time en route to the court of Diocletian.

Members of western emperor Maximian's family were also staying at the Aquileian palace. Maximian himself is likely to have been present, for, at Maximian's suggestion, Constantine modeled for a new portrait being painted on the wall of the palace's public banqueting hall. In that painting, the eighteen-year-old Constantine was being handed a helmet by a cute, noble-looking little girl of three of four. We are told that the helmet sparkled with gold and jewels and was decked with the feathers of a beautiful bird, probably a peacock. The cute little girl was Flavia Maximiana Fausta, daughter of Maximian and his wife Eutropia, a Syrian beauty. Little Fausta had been born in Rome, where she lived until she was five, so may have been in Aquileia for a vacation with her family or was residing there.

Constantine, despite his youth, was already a married man by this time. According to an official speech delivered at his second wedding in 307, that first marriage had taken place at "the precise moment" Constantine came of age.[16] Roman men officially came of age at sixteen, then the legal marrying age for males (for centuries, Roman females could become engaged at twelve and marry at thirteen). The coming of age of young Roman men was commemorated by a ceremony, the *deposito barbae,* held during the March 17 Liberalia religious festival that was closest to the youth's sixteenth birthday. Everything points to Constantine celebrating his sixteenth birthday on February 27 in the year 291, with his coming of age taking place at the Liberalia that occurred less than three weeks later. The orator of 307 indicates that Constantine's first marriage took place the same day as the Liberalia, March 17, 291.

On the Liberalia, a festival dedicated to the fertility god Liber Pater and his consort Libera, the young Roman man donned the formal white toga for the first time and had his beard shaved in front of gathered guests. The hairs from his beard were placed in a small casket, the *deposito,* which the young man's father then deposited as an offering to Capitoline Jupiter. Leading

Romans made this deposit at a temple to Jupiter. For other families, it was made in the small shrine to the *Lares* or household gods that Romans maintained in their homes. In the first-century novel the *Satyricon,* author Petronius Arbiter had his hero place his son's *deposito* between the silver statuettes of his two Lares and a statuette of Venus, goddess of love.[17]

Some writers today speculate that Constantine's first wedding took place not at the time of his coming of age, but in March 303, twelve years later, when Constantine's father Constantius was declared Augustus of the West. On the other hand, the panegyrist recalling Constantine's first wedding when he delivered a 307 speech in front of Constantine and his new second wife, quite emphatically stated that it had taken place as soon as Constantine entered manhood at the age of sixteen, in 291. There is absolutely no reason to disbelieve the panegyric on this point.

All authorities acknowledge that Constantine's first wife would bear him a son, Crispus, by 295. If he had not married until 303, Crispus would have been illegitimate when Constantine made him his Caesar in 317. Late in his life, Constantine would promulgate a law retrospectively legitimizing bastard children of leading men if the parents subsequently married and the father had no existing legitimate children. Some claim Constantine did this to legitimize Crispus, but Constantine had several existing legitimate children by 317, so the law could not apply to him. It is likely that the legitimizing law, like another from 336 concerning natural children and their mothers, originated some time after Crispus's death—the precise wording of the law and its date have not come down to us.

We know that Constantine's first wife was a young woman by the name of Minervina, and their wedding is believed to have taken place in Trier, where Constantine's father was based. Minervina was a woman of whom we know little other than the fact her name meant Little Minerva. Minerva was the goddess of wisdom, arts and crafts, healing, and defensive war. It has been suggested by some latter-day historians that Minervina may have been the niece of Diocletian, although there is no corroborating evidence of this. Some scholars think she was merely a concubine, or mistress, not Constantine's legally wedded wife, and certainly Minervina was the type of name borne in Roman times by the lower classes, slaves, and freedwomen. According to Zosimus, in his *New History* a century later, Maxentius, brother of Constantine's second wife, would mock Minervina as a "harlot," implying that she was a common prostitute.

It should be noted that the Roman middle and upper classes did not name their children after gods or goddesses. They gave their daughters names derived from that of their fathers and mothers. For example, Constantius's eldest daughter, Constantine's half-sister, was named Constantia. Similarly, Galerius named his daughter Galeria. However, a high-status *alienus*, or foreigner, living in the Roman Empire and commanding foreign units such as the *Numeri* in the Roman army—more than twenty *Numeri* units were stationed in Britain alone—may have named his daughter after a Roman goddess to advertise that he was Romanized. And there is a possibility that Minervina had a strong British connection, as will be explained.

In the twelfth century, British writers Henry of Huntingdon and Geoffrey of Monmouth would separately write that Constantine's mother Helena, first wife of Constantius, was a British princess, the daughter of a British tribal leader named King Coillus—also written Coil and Coel. However, Henry's *History of the English* and Geoffrey's *History of the Kings of Britain*, while influential in the Middle Ages, are today dismissed as works of romantic fiction whose numerous historical claims rarely have a provable basis in fact, or have been disproved by more reliable and authenticated sources.

More importantly, it is accepted by historians that Constantine's mother Helena was of Greek background and hailed from Bithynia in the East, where her father was an innkeeper and far from royal—innkeepers were then considered so inferior in status that, like slaves, freedmen, and cooks, they were banned from enlisting in Rome's legions.

But consider this. Constantine's wife was named for the goddess Minerva. That goddess had a major shrine in Britain, at today's city of Bath in north Somerset, where she was worshipped as Minerva Sulis, goddess of healing, after Roman Britons combined Minerva with their own Celtic goddess Sulis in the first century. More importantly, in the north of England, Minerva was worshipped at the forts of German cavalry units serving in the Roman army, in her healing guise as Minerva Medica. Many German cavalrymen serving Rome worshipped Minerva, as demonstrated by the fact that at one of the forts at Rome of the Singularian Horse Guard, the primarily German mounted bodyguard of the emperors, no fewer than forty-four dedications to Minerva by the unit's troopers have been found.

It is possible that in the twelfth century Henry and Geoffrey heard folk tales that, in passing down through the ages, had confused Constantius's first wife with Constantine's first wife. And Minervina may well have been the daughter of a British king, or more precisely, a king who would settle in Britain. The King Coillus of legend, said to be father of the wife of a Roman emperor, may in fact have been King Crocus (also written Chrocus), of the Alemanni Germans, who, we know, served under Constantius in Britain.

Crocus had once been a major thorn in Rome's side. In about 260, as a new, young king, he had been persuaded by his mother to lead a combination of German tribes in a raid across the Rhine from his homeland in the Main River valley to devastate northern Gaul.

Driving as far south as Augusta Nemetum, today's Clermont-Ferrand in central France, and, some believe, even going as far as Ravenna in northern Italy, Crocus and his army had made a point of destroying every Roman temple and killing every Christian they encountered. But by the time of Constantius's reign, aged in his fifties or sixties, Crocus was marching for Rome, the same way that Frankish Germans marched for Carausius, for money, status, power, and security for their families.

How Crocus came to change sides is not recorded, but like earlier German princes who served Rome, such as Arminius and his brother Flavus in the first century, he would have had an original German name that preceded his Roman name—Crocus may have taken the name of the purple crocus flower because purple was the color of royalty among the Romans. We know that by 306, Crocus was serving under Constantius in Britain in a very senior capacity, and would be so highly regarded by Constantius that his legions would demonstrate that they considered him their commander's trusted friend.[18]

Following his Gallic raid in 260, Crocus does not again appear in recorded Roman history until 306 as either an enemy or an ally. Equally, there is no record of how or when he changed sides. He had to have been an active ally of Rome since the 270s at the most recent, in order to name his teenage daughter after a Roman goddess and to be serving under Constantius in 291 at the time of Constantine's wedding.

There were two battles at which Crocus could have been captured by a Roman emperor. One was the 271 Battle of Pavia, where the emperor Aurelian defeated a combined Alemanni/Juthurgi invasion force. It was following the scare of this German incursion that Aurelian constructed his Aurelian Wall to encompass the suburbs of Rome that had grown beyond the old Servian Wall. However, the more likely occasion for Crocus's capture was the earlier 268–269 Battle of Lake Benacus, near today's Lake Garda in northwest Italy, when another invading Alemanni force was delivered a resounding defeat in Italy, this time by the emperor Claudius II Gothicus—the same Claudius Gothicus from whom Constantine was to claim descent. The possibility that Constantine named his first son after Claudius Gothicus's brother Crispus, which is discussed below, may indicate that it was the original Crispus, serving as one of his brother's generals, who gave quarter to Crocus on the battlefield at Lake Benacus, after which Claudius spared the king.[19]

Certainly, through the late third century and early fourth century, up until Constantine's rule in Gaul when he overturned the custom, it had long been the Roman rule to spare captured German kings and settle them in Roman territory. The custom would be resumed in 357 by Constantine's nephew Julian, when Caesar to Constantius II. After thrashing a large Alemanni army on the Rhine, Julian would capture then-Alemanni king Chnodomar, along with 200 of his men. Julian spared the king and his retainers and sent them to Constantius II, who likewise let the king live.

But why would Constantius marry his son and heir to a German princess when it was the habit of the members of the Tetrarchy to intermarry their sons and daughters? We know that Galerius, Diocletian's Caesar, had great influence over Diocletian and increasingly dictated who would marry whom among the imperial families. And we know that there was no love lost between Constantius and Galerius. In fact, each deeply distrusted the other, to the point of despising each other. In all probability, Constantius chose to thwart any attempt by Galerius to impose a wife on his son, a wife whose loyalty would be to Galerius, by marrying off Constantine *on the very day* he came of age and was eligible to marry. That would certainly explain the rush to wed.

King Crocus was to prove firmly loyal to Constantius, and Constantine was, we know, genuinely fond of Minervina. If Crocus had been an ally of Rome since 269 or 271, he, his daughter Minervina and the rest of his resettled family would have lived in Gaul or Britain for some years by the time of Constantine's wedding, suggesting that they mixed with the court of Constantius and that Constantine and Minervina knew each other while growing up.

Subsequent events in 295 and 306 lend weight to the distinct possibility that Minervina was Crocus's daughter, as will shortly be explained.

Whatever Minervina's background, by 295 she would give birth to Constantine's first child, Crispus, whose name literally means curly-headed. Later coin images show Crispus, when a young man, as straight-haired. However, according to the *Excerpta Valesiana*, written by an otherwise unknown Roman author around 390, Constantine was the great-grandson of theCrispus who was the brother of the emperor Claudius Gothicus, and this provides a sound reason for naming the boy Crispus, advertising an enhanced royal lineage.

Why go back as far as the brother of Claudius Gothicus for the child's name? Well, if Claudius Gothicus's brother had been the one who initially saved King Crocus's life, the naming of the grandson of a descendant of the Claudian line and close relative of the king who spared Crocus would have seemed a very appropriate way to link the families of Constantine and Crocus. Constantine always recognized Crispus as his legitimate firstborn son and heir, indicating a formal marriage with Minervina. And the orator at Constantine's second wedding in 307 would not only be quite clear that Constantine had previously gone through a formal marriage with Minervina; he actually described it as a love match.[20]

Minervina would not have traveled with Constantine in 293 as he made his way from Gaul via Aquileia to Nicomedia. She must have remained in Gaul, for, when she gave birth to their son Crispus in 295, it was at Arelate in southern Gaul, today's Provençal city of Arles. British historian Timothy Barnes feels it likely that Maximian's son Maxentius also joined Diocletian's court in Nicomedia at this time. In fact, it is probable that Maxentius, who was only a year or two younger than Constantine, had also been present at Aquileia at the time of the portrait-painting episode, and thereafter accompanied Constantine to Nicomedia.[21]

Once Maxentius reached Nicomedia, he was due to take part in a dual wedding ceremony. Galerius, forty-three-year-old deputy emperor of the East, was to marry Diocletian's daughter Valeria, having annulled his first marriage to enable the union. At the same time, Galerius had arranged for teenager Maxentius to wed Galeria Maximilla, Galerius's own daughter from his first marriage.

Little did either Constantine or Maxentius know that, one day, Constantine would marry Fausta, the little girl depicted with him in the painting on the Aquileian palace wall, or that Constantine and Maxentius would be brothers-in-law, only to go to war with each other.

III

SOLDIER IN WHITE

Just months after Constantine settled into the palace at Nicomedia and commenced his studies under tutors approved by Diocletian, an opportunity for adventure reared its head, and Constantine grabbed it. Word had reached Diocletian of an uprising in Egypt that summer of 293. The Egyptian residents of two prosperous cities—Coptos, which sat on the most easterly branch of the Lower Nile close to Thebes; and Boresis, also sometimes written as Busiris, located in the middle of the Nile Delta—had taken up arms against Rome, just as their ancestors had done back in 30 B.C. Both rebel cities would have to be stormed to terminate the revolt, and Diocletian delegated the task to his new deputy emperor, Galerius.

On hearing this, Constantine appears to have put up his hand to serve with Galerius. "You wanted to become great by serving in the army and by facing the risks of war," a member of Constantine's staff would say to him eighteen years later. With Diocletian's approval, Constantine now commenced his Roman army track as a junior tribune, or subaltern, serving in the mounted *Divine Comitatus* bodyguard of Galerius.[22]

Under the old system for training Roman officers established by Augustus, at the age of eighteen Constantine would have been eligible to take part in the *semestri tribunata*, the officer cadet scheme whereby the sons of the Roman elite served with the army for six months as a *tribunus laticlavius,* or tribune of the thin stripe, as their first step on the ladder to the Senate and senior government appointments. Constantine would, once he was emperor, establish a new system for training junior officers, creating the *Candidati Militares,* a dedicated officer training unit attached to the emperor's bodyguard. Their title literally meant "soldiers in white," referring to the white tunics traditionally worn by all tribunes, as opposed to the red tunics of the Roman army's rank and file. These military candidates of the officer cadet unit were required to be tall, fine-looking young men aspiring to be officers. The duration of their service with *Candidati Militares* before promotion to tribune and posting to other units is unknown.

The old subaltern training system was still in place during Constantine's youth, and, as Diocletian lifted the minimum age for all fulltime army recruits from eighteen to twenty during his reign, it is likely that he similarly moved the semestri tribunata age to nineteen to enable subalterns to move on to fulltime service at twenty. And by the time that Galerius would have readied a force to take on the Egyptian rebels in the spring of 294, Constantine would be nineteen.

In the past, this six-month semester as a junior tribune had either been with a legion or on the staff of an army commander, and had often involved little more than acting as a messenger or secretary. Agricola, one of the best-known Roman governors of Britain, had first arrived in Britain in A.D. 60 as a junior tribune assigned to the staff of the province's governor, Paulinus, only to find himself fighting for his life in the largest battle ever to take place on British soil, the Battle of Watling Street, during the British Revolt led by war queen Boudicca.

In the 80s A.D., noted Roman civil servant Pliny the Younger spent his six-month semester as a junior tribune peaceably with the 3rd Gallica Legion at Raphanaea in Syria, diligently conducting an audit of the base's financial records and finding significant discrepancies. Not many years later, Pliny used his influence to organize a *semestri tribunata* for the future biographer Suetonius on the staff of the governor of Britain, but Suetonius chose not to accept it, instead pursuing a career as a writer.

Constantine was keen to use the opportunity of his junior tribuneship to make a name for himself as a soldier, wielding a sword, not a pen; and in the fall of 293, Diocletian dispatched him to join Galerius at his capital, Antioch in Syria. There, Galerius was preparing for an Egyptian operation that would be launched in the new year. Late that fall, as Galerius marched down the Mediterranean coast from Antioch to Caesarea, the staging post for his operation, Constantine would have accompanied him.

At Caesarea, Alogius, a records clerk with Galerius's *Divine Comitatus* bodyguard—his Latin job title literally meant memory assistant—fell ill and was consigned to the hospital in Caesarea's legion barracks. Alogius remained in Caesarea following Galerius's departure, and on December 6 was issued with a government warrant to cover his rations until he recovered and caught up with Galerius in Egypt. Galerius reached Egypt by December 26, and Alogius rejoined the bodyguard shortly after, losing his papyrus ration certificate once in Egypt; it was found in modern times, in almost perfect condition.[23]

The Mediterranean sailing season would normally have been suspended for the winter. This fact, and the time taken to reach Egypt, indicate that when Galerius and Constantine left Caesarea that December, accompanied by Galerius's personal household and bodyguard troops, they traveled overland to Egypt, to base themselves at Alexandria until all the units assigned to Galerius's punitive operation came together there.

At the very same time that Constantine was heading for Egypt, on the other side of the Roman world in Gaul his father was also heading for war. In late 293, Constantius marched into Gaul with a Roman army made up of troops from the legions on the Rhine. Arriving outside Boulogne, he lay siege to the port, as Carausius's forces made a stand there. Setting his legionaries to work, Constantius built two earth dikes out into the English Channel, which, when they linked up, cut off the port from the sea.

Constantius was killing two birds with one proverbial stone—preventing the rebels from escaping by water, and preventing their resupply and reinforcement from Britain. Once surrounded, the rebels surrendered Boulogne. We know the identities of two of the legionary units that surrendered to Constantius—the entire 4th Flavia Legion and the cohorts of the 7th Claudia Legion that had gone over to Carausius here at Boulogne seven years earlier.

Once Constantius captured Boulogne, he would have executed the leading tribunes and centurions of the 4th Flavia and 7th Claudia, replacing them with officers from his own legions. He then ordered the 7th Claudia cohorts and several cohorts that he detached from the 4th Flavia to make their way across the empire to Egypt, to join Galerius's task force for the 294 campaign against the Egyptian rebels alongside cohorts from the 11th Claudia Legion, which were en route to Egypt from its base on the Danube.

We know this because papyri discovered in Egypt list vexillations from the 4th Flavia, 7th Claudia, and 11th Claudia taking part in Galerius's Egyptian campaign. The formerly rebellious legionaries would have marched from Boulogne to the Mediterranean coast to board ships that would take them across the sea to Alexandria come the spring. The remaining cohorts of the 4th Flavia Legion returned to the Danube and their old base at Singidunum, today's Belgrade in Serbia. All these troops' movements, which involved units from both the West and East of the Empire, would have required coordination by Constantius with Diocletian and Galerius in the East.

It is highly likely that the four Praetorian Guard cohorts that had gone over to Carausius back in 286 were also among the units that surrendered to Constantius at Boulogne. We know that Diocletian ordered the disbanding of several Praetorian cohorts during this period, and he had probably sent Constantius orders to disband the Praetorian cohorts that had gone over to Carausius once they fell into his hands. In that case, the 4,000 men of these four cohorts—Praetorian cohorts consisted of a thousand men, unlike legion cohorts, which contained 480 men—were discharged by Constantius, stripped of their arms and equipment, and left to their own devices to return home to their families in Italy.

Meanwhile, when news of the loss of Boulogne reached troops serving under Carausius in Britain, they revolted and assassinated him. But instead of returning their allegiance to Rome, they made Carausius's deputy Allectus their new leader and new emperor of Britain. Allectus, who held the post of Carausius's treasurer, had, according to legend, been a smith prior to his army service and personally made the sword he wore. Now, the blacksmith with pecuniary skills ruled Britain. But Carausius's short-lived empire had been primarily funded by plunder from Gaul, and with access to Gaul now cut off by Constantius's army, the only way that Allectus could pay for the continued loyalty of his troops was by plundering the Britons, which he proceeded to do.

Across the Channel, with Boulogne and Carausius's ships in his hands, Constantius ignored Britain for the moment. Instead, he secured his rear, over 294 to 296 systematically retaking northern Gaul from the Franks and defeating Alemanni German forces at the mouth of the Rhine, restoring Gaul to Roman control. His greatest success came after German tribes flooded across the frozen Rhine that winter of 293/294 to invade Batavia, which occupied the island formed by two branches of the Rhine on the great river's last leg to the sea.

When the ice thawed in the spring of 294, the Germans were isolated on the island, which Constantius surrounded with the light warships of Rome's Rhine Fleet. Constantius offered to allow the Germans to depart the island if they handed over part of their number, including men "of great nobility." The Germans drew lots to decide who surrendered to the Romans, before the remainder retreated back to where they had come from, taking to their tribes "the shameful news of their betrayal of their fellows," as an official who knew Constantius would record. The surrendered German prisoners are believed to have been settled by Constantius in southern Gaul.[24]

IN THE SUMMER OF 294, young novice bodyguard officer Constantine witnessed the legion cohorts sent from Gaul by Constantius and from the Danube by Diocletian assemble in Egypt as they joined deputy emperor Galerius's task force for the counteroffensive against Coptos and Boresis.

Back in the winter of 30/29 B.C., the Egyptian rebels had been defeated in fifteen days by the resident Roman prefect of Egypt, Gaius Cornelius Gallus. But here, now, Galerius, an outsider, seems to have been unaware that, like clockwork, the Nile River flooded between June and September every year, making the Nile Delta difficult to cross. In fact, the Egyptian name for the Nile, Ar, or Aur, meant "black," from the color of the river sediments that filled the annual floodwaters in the Delta.

As Galerius's force, made up of his bodyguard, auxiliary cavalry, and some 15,000 legionaries from the three European legions and the resident 3rd Cyrenaica Legion, marched southwest from Alexandria, they would have found the Delta awash with floodwaters. Following the initial flooding, land either side of the eight branches of the Lower Nile became marshland, and as the Roman troops slowly, warily advanced, Egyptian rebels, knowing the local terrain and conditions, would have harassed them with ease.

Biased early pro-Constantine sources such as Eusebius and Lactantius claimed that Galerius hated Constantine. This would assuredly be the case in later years, when the pair were direct rivals for power. But, those same sources claim, even when Constantine was a teenaged junior tribune in Galerius's mounted bodyguard, Galerius wanted him dead, and he now ordered the green, inexperienced Constantine to lead a cavalry charge through the marshland to break up the enemy force.

Seventeen years later, a member of Constantine's personal staff would state that Constantine gained fame as a result of his very first military campaign as a junior officer by "joining battle with the enemy even in an unusual engagement."[25] This unusual engagement was the charge through the Delta marshes. Even Eusebius would admit that, in his early military career, Constantine was rash and impulsive.[26] So it is highly likely that eager beaver Constantine volunteered to lead this charge, the first action of his military career, and Galerius happily agreed.

Constantine proceeded to turn the charge into a great victory. Soon, as the story spread that the teenage son of the Caesar of the West had earned himself glory in Egypt with the Caesar of the East, comparisons were spawned between Constantine and past heroes who had become conquering soldiers in their youth, men such as Alexander the Great and Pompey the Great.

Galerius put down the Egyptian revolt by February 295, after laying siege to the rebel cities. Once Coptos and Boresis fell, Galerius executed the populations and had their cities leveled, transferring the trading center from Coptos to a new city he created nearby, naming it Maximianopolis, after himself—his full name as Caesar was Gaius Galerius Valerius Maximianus. He had a fort built where Coptos had stood, stationing a detachment of resident Roman troops there.

The final defeat of the Egyptian rebels occurred after Constantine had completed his semester as a junior tribune. He would have gone home before the sailing season ended in October 294, heading back to Gaul and reuniting with Minervina, who fell pregnant to him, after which she went into confinement at Arles, where she would give birth in 295. Come the spring of 296, new father Constantine was on his way back to Nicomedia, to join the army full-time now that he was twenty, taking up an appointment as a military tribune with the mounted bodyguard of the emperor Diocletian, and to further his study.

IV

THE YOUNG WAR HERO

Through this period, in Gaul, Constantine's father had added to the ships he'd captured at Boulogne to create two invasion fleets, one based at Boulogne, the other near the mouth of the Seine River in Normandy. In all probability, Constantius bolstered his navy with Liburnians from the Rhine Fleet that had helped him humiliate the Germans at Batavia. Spring was the customary time for launching Roman military campaigns, and western emperor Maximian marched from Italy in the first half of 296 with an army whose role would be to cover the Rhine while Constantius did the heavy lifting in Britain.

This freed up Constantius to launch an amphibious operation against Allectus. Constantius's deputy for this operation was Maximian's new Praetorian prefect Julius Asclepiodotus. Of Greek heritage and a consul of Rome four years prior to this, Asclepiodotus had previously served as Praetorian prefect to three emperors—Aurelian, Probus, and Diocletian—and seems to have been foisted on Maximian by Diocletian. Constantius gave Asclepiodotus command of the southern invasion force at the Seine, with orders to land in the vicinity of today's Southampton, perilously close to Allectus's fleet, which was stationed at the Isle of Wight. At Boulogne, Constantius himself took charge of the northern landing force, with the Thames River and Allectus's capital, London, as his objective. It is highly likely that King Crocus and a force of his Alemanni, serving as Numeri in the Roman army, were part of Constantius's invasion force.

As both fleets set sail with the tide, the English Channel was flat calm but filled with a thick fog that severely reduced visibility. We do not know what month this was, but the presence of fog does not necessarily narrow it down—fog at Southampton is common in winter but can also manifest in August, in midsummer. This fog proved a barrier to Constantius's ships, which lost contact with each other and became separated. But to Asclepiodotus it proved a boon, enabling him to slip by the enemy fleet and land his troops near Southampton, probably at Calshot Beach.

Dividing his force into two divisions, giving the second division the task of cutting off the enemy's retreat, the prefect set out to find the foe. Allectus was in the vicinity and, learning of the landing, led his troops to counter the invasion. Running into one of Asclepiodotus's divisions in the fog, the rebel troops put up a brief fight before turning and running. Allectus fled along with his men. As he ran, he threw away his *cincticulus*, his insignia of rank—a knotted golden waistband that identified commanding generals. Near the town of Callevra Atrebatum, today's Silchester, Allectus and his men ran into Asclepiodotus's second division, and the second self-declared emperor of Britain died in a slaughter of his men.

Meanwhile, several ships from Constantius's fleet located the Thames in the fog, made their way upriver, and landed troops at London. There, leaderless Frankish mercenaries garrisoning the city surrendered. Once the fog cleared, Constantius's flagship pulled up beside the London wharf. The story goes that he was greeted by a crowd of Londoners, who, relieved to be rid of the depredations of the rebels, welcomed the deputy emperor with joy. According to one legend, the locals even took pieces of the sail and mast of the ship that had brought Constantius, as souvenirs. A medallion subsequently minted by Constantius to celebrate the event shows him riding victoriously into London after leaving his ship.

As for the Frankish prisoners taken in London, they were massacred. According to Geoffrey of Monmouth's *History of the Kings of Britain*, they were decapitated beside the Walbrook, the stream that ran through Roman London from north to south between Cornhill and Ludgate Hill, with their heads then tossed into the river. Hundreds of skulls were indeed found in the bed of the Walbrook in 1838, but these were subsequently dated to the second century—although no recorded second-century event at London explains why they ended up in the stream.

Constantius remained in Britain for several months after defeating Allectus. There he "restored what had been lost to those who had been despoiled" by Carausius and Allectus, and reorganized and put his stamp on the administration across Britannia as he installed new governors answerable to him. It is also possible that Constantius left Praetorian Prefect Asclepiodotus to govern a British province, or even put him in overall charge in Britain; we do not hear of him again. In Geoffrey of Monmouth's later mangled account, Asclepiodotus was a British-born king who ruled the island for ten years. Perhaps the truth of the matter was that Prefect Asclepiodotus indeed ruled in Britannia for a decade, as a Roman governor.[27]

As Constantius departed London, he left behind a number of small auxiliary units that he'd brought to Britain, including a Dalmatian cavalry formation. These newly introduced units were based in the hinterland south of Hadrian's Wall, as "a mobile reserve" in support of units on the wall itself. It is possible that King Crocus and his Alemanni similarly remained in Britain and were based south of Hadrian's Wall, to help combat incursions of the Picti from Scotland and to ensure that no new Carausius arose in the British provinces to threaten Roman control.[28]

Constantius returned most of the remaining troops who had followed Carausius and Allectus to their original bases. The three legions resident in Britain prior to the rebellion remained there, although the indications are that at least the 2nd Augusta was punished for its role, perhaps for too enthusiastically embracing the oppression of the Britons. It was reduced in status, substantially reduced in size, and posted to coastal defense duties at Richborough in Kent, where the unit would still be found a century later.[29]

That same year, 296, Constantius returned to Gaul. There he would be occupied for several years to come leading his troops against Germanic pushes across the Rhine, gaining several notable victories against the Alemanni and Franks. He finally conciliated the Franks by allowing numbers of them to settle in the rural areas of Gaul that had been depopulated by the Bacaudae Revolt.

IN THE EAST, Constantius's son Constantine was paying less attention to his studies than his father would have liked. At Nicomedia, a city with a population exceeded only by Rome, Alexandria, and Antioch, and endowed by Diocletian with grand buildings—imperial palace, drama theater, amphitheater, hippodrome, temples, and basilicas—Constantine the military tribune begrudgingly used his spare time to attend lectures in Greek, literature, and rhetoric or public speaking.

Constantine's low-born father Constantius clearly regretted that he could not speak Greek, and wanted his son to become fluent in the language of classical authors, educated Romans and emperors, and the Roman civil service. But Constantine showed little interest in literature and acquired only a passing acquaintance with Greek, which he would never be able to read, write, or speak fluently. Constantine's focus was on military skills and horsemanship, in which he excelled. He undertook his "military service in the ordinary way," says the orator of 307, "passing through the various stages of a military career."[30]

However, the ordinary course for a young tribune was to serve with the legions and then hold a command with several auxiliary units before taking command of a legion. Tribune Constantine remained with Diocletian's bodyguard for the next several years, and while he attained the rank of first-class tribune he was not promoted to prefect or given a field army command of his own. Under Diocletian's army reforms, prefects, who, like tribunes, were members of the Equestrian Order, now commanded legions. In the system established by Augustus three centuries earlier, a more senior officer, a member of the Senatorial Order with the rank of legatus, or legate, had held legion command.

The fact that Constantine remained in Diocletian's bodyguard—despite the glorious reputation gained from his exploits in combat to date—is suggested by some writers as a desire by Diocletian to either shackle or protect the young man. And knowing the reckless nature Constantine showed in his youth, it was possibly the latter.

However, Diocletian was no shrinking violet when it came to campaigning to protect his empire's borders, and when he went to war, Constantine went with him. While Constantine's father was dealing with Allectus and his rebels in Britain in A.D. 296, that same summer his son is believed to have been a member of Diocletian's mounted bodyguard when the emperor did battle with, and soundly defeated, Sarmatians of the Carpi tribe on the Danube. Natives of Dacia, the Carpi were demanding the right to settle in Roman territory south of the river.

According to Eusebius, a mounted Constantine grabbed a Sarmatian leader by the leg, dragged him off, and dumped him at his emperor's feet. This is likely to have occurred during this 296 campaign, not later as some writers suggest.[31]

Meanwhile, in the East, Narseh, new king of the Persians, had abandoned his late father's policy of conciliating the Romans, and invaded Roman Mesopotamia. Diocletian's deputy Galerius subsequently led Roman troops to a defeat at the hands of the Persians, which led to Diocletian humiliating Galerius in the Syrian capital Antioch before sending him back against King Narseh with reinforcements, primarily from legions on the Danube.

Constantine was now released from Diocletian's bodyguard to command a cavalry unit among these reinforcements sent to Galerius in the spring of 298. Galerius, a cattle herder as a youth in Dacia—from which he'd gained the unflattering nickname of the Herdsman—had risen to power via a career as an indomitable soldier. Trusting only men he'd grown up with, and, furious with his master Diocletian's treatment in Antioch, Galerius would have been particularly suspicious of confident young Constantine being foisted back on him from Diocletian's personal staff.

To outwit the Persians, Galerius this time marched into their territory via Armenia. In a surprise attack, Galerius was able to take King Narseh's camp, complete with his wife, harem, and treasury, before marching south to the Persian capital, Ctesiphon, and to gaze on the ruins of Babylon. As a result of Galerius's campaign, Narseh sued for peace in 299, with the subsequent negotiations resulting in the cessation of hostilities and Persian surrender of territory to Rome.

A legend from this period has Galerius pitting Constantine against a lion in single combat. If true, Galerius may have dared Constantine to go against a lion on horseback in the arena as part of victory celebrations in Antioch in 299. Rash young Constantine was to repeatedly dive into perilous circumstances on the spur of the moment, so accepting such a dare would have been as natural as breathing to him. And of course, as with all good heroic legends, the story has Constantine surviving the encounter and dispatching the lion.

Constantine, aged twenty-five in A.D. 299, a daring, dashing young war hero and a popular favorite at Diocletian's court, still had much to experience before his appointment with destiny at the Milvian Bridge thirteen years later.

V

THE GREAT
PERSECUTION

ETWEEN THEM, BY LATE A.D. 299, eastern emperor Diocletian,
western emperor Maximian, and their deputies Constantius and Galerius had regained Gaul and Britain and succeeded in securing the Roman
Empire's borders on the Rhine and the Danube and east of the Euphrates,
with decisive military campaigns. The Roman Empire was in a rare state
of peace.

At Antioch, capital of the province of Syria, Galerius joined his emperor
Diocletian as the pair officiated at sacrifices of thanks at a temple. This was
possibly Antioch's hilltop Temple of Jupiter Capitolinus—Jupiter was Diocletian's patron deity—or the Temple of the Pythian Apollo at Daphne, a
religious sanctuary four miles west of Antioch considered an appendage
of the great city. At Daphne, location of the first-century death of Roman
hero Germanicus Caesar, Diocletian had constructed a companion sanctuary to the sprawling garden of Apollo, an underground grotto dedicated
to Hecate, goddess of light and protector of the household.

Now, in the presence of Diocletian and Galerius, the chief haruspex
conducting the sacrifice declared that after repeated attempts he was
unable to read the entrails of the sacrificial animals to offer auspicious signs
for the future, blaming the presence of Christians. According to Bishop

Eusebius of Caesarea, writing several decades later, these Christians had made the sign of the cross during the sacrifices. For at least a century, Christians had used their right thumb to discreetly make the sign of the cross on their foreheads. "We Christians wear out our foreheads with the sign of the cross," joked Christian writer Tertullian in Carthage early in the third century.[32]

Up to this point, Diocletian had tolerated members of this sect, who, incidentally, had first gained their "Christian" appellation in Antioch, as a derogatory term imposed by critics. The last emperor to act against Christians had been Valerian. Over 257–258, he had issued a series of edicts banning Christians from their places of collective worship and requiring Christian senators and equites to sacrifice to Roman gods on pain of exile, or, after repeated refusal to sacrifice, execution. With Valerian's capture by the Syrians, anti-Christian measures had been abandoned by his son and successor Gallienus. Prior to Valerian, the emperor Trajan Decius had, in 249, ordered Christians to be tested on the rack for their faith, only for that practice to cease shortly after, with his death.

Diocletian's toleration would have had much to do with the fact that his wife Prisca and daughter Valeria were, according to Lactantius, Christians. A small number of Christians served on Diocletian's personal staff, and others were employed by Diocletian as tutors at Nicomedia; Constantine had likely attended lectures by some of them. But Diocletian's deputy Galerius had no time for the Christian sect's members. No doubt he was influenced in this by his mother, Romula, a onetime priestess at a Roman temple in Dacia. Galerius adored his mother, renaming his Dacian birthplace Felix Romulana in her honor.

But Galerius's dislike of Christians had less to do with religious beliefs than a fear that the organized Christian Church represented a threat to stable imperial government. While the members of other Roman sects observed Roman law, Galerius was concerned that Christians "made laws unto themselves . . . and collect various peoples in diverse places in congregations." Christians, to him, represented a subversive threat to the emperor's power and wishes, and Diocletian was now beginning to agree.[33]

To flush out Christians who might hinder the efficient workings of the state, Diocletian, irritated by apparent Christian interference in sacrifices, now followed Valerian's lead by ordering all members of his staff and all members of the military throughout the empire to make ritual sacrifices to

Rome's gods. Those who failed to do so would lose their jobs. According to Lactantius, even Diocletian's wife Prisca and his daughter Valeria, wife of Galerius, were made to perform sacrifices against their will.

This brief anti-Christian storm passed. Many Christians, even bishops, apparently performed pagan sacrifices to escape punishment, but within several years Christian bishops would implement a policy whereby any baptized Christian who was known to have sacrificed to pagan gods to avoid persecution would only be granted admission to the Christian congregation after a long period of penance—in some cases a lifetime of penance.

The next few years were, for Diocletian, and apparently also for his senior bodyguard officer Constantine, filled with travel. Over the winter of 301/302, Diocletian visited Egypt, basing himself in Alexandria for several months and officiating at the doling out of a grain allowance to needy citizens. Constantine accompanied the emperor on this trip. Eusebius of Caesarea, then a Christian presbyter, or elder, in his home city, would later recall seeing Constantine standing to the emperor's immediate right in Caesarea during this trip, and looking conspicuous by his size and presence. This was most likely as Diocletian received an address of welcome from Roman dignitaries, with Caesarea a stopover for the emperor's fleet going to and returning from Alexandria on this 301/302 sojourn.

While in Alexandria, Diocletian had dealt with a religious sect called the Manicheans, which was disrupting Roman religious life in Egypt. The Manicheans were adherents of the third-century Parthian priest and self-proclaimed prophet Mani (A.D. 216–274), whose influences included the teachings of Jesus Christ. With a decree issued at the end of March, Diocletian ordered the extinction of this new sect, with the result that Manichean scriptures were burned, low-status disciples of Mani were executed by the sword, and higher-status Manicheans were sent to quarries and mines.

By the autumn of 302, Diocletian and Constantine had returned to Nicomedia via Antioch. Late in the year, Romanus, a deacon of the Christian church in Nicomedia, Diocletian's capital, interrupted sacrificial preparations at a Nicomedian temple, loudly decrying traditional religious practices. Romanus was arrested, and a judge sentenced him to death by fire, but Diocletian commuted his sentence—Romanus was cast into prison, after his offending tongue had been cut out.

Diocletian's deputy Galerius was unhappy with this reduced punishment, arguing with the emperor and declaring that all Christians should be burned to death. To settle the matter of what to do with the Christians, over the winter of 302/303 the pair sent an envoy to the oracle of Apollo in Didyma for heavenly guidance. Located just outside the Ionian city of Miletus on the west coast of today's Turkey, this oracle's past clients had included Alexander the Great and the Roman emperors Trajan and Hadrian.

Roman writers of the first century A.D. half joked that the several oracles of Apollo throughout Greece and Asia Minor had shown a tendency to predict an early doom for notable figures such as the emperor Nero and Germanicus Caesar, father of Caligula and brother of Claudius, when they consulted them. In both cases, an early doom had certainly followed. The best known of the oracles of Apollo was at Delphi in western Greece, whose prophesies were famously cryptic. It was that oracle, 850 years before the application by Diocletian and Galerius to the oracle at Didyma, that King Croesus, the fabulously rich ruler of the Lydian Empire in Asia Minor, had asked whether he should go to war with Cyrus, founder of the Persian Empire. The oracle had replied that if he did so, a great empire would fall. Based on this, Croesus had launched his war against the Persians, and sure enough, a great empire did fall—Croesus's own.

Young Constantine would later recall that he was at the palace in Nicomedia with Diocletian when the envoy returned from Didyma in early 303, bringing a response from the oracle of Didyma. The messenger also brought news that the leading people of Miletus were complaining that Christians had set up residence outside Apollo's huge temple at Didyma, the fourth-largest Greek temple in the world, and were interfering with, and discouraging, pilgrims who came to Miletus to walk the twelve-mile-long Sacred Way to Didyma to seek the help of Apollo. The thousands of annual pilgrims attracted to the shrine every year were a boon to the economy and prestige of Miletus, whose businesspeople were incensed by the Christian interference.

Not only was Apollo a god of war, he was the god of sun and light, the god of healing and protection, the god overseeing truth and prophesy. Apollo's link with prophesy went back to an ancient Greek myth in which he had killed the giant serpent Python guarding the Castalian Spring at Delphi. Apollo had subsequently stood guard while a prophetess gave out her prophesies as she inhaled vapors from an open chasm near the spring. And so it was that Apollo was believed to continue to protect and guide the priestesses delivering prophesies at sacred springs such as that at Didyma.

Usually, the prophetess serving as Apollo's intermediary at Didyma fasted for three days beside the sacred spring in the temple complex before verbally giving answers to pilgrims' questions. Priests wrote down the answers, which often took the form of riddles, in verse form, then passed them on to the supplicants, who paid for the privilege via a donation to the temple. But the priests of the Temple of Apollo at Didyma had told the imperial envoy that the prophetess was unable to provide an answer to the question from Diocletian and Galerius, due to "the righteous on earth." Diocletian subsequently confided to Constantine, who later told Bishop Eusebius, that he interpreted these interfering self-righteous men to be Christians.

For centuries, Rome had not only tolerated the worship of foreign gods, it had brought those gods into its own pantheon, often identifying new deities with existing Roman gods and fostering their cults. Only the Jews, with their insistence on the existence of just a single god, had defied that policy, and under different emperors Jews had at times been banned from Rome. Yet Jews had not prevented Romans from worshipping their own gods. Jews had merely sought to observe their own faith unmolested. Never before had adherents of a foreign cult actively interfered in the religious observances of pious Romans.

Diocletian was furious that Christians had crossed the boundary of acceptable behavior by preventing a Roman emperor from receiving the guidance of Apollo. Goaded by Galerius, on February 23, day of the Terminalia, feast of Terminus, Roman god of boundaries, Diocletian acted to terminate Christian interference in Roman religious observance. He began by calling in his Praetorian prefect and giving him explicit orders concerning the recently built Christian church in Nicomedia, which overlooked Diocletian's palace.

According to Lactantius, who was living and working in Nicomedia just prior to this, "The prefect went to the church with generals, tribunes, and accountants." While the accountants compiled a list of the church's valuables, the officers burned its holy books. It is highly likely that Constantine was among the tribunes in this party. Troops of the imperial bodyguard were then sent into the church. First confiscating the contents, the soldiers then razed the building to the ground, stone by stone.[34]

There was more to follow. The very next day, February 24, 303, Diocletian and Galerius issued a joint *Edict Against the Christians*. This banned Christians from gathering in their places of worship or in cemeteries for funerals, and decreed the confiscation of Christian churches and the burning of their holy books. Senators, members of the Equestrian Order, city decurions, and soldiers who professed Christianity were to be deprived of their rank, and Christian imperial freedmen were to be returned to slavery. But, Diocletian added, perhaps influenced by his Christian wife and daughter, this was all to be done without bloodshed.

In addition to eventually being distributed to every provincial governor in the East, this edict was sent to eestern emperor Maximian in Milan, who circulated it throughout the Western Empire via his deputy Constantius and provincial governors. As Christianity had first taken root in the East, the congregation there was larger than in the West. There, too, the first dedicated church buildings had begun to be built around 230, with fewer church structures existing in western provinces. There were then none at all in Britain.

Edward Gibbon estimated that by this time, 5 percent of the population across the entire Roman Empire had embraced Christianity. In the second century, the faith had been strongest among slaves, former slaves, and women. Over the following two hundred years, Christianity had spread into the Roman civil service, and, to a lesser degree, into the army. But even by 303, the number of avowed Christians in influential posts was small, and the number among Diocletian's staff even smaller.[35]

Within fifteen days of the anti-Christian edict, two fires had broken out in Diocletian's palace at Nicomedia, one in his bedroom. Despite a thorough investigation, the causes could not be ascertained. Lactantius would credit the fires to "lightning and divine wrath," while Eusebius expressed ignorance of the cause.[36] Constantine himself later wrote that "it was kindled by the malice of Galerius," being convinced that the deputy emperor had instigated the fires to cast blame on the Christians.[37]

According to Christian sources, four members of Diocletian's staff suffered as a result of the February edict, probably charged with lighting the fires. Eusebius and Lactantius say that Peter, a eunuch at the Nicomedian palace and one of Diocletian's personal chamberlains, refused to sacrifice to Rome's gods and was arrested and tortured. Peter's superior, the eunuch Dorotheus, and Gorgoneus, a soldier of the imperial bodyguard, both protested his treatment. This pair was executed, along with another imperial servant named Midgonius.[38]

Christian tradition has the latter three victims receiving a quick death on or about March 12, with all three beheaded, as was the right of Roman citizens. Peter, apparently not a citizen, was burned alive, suggesting a link with the fires at the palace. The same fate was suffered by an unidentified Christian who ripped down the edict when it was first posted on the public notice board in Nicomedia's forum. Although only Peter identified himself as Christian, the Church fathers, assuming Dorotheus and Gorgoneus were also Christians, would later make saints of all three. Some authors claim that Anthimus, Bishop of Nicomedia, was also executed that spring, although his death seems to have come in 311 or 312.

Historian Gibbon felt that only one senior member of Diocletian's staff perished for being an unrepentant Christian during the Great Persecution, as it became known—Adaucus, Treasurer of the Private Estates, who managed Diocletian's extensive personal properties and landholdings throughout the Empire. Gibbon also tells of the recorded fate during this time of much of the population of a small, unnamed town in Phrygia, a landlocked district some distance southeast of Nicomedia. Several hundred at most, these people refused to sacrifice to the old gods. When troops were sent by the provincial governor to deal with them, the people locked themselves in their church. The troops subsequently burned the church to the ground, with the Christians inside. Today, the Eastern Orthodox Church claims this massacre involved twenty thousand victims and took place in the church in Nicomedia. However, no classical account supports this, and according to Lactantius, the Nicomedian church had already been demolished by this time.

Historian Gibbon had his doubts about the veracity of Eusebius and Lactantius, especially when they told lurid tales of heinous crimes committed by Rome's pagan emperors against Christians. "What degree of credit," asked Gibbon, himself a devout Christian, "can be assigned to a courtly bishop [Eusebius] and a passionate disclaimer [Lactantius], who, under the protection of Constantine, enjoyed the exclusive privilege of recording the persecutions inflicted on the Christians by the vanquished rivals or disregarded predecessors of their gracious sovereign?"

Gibbon, in his *Decline and Fall*, declared that Eusebius quite deliberately bent the truth and was prepared to repeat any rumor that reflected badly on pagan Romans, while hiding the less edifying acts of Christians. Later academics would support Gibbon's view, among them noted nine-teenth-century Swiss historian Jacob Burckhardt, himself the son of a clergyman, who railed against Eusebius's "contemptible inventions" and described Eusebius as "the first thoroughly dishonest historian of antiqui-ty."[39] In fact, both Lactantius, who displayed a woeful knowledge of the scriptures in his writings, and Eusebius were dismissed by the Church and labeled heretics up until the Middle Ages, when their fictions were adopted by Church zealots and flat-earth proponents.

W. H. C. Frend, in *The Rise of Christianity* in 1984, estimated that between 3,000 and 3,500 Christians died in the Great Persecution. Other authors believe this to have been the entire number of Christian martyrs killed for their faith over three hundred years between the first and fourth centuries. Yuval Noah Harari, in *Sapiens: A Brief History of Mankind*, wrote, in 2014, "It turns out that in these three centuries, the polytheistic Romans killed no more than a few thousand Christians."

To this day, the Vatican treats Rome's Colosseum as a shrine to Chris-tian martyrs, yet no records exist to confirm the oft-quoted claim that eighty thousand Christians were condemned to die in the Colosseum for their faith. In fact, while the occasional Christian must have been con-demned to the beasts in the Colosseum over the centuries for capital crimes along with thousands of non-Christians, as British classical histo-rians Mary Beard and Keith Hopkins point out, not one Christian is on record being sent there for professing their faith. And we can be certain that no Christian was killed in the Colosseum during the emperor Nero's infamous purge following the A.D. 64 Great Fire of Rome, because the Colosseum would not be built for another seventeen years.[40]

Despite the deaths of numerous notable martyrs being attributed by Christian writers to Diocletian's colleague Maximian, emperor of the West, the persecution in his half of the Empire was mild compared to that in the East. Despite this, in the sixteenth century, Maximian's reputation as a Christian-hater reached its peak with self-proclaimed English "marty-rologist" John Foxe publishing three volumes of lurid and highly fictional deaths of Christian martyrs and claiming that Maximian was among the most bloody of the persecutors.[41]

American author John Watts de Peyster, writing a defense of British "emperor" Carausius in 1858, claimed without evidence that seventeen thousand Christians died at Maximian's command. Watts de Peyster listed six prominent Christian saints who, he said, were executed by Maximian during the Great Persecution; however, of these, four—Christyne, Fey (Faith), Fabian, and Sebastian—are known to have actually died the previous century, prior to Diocletian's persecution.

Another listed by Watts de Peyster, Saint Alban, is believed to have died in Britain either in the third century but prior to Diocletian's reign, or in 304—in which case it would have under the auspices of Constantine's father Constantius. The very existence of some, even all, of these martyrs, including Alban, is questioned by some modern historians.[42]

Similarly, following the edict of Diocletian and Galerius, the later tales originating centuries after the fact of Christian persecution in North Africa, which came under Maximian's direct control, are riddled with colorful but questionable examples of gruesome, often sadistic tortures and executions. Gaius Annius Anullius, the Roman proconsul of Africa appointed by Maximian who served there between 302 and 305, is said by much later Christian writers to have ordered the executions of numerous Christian martyrs, such as Felix, Bishop of Thubiuca and four members of his congregation, condemned for refusing to hand over Christian scriptures for burning. Closer examination of Felix's story shows that a local magistrate was responsible for their sentencing.

Anullius is also blamed for the deaths of the so-called Forty-Nine Martyrs of Abitinae, who are said to have assembled for worship even after their bishop, Fundanus, had handed over the church's scriptures for burning. Saint Ambrose, much of whose writing would later be contested, would a century later attribute the martyrdom of Saint Crispina in Africa to Anullius. John Foxe, writing the tale of the executions of the Three Virgins of Taburga—the canonized Maxima, Donatilia, and Secunda—also blamed Anullius, even though the trio is recorded as having died in 257, which was most likely before Anullius was even born. Saint Perpetua, yet another supposed victim of Anullius, died in 203, a century before Anullius's term; her story became known via a book, purporting to be her diary, published anonymously centuries later by inventive Christian sources.

Anullius seems to have been slandered by Christian historians, especially when we know that monuments honoring Anullius' public service were raised by local communities in Africa, where Anullius's family originated, and that Constantine, once he took Rome, would give Anullius several senior appointments, including a return to Africa as governor in 313–314, during which time Constantine referred to him in several letters as "most esteemed Anullius," a term he did not apply to others.[43] Would Constantine, who was by that time favoring the Christian community, have sent Anullius back to Africa if the man had a reputation as a slayer of Christians during his last posting there? Certainly, there is no record of the bishops of Africa complaining about Anullius's return, yet they are on record via Constantine's extant letters being most vocal in their complaints to the emperor on other Church matters.

There can be no doubt that some local Roman officials enthusiastically enforced the *Edict Against the Christians*, but both Maximian and senior appointees such as Anullius seem to have done the minimum to satisfy the edict, requiring sacrifices to the gods and burning of Christian scriptures. Indeed, following the first edict of Diocletian and Galerius, Maximian did not even circulate the pair's two subsequent edicts concerning measures against Christians in his western half of the empire.

Meanwhile, it is believed that, under orders from Maximian, Marcellinus, the Bishop of Rome, sacrificed to the Roman gods. Bishop Marcellinus died the following year, apparently from natural causes. Despite his having apparently sacrificed to Roman gods, Marcellinus would be made a saint by the Church. With the Bishop of Rome's death, Maximian banned the election of a successor, and the post fell vacant.

Diocletian did not escape the martyrologists. His mausoleum at Split would be incorporated into a Catholic cathedral named for Saint Domnius, a Dalmatian bishop who was canonized for supposedly being executed for his faith by Diocletian in 304, despite Domnius having lived in the first century. Then there is the case of Saint Pancras. According to Christian legend, the fourteen-year-old Pancras was brought before Diocletian at Rome in May 303, and after refusing to sacrifice to the gods was condemned by Diocletian to decapitation. But Diocletian was only in Rome over November–December 303, and children did not make sacrifices. Plus, according to the Saint Pancras legend, Bishop Cornelius was Bishop of Rome at the time of Pancras's death in 303, but Cornelius had ceased to be bishop in 253.

Neither Eusebius nor Lactantius would accuse Maximian's deputy Constantius of persecuting Christians in any form, giving the impression that he even failed to implement the first edict. But when this pair was writing, Constantine, son of Constantius, was their emperor and patron, and they were not going to antagonize him by accusing his father of crimes against the Christians. So we do not know with any certainty whether or not Constantius participated in the persecution of Christians. We do know that, unlike Diocletian, neither Constantius nor Constantine employed known Christians on their staff during this period.

As regards Christian influence on father and son, there is the matter of Constantius's first wife Helena, Constantine's mother, to consider. Eusebius stated that Constantine converted his mother to Christianity after he became emperor. Gibbon and other historians believe this to be pure propaganda, to give Constantine the credit as the Christianizing influence, and that it was the other way round. They suggest that Helena was probably a Christian long before her son came to the throne, as were other women in the imperial family. Helena was certainly a far more outwardly devout Christian than her son in later years, and it is entirely possible that Helena was at the very least a restraining hand on her former husband and her son when it came to their dealings with Christians.

Eusebius, writing Constantine's biography after the emperor's death, when Constantine was not around to correct or admonish him, claimed that Constantine's father was a covert Christian who pretended to worship the old gods, and that he influenced Constantine's conversion to Christianity. Against this we have the statement by Constantine's nephew, the erudite future emperor Julian, that all previous members of his line including Constantius had been adherents of the god Sol Invictus, the Unconquerable Sun. This is supported by a remark from a speech delivered at Constantine's 307 wedding, the year following Constantius's passing, in which the orator speaks of Sol reaching out from heaven for Constantius as the emperor lay on his deathbed.[44] Certainly, Constantius's coinage occasionally depicted Sol, along with Hercules—or, more often, Victoria, goddess of victory. Minor female deities also appeared on his coins, among them Moneta, Concordia, and Providentia.

The most substantive evidence of his son Constantine's religious affiliation during this period comes from the coins Constantine issued once he was Caesar. Minted at Trier, Arles, and London between 307 and 312, these declared the war god Mars to be Constantine's protecting deity. Mars would still be appearing on Constantine's coinage in 317, following a significant military victory. There was good reason for Constantine to have adopted Mars as his patron god from an early age—February 27, Constantine's birthday, was the date of the Equirria, the first of two major annual religious festivals on the Roman calendar that were dedicated to Mars. It was only after 312 that Sol Invictus started to regularly appear on Constantine's coinage.

The Sol sect had originated with the Syrian sun god Elagabalus, who had a temple at Emesa in Syria housing a sacred black meteor. Syrian legionaries, notably the men of the 3rd Gallica Legion, traditionally worshipped Elagabalus, and their pay was minted at the temple in Emesa. The meteor was transferred to Rome by the young emperor Elagabalus, who was himself named for the sun god, and whose family traditionally provided the cult's high priest. To house the meteor, the boy emperor built a large new temple in Rome, the Elagabalum, on the northeastern corner of the Palatine Hill in the Palatium, the palace complex that occupied the hill.

Following the death of Elagabalus in 222, the sect lost official favor. The black meteor was returned to Emesa and the emperor Severus Alexander rededicated the sun god's Palatine temple to Jupiter. Elagabalus had eschewed the Palatine as his imperial Roman residence, instead favoring the Sessorium, or Sessorian Palace. This complex on the Via Labicana outside the Servian Wall east of Rome had been commenced by Septimius Severus and completed by Elagabalus, who expanded it into the sprawling Varian Gardens owned by Elagabalus's father, Sextus Varius Marcellus. Because the gardens also contained an ancient temple dedicated to Spes, the goddess of hope, which dated back to 477 B.C., they were colloquially known as the Gardens of Old Hope.

The Sessorium complex, later built into the Aurelian Wall so that it came within the protection of the city's outer defenses, also included a vast country villa, an amphitheater, and a private hippodrome. That hippodrome, the Circus Varianus, was where young Elagabalus loved to compete against the best charioteers of his day. The Sessorium also featured a small temple to Elagabalus's sun god. Half a century after Elagabalus's death, on December 25, 274, the day of the deity's annual feast, the emperor Aurelian made worship of the sun god Sol Invictus an official Roman cult alongside all other cults.

In the East, while only a handful of Diocletian's staff fell victim to the crackdown on Christians, perhaps others in his favor had gotten wind of the crackdown and left their posts. This certainly seems to have been the case with Lactantius, who was able to leave his teaching post in the city by the time of the persecution program and go into seclusion, where he penned several Christian books, such as *The Works of God*, which was written between 303 and 304, dedicating the work to Demetrianus, a Christian and former student of his who most likely hid and supported him through this period.

Six years after the anti-Christian edict of Diocletian and Galerius, Constantine would appoint Lactantius tutor in Latin to his son Crispus in Gaul. Many historians believe that Constantine had attended Lactantius's lectures on rhetoric in Nicomedia, and it is not impossible that Constantine subsequently slipped his former tutor a warning about Diocletian's coming crackdown on Christians, allowing him to go into hiding. With the Christian problem seemingly dealt with, Diocletian moved on, heading west for a spring military campaign; and while there is no record of it, there is every reason to believe that Constantine, by this stage a senior tribune in the mounted imperial bodyguard, traveled with his emperor as Diocletian headed for the Danube.

In June, Diocletian was locked in a campaign with the ever-troublesome Carpi on the Danube. But, feeling increasingly unwell, he was no longer riding and was being carried everywhere in a litter. The pain and discomfort of his condition probably contributed to his irritation with Christians, for that summer he issued two more edicts against them. One ordered the arrest and imprisonment of troublesome Christian clerics, while the second, seemingly an afterthought, or perhaps again driven by Diocletian's wife, authorized the release of these men if they performed traditional sacrifices to the Roman gods. These latest edicts were only circulated in the East.

Throughout this period of Christian persecution, young Constantine neither did nor said anything that indicated he favored Christianity, and he certainly never overtly helped persecuted Christians. Constantine's biographer Eusebius wrote that Diocletian kept Constantine in his retinue as a hostage to Constantius's loyalty. Diocletian clearly liked the affable young man, confiding in him more than once, but Constantine would have been on his guard so as not to do or say anything that jeopardized his father's position.

Come the autumn of A.D. 303, Diocletian joined his imperial colleague Maximian and his deputy Galerius on a rare visit to Rome, and there is every reason to believe that Constantine, as an officer of his bodyguard, accompanied him. All were there to celebrate Diocletian's *vicennalia,* the twentieth anniversary of his reign, and the *decannalia,* the tenth anniversary of the Tetrarchy, of which Constantine's father was a member. As part of those celebrations, the imperial party enjoyed the street parade and circus games of a Triumph for the victory over the Persians, with Diocletian claiming Galerius's ultimate success against King Narseh as his own. On December 20, offended by the lack of reverence shown to him by the people of Rome, Diocletian cut short his stay in the city and set off for Ravenna, where he spent the early part of the new year before returning to Nicomedia.

Almost a year later, on November 20, 304, on the latest anniversary of his reign, Diocletian appeared in public for the first time in many months, for the opening of a new hippodrome beside his palace in Nicomedia. Those who saw him were shocked: as a result of a mysterious illness, which was likely to have been cancer, he had lost so much weight and was so emaciated that he was almost unrecognizable. The end of an era was fast approaching, and Constantine's time in the spotlight was near at hand.

VI

THE ROAD TO POWER
BEGINS IN BRITAIN

IN THE EAST AND IN THE WEST, history-making ceremonies were
taking place at the two capitals of the Roman Empire on the same day.
It was May 1, in the year 305, and two emperors were voluntarily abdicat-
ing and going into retirement, an event that was unprecedented in Roman
history. Diocletian's illness had deprived him of the strength to carry on,
and he had convinced his co-emperor Maximian that they should step
down together.

Not that Maximian needed much convincing; effectively sidelined by
Diocletian's dictating military decisions in his western half of the empire
and giving significant responsibility to Constantius, Maximian had been
taking lengthy breaks at his country villa in Italy over the past few years,
and this would become his retirement home. Diocletian had prepared his
own retirement place and mausoleum, a massive palace beside the Adriatic
outside the town of Spalatum. Today's Croatian city of Split would grow
around Diocletian's palace, which stands to this day.

The first day of May was the day when Roman priests annually celebrated the rites of the Lares Praestites, guardian spirits of Rome, and this
same day Diocletian and Maximian conducted formal public handover
ceremonies in their respective capitals, with Diocletian to be succeeded

as emperor by his Caesar, Galerius, and Maximian to be succeeded by his Caesar, Constantius, as per the succession plan established at the creation of the Tetrarchy. In the ceremony at Nicomedia, Diocletian anointed Galerius as his successor and called upon Galerius's chosen Caesar to remove the purple cloak of the Augustus from his shoulders and drape the garment over the shoulders of Galerius.

It had been long been widely assumed that, as neither Diocletian nor Galerius had a son old enough to become Caesar, Constantine and Maxentius, the sons of Constantius and Maximian, would fill that role in the new Tetrarchy. With this expectation, in Nicomedia, says Lactantius, all eyes turned to young Constantine, who stood on the dais with Diocletian, Galerius, and other officials, expecting him to perform the cloak transfer as Galerius' newly appointed Caesar.

Instead, another man stepped forward—Daia, thirty-four-year-old nephew of Galerius, who had the same Dacian birthplace and background as his uncle. Newly adopted by Galerius as his son and taking the new name Galerius Valerius Maximinus, although he would continue to be known as Daia by contemporaries, he was now Caesar of the East. And it was Daia who performed the cloak transfer that anointed Galerius as the new Augustus, and emperor of the East.

Similarly, in Milan, it was not Maximian's son Maxentius who stepped forward as new Caesar of the West, it was Flavius Valerius Severus, a noted general and close friend of Galerius. Clearly, Galerius had worked on the increasingly frail Diocletian and persuaded him to sideline Constantine and Maxentius and instead appoint his own loyal lackeys as Caesars of the East and West. This gave Galerius power across the empire and undermined the authority of Constantius, his new fellow emperor in the West. When Diocletian went into retirement at Split, he sent his Christian wife Prisca to live at Galerius's court with their daughter Valeria, Galerius's wife. There, she could be watched over by the likes of Galerius's anti-Christian mother Romula.

The sidelined Constantine knew that Galerius, who kept him close at his court, was far from his friend. In fact, Constantine's father Constantius clearly feared for his son's life, for in the late spring he sent Galerius a polite request for Constantine to be sent to join him for a campaign north of Hadrian's Wall in Britain. Galerius turned down the request. So Constantine waited until Galerius had had too much to drink at dinner one night, then told the new emperor that he'd just learned that his father was very ill and sought permission to go to him. Whether Constantine was aware that the founder of the Persian Empire, Cyrus the Great, had used the same ploy to escape the King of Media and join his father nine hundred years before is unknown. But in both cases, the ploy worked. The merry Galerius agreed. And Constantine departed at once.

Constantine traveled alone. Of his wife Minervina and young son Crispus, we hear nothing. Crispus was possibly still at Arles in southern France, his birthplace, or at Trier. As for Minervina, she disappeared from the record after Crispus's birth. It is possible she had died in childbirth—sadly, a common fate for many women in ancient times.

The fleeing Constantine traveled aboard a carriage of the government courier system, the *Cursus Publicus Velox*, sitting beside the driver. Originally known as "the state's very fast runner," the Fast Public Way had been established by Rome's first emperor, Augustus. This organization, known colloquially as the state posting service, used fast, four-wheeled, two-horse carriages carrying government mail between staging posts set along Roman highways from one end of the empire to the other. With imperial permission, a high-status passenger could travel beside the Cursus driver—Pliny the Younger's wife had done so when Pliny was governor of Bithynia-Pontus in the second century.

To be sure that no message from Galerius cancelling his permission to travel overtook him, Constantine took preventative action at each Cursus station on his route, hobbling every horse in the stable apart from those used for his carriage's change of steeds—forty horses per posting station was the norm. Via the Cursus, Constantine would have travelled fifty miles a day, and the speed with which he reached Boulogne amazed all of Gaul when they learned of his journey.

"You did not seem to have traveled by the state posting service but to have flown on some divine chariot," a member of Constantine's staff would remark to him several years later. The arrival of the popular young prince "lit up the fleet, which was already setting sail," according to the same source.[45]

Eusebius of Caesarea, writing his *Life of Constantine* decades later, stated that Constantine's father was on his deathbed when he reached him, with all of Constantius's other children gathered around him. No modern historian accepts this. For reasons that will shortly be made clear, all agree that Constantine linked up with his father at Boulogne and together they sailed for Britain aboard the Britannic Fleet, taking a sizable force of troops with them. A member of Constantine's staff would say that Constantius had set his sights on also conquering lands farther afield, including Ireland, and other islands to the north of Britain, among them Iceland, known to the ancients as Thule.

Once they landed in Britain, Constantius and Constantine would have hurried north. It is likely they were met on their arrival in York, capital of Britannia Secundus, by the Alemanni German King Crocus, who was now in his seventies, leading a company of Alemanni from northwest England to again serve Constantius. The only other unit in Constantius's force that we can identify with some degree of certainty is the Ala Herculea, the relatively new cavalry unit raised by Maximian. The 500-man wing had probably been enlisted in Gaul, and originally served as the mounted bodyguard of the emperor of the West. Subsequently, Constantius would leave the unit in Britain, where it would be permanently based thereafter.

Eusebius's account of the scene at Constantius's eventual deathbed suggests that the emperor also took all his children from his marriage to Theodora, daughter of Maximian, with him to Britain, probably to keep them safe from his own deputy, the Caesar Severus, appointee and tool of Galerius. These six children, Constantine's three half-brothers and three half-sisters, were still only infants and juveniles.

Constantius and his family based themselves at the Roman governor's palace in York, from where the Western emperor, his son, and King Crocus mounted a military campaign in Scotland that summer against the Picti, "the painted ones," a confederation of Celtic tribes living in eastern Scotland north of the Forth-Clyde isthmus. The campaign probably resulted in the destruction of numerous Celtic villages, but ever since their ancestors had been slaughtered in a battle with the Romans at Mons Graupius in northeast Scotland in A.D. 84, the locals had been wary of engaging in a major set battle with Roman forces. There would be no major battle during this campaign.

Over the centuries, the tribesmen of Caledonia had generally melted into forests and mountains at the approach of Roman armies, using guerrilla tactics to harass Roman incursions, although in the second century they were likely to have lured the 9th Hispana Legion into an ambush and annihilated it.[46] As modern historians and archaeologists have concluded,

Scotland north of Hadrian's Wall had become "Rome's Afghanistan," a land that outside forces could never, and would never, conquer. Constantius nonetheless claimed a victory over the Picti, and, back in York for the winter, is recorded on January 7 adding the titles *Britannicus Maximus,* Britain's Greatest, to his existing titles.[47]

It is likely that the reported poor state of the health of his father used by Constantine to facilitate his escape from Galerius's grasp in 305 had a basis in fact, and that poor health had stayed with him in the form of an underlying or chronic condition. For, when the spring of 306 arrived and the army prepared for a renewal of hostilities in the north, Constantius was too unwell to lead the campaign. Constantine led the legions north for the new campaign, but was called back to York in late June as his father's condition worsened.

Eusebius's description of the dying Constantius on his couch, surrounded by his other children, when Constantine arrived from Nicomedia, appears to more accurately depict the moment of Constantine's return to York from the latest Scottish campaign. The previously quoted member of Constantine's staff, speaking ten years after the event, tells us that when Constantine arrived back at York he found "the emperor on the point of passing over to heaven," and Constantius lived long enough to see "the man whom he was leaving as heir."[48]

Constantius in fact lingered for weeks until, on July 25, 306, he died at the York palace. His troops were then assembled in their camp and his death announced. A written message from the dead emperor was then read by the officer serving as camp "announcer," commending Constantine as his successor. King Crocus, the Alemanni German, then stepped onto the tribunal and called on the legions to hail Constantine as his father's successor as emperor of the West.

This was unprecedented in Roman history—a foreign king leading Roman citizen soldiers in hailing a new Roman emperor. There was also the fact that, apart from being highly irregular, this was quite illegal. Under the Tetrarchy's succession plan devised by Diocletian, the Caesar of the West would now automatically take the place of Constantius as Augustus of the West of the Roman Empire. That particular Caesar was the emperor Galerius's old friend and lackey Severus, who should have automatically succeeded Constantius as emperor.

The Roman troops at York should have ignored the German king. But if

Crocus truly was Constantine's father-in-law, as postulated earlier, he had every reason to lead the call for Constantine's elevation, and the men of Constantius's legions, who had great affection for Constantine, had every reason to follow Crocus's lead, which is exactly what they did.

The voices of thousands of legionaries boomed out around the stone walls of York's military fortress. "Hail Constantine Augustus!"

"The whole army gave you its approval," said Constantine's staff member a decade later. But Constantine, now thirty-four, did not want to be emperor. Hurriedly leaving his father's palace, he mounted up and went to ride away. But soldiers chased him and draped his father's purple emperor's cloak around his shoulders, leaving Constantine sobbing. "The soldiers immediately threw the purple on you, who were in tears. In trying to escape the enthusiasm of the army as it called out for you, [you] urged on your horse with your spurs." This, said the staff member, excusing Constantine's attempt to avoid the responsibility of the highest office, was merely "an error of youth."[49]

This reluctance to take power may have been feigned, to assuage Galerius, the empire's powerbroker. Certainly, those historians who have attributed unbridled ambition to Constantine have thought so. But several more times during his career, when the door to the advancement of his career opened, Constantine would choose not to walk through it, to avoid confrontation with a powerful rival, making this "error of youth" in York seem in character. However, unable to escape the enthusiasm of his army, Constantine, who seems to have been more interested in soldiering than power, reluctantly acceded to his clamoring troops' wishes.

But, for his appointment as emperor of the West to be official, it would have to be endorsed by the emperor of the East, Galerius. So Constantine composed a letter to Galerius in Nicomedia, telling him that "the purple" had been forced on him by his troops, and that he had only accepted the Western throne to serve the army and the Roman people as Constantius's son and heir.

He made no attempt to hurry to dispatch the letter. First, once he had conducted his father's funeral and cremation, Constantine had a court artist paint several portraits of him, in Constantius's ankle-length imperial purple cloak and vestments. Constantine sent one copy of the painting to Galerius together with the letter. According to Zosimus in his *New History*, written a century later, Constantine also sent a portrait to Rome. He is in fact likely to have sent copies to every imperial capital, including Milan and Trier, and to the Spanish provinces, which had come under Constantius's rule the previous year. He certainly wrote to the Roman governors in Spain notifying them of his assumption of power, for they promptly declared that they did not recognize his legitimacy, throwing their support behind Severus, the legitimate claimant.

Although Constantine would later show a love for ostentatious display, this distribution of portraits was not entirely a vanity exercise—for, at the commencement of the *ludi*, the games on the annual Roman religious calendar that involved chariot races and gladiatorial shows, there was a parade, and the carved busts or painted portraits of the emperors and Caesars were carried around the stadium at the head of that parade.

Constantine did add one unique touch, a personal statement, to the portraits. He had himself shown wearing a crown of bay laurel leaves. Although the daily wearing of such a crown had been an affectation of Julius Caesar, the members of the Tetrarchy did not typically have themselves depicted wearing such an adornment. The bay-leaf crown was traditionally worn by Roman generals when celebrating a Triumph, and Constantine's use of it was his statement that first and foremost he was a soldier, a triumphant general. The bay-leaf crown was also worn by the god Apollo, and later events suggest that the association with Apollo could have also played a role in Constantine's use of the laurel crown in these paintings.

After Galerius saw the portrait and read Constantine's missive, delivered by a messenger from Britain—a centurion from one of Constantine's legions would have been entrusted with this mission—the emperor of the East exploded with rage, threatening to burn the painting, the message, and the messenger. Once he'd calmed down, Galerius thought better of such precipitous action.

Writing back to Constantine, Galerius failed to recognize him as his father's successor, instead conferring the lesser post of Caesar of the West on him, at the same time elevating his old friend Severus from Caesar to Augustus to replace Constantius, following the Tetrarchy's established succession plan. Severus, who would be called Severus II by later historians to distinguish him from third-century emperor Septimius Severus, was now emperor of the West. From this point forward, in all official communications Galerius would rank Constantine last, after himself, Severus, and then Galerius's Caesar, Daia.

Had Constantine truly wanted the purple, he would not have accepted this rejection and demotion. He could have taken his ardently loyal troops to Italy to take what he saw as his birthright by force. But he meekly accepted Galerius's ruling and, as Severus made Milan his capital and took overall control of the West, Constantine returned to Gaul with his family members, taking up residence at Trier as Severus's Caesar and subordinate, and focusing on campaigning against German tribes.

According to Lactantius, Constantine's first official act as Caesar was to grant Christians freedom of worship in his realms of Gaul and Britain. The fact that the Christian bishop of Trier, Miletus, had been serving in his post since 300, and would continue to serve in that role for many more years to come, suggests that Christians had been granted freedom of worship by Constantine's father, and Constantine was merely confirming his father's measure.

As for King Crocus the German, possibly Constantine's father-in-law, we never hear of him again in Roman accounts. The likelihood is that he remained in Britain, where he lived out the rest of his life and died fighting. This is suggested by the folklore of England, Wales, and Scotland, which contained colorful tales of a King Coel—also called Coillus, known as Coel the Old and progenitor of a noble line of locally born princes—who may in actuality have been old Crocus. According to the folklore of Ayrshire in lower Scotland, King Coel and a force of Britons were killed by a joint force of Picti and Scoti north of Hadrian's Wall in the fifth century.

The story goes that King Coel initially escaped a surprise night attack on his camp, in what came to be called the Battle of Coilsfield (Coel's field), but subsequently drowned with a number of his men while attempting to cross the River Doon. A mound in Ayrshire is said to contain his tomb. Ayrshire, it should be noted, is directly to the north of the Lonsdale area where English folklore placed the death of King Coel in the fourth century. English and Welsh folklore in fact both firmly date King Coel to the fourth century during the reigns of Constantius and Constantine.

The remains of Constantine's father would also excite British folklorists, with several different sites in Britain later laying claim to the location of Constantius's tomb. Today, scholars believe, as Constantius's grandnephew Julian was to write, that Constantine interred his father's remains back at his capital, Trier—although no tomb or inscription at Trier has to date been found to confirm this.[50]

It is likely that, with Constantius dead, Constantine's mother Helena now joined her son at Trier. Here she would become involved with the local Christian community, later ensuring that honors and favors were showered on Trier by her son. That Helena's influence over Constantine was now considerable can be gauged from the fact that, at his mother's behest, Constantine removed his six half-brothers and half-sisters from Trier and sent them to southwest Gaul, to the city of Tolosa, today's Toulouse. Of Constantine's stepmother Theodora we hear nothing through this period, but in all probability, with Helena now ruling the Trier roost, Theodora was also exiled to Toulouse to care for her brood.

After Rome, Trier, and Arles, Toulouse was then the largest city in the Western Empire and contained all the features of a cultured metropolis, from drama theater to large public baths, amphitheater, and hippodrome. But it was out of the way, and that is where Helena wanted these children of the woman who had replaced her in the affections and bed of Constantine's father. Of Constantine's siblings, Julius Constantius was the eldest. Julius, who would later father the future emperor Julian, was eighteen years of age at this point. Despite being soon eligible for a semester as a junior tribune in the army, he seems not to have been permitted to leave Toulouse. The other siblings, including Constantine's eldest sister Constantia, were in or approaching their teens. But, at Helena's insistence, these children of the woman who had replaced her as Constantius's empress were all deliberately kept away from their brother, and away from Trier's corridors of power.

Meanwhile, within three months of the death of Constantine's father, upheaval in Italy, from a totally unexpected source, quickly changed the face of the Roman West. This would elevate a new player into the Tetrarchy's mix, and into Constantine's line of fire—Maxentius, his future brother-in-law, ally, and then archrival.

VII

ENTER MAXENTIUS

MARCUS VALERIUS MAXENTIUS WAS A PRINCE, the son and heir of the retired emperor Maximian. Today we might call him Mark Maxenti—in the same way that Shakespeare gave Marcus Antonius the Anglicized name of Mark Antony. Maxentius was born around the year 276 in Rome, where he spent his childhood. He grew into a handsome young man. His coins and a statue of Maxentius found at Ostia show him with a stubbly beard, as he set himself apart from his heavily bearded father and cleanshaven brother-in-law Constantine. The statue depictss him as being of medium height and build, and with thick, curly hair. His coins indicate that he usually kept his hair very closely shorn, and, while Italian artists in the sixteenth and seventeenth centuries would depict him as a blond, no contemporary source confirms his hair color.[51]

The young Maxentius was a good-for-nothing. Constantine's nephew Julian would describe him as "untrained in war and effeminate."[52] Maxentius certainly seems not to have had any interest in manly pursuits, and his father Maximian appears not to have required him to follow a military career like himself, for Maxentius neither undertook military training nor performed any army service. Neither did he serve in any of the posts on the old Roman civil service ladder that the young Roman elite usually occupied. An archetypal spoiled rich kid, this emperor's son appears to have been principally interested in architecture and chariot racing.

According to the historian Aurelius Victor, a provincial governor and city prefect of Rome in the second half of the fourth century, "no one liked Maxentius, not even his father or father-in-law."[53] That father-in-law was the Eastern Roman emperor Galerius. According to Zosimus, Galerius hated Maxentius, but he had shrewdly married his daughter Valeria Maximilla to him in 293, at the commencement of the Tetrarchy, when Maxentius was still in his teens. This cemented the young man into Galerius's circle of power and kept him under his watchful eye. Maxentius did his princely duty and produced an heir, with Maximilla soon giving him a son, on whom Maxentius would dote. This was Flavius Romulus, born around 295, the same year that Constantine's first son Crispus was born.[54]

When Maxentius's father Maximian retired in the spring of 305 and Maxentius was overlooked for the post of deputy emperor, the young man withdrew to a Republican villa just to the south of Rome that was owned by his family and may have been his birthplace. Sitting in lush countryside on a rise between the second and third mileposts on the Appian Way, and looking toward the Alban Hills, the villa was within easy reach of Rome, yet away from the noise, bustle, and intrigues of the city that never slept. To keep himself amused, Maxentius proceeded to dabble with designs for extensions to the villa, for the creation of a chariot-racing circus on the flat below the villa, and for massive buildings that would add to the glory of Rome, if only he'd had the money and the power to implement them.

Little more than a year later, in October 306, Maxentius was secretly approached by a conspiratorial delegation of senior military officers from Rome's garrison. At the time of their first meeting, Maxentius was residing at a city house on the Via Labicana, in Rome's outer east, almost certainly to attend the Ludi Augustales, the October 3–12 religious festival dedicated to Augustus, Rome's first emperor. This festival culminated in the October 12 Augustalia, one of the biggest chariot-racing competitions of the year, held at the Circus Maximus before hundreds of thousands of excited, cheering, gambling spectators. It was an event that racing fan Maxentius would never have missed.

The house where the covert meeting took place was, perhaps not coincidentally, located not far from the barracks of the Praetorian Guard and the two Caelian Hill barracks of the Singularian Horse, the imperial horse guard. During this era, the Singularians would have been based at Milan with the emperor for the West, but their Rome forts continued to be maintained by *remansores*—literally "the remainder"—Singularians nearing retirement or nursing old wounds.[55]

Maxentius's younger sister Fausta owned a house known as the Domus Faustae in the vicinity of the Via Labicana, abutting the newer of the Singularian Horse barracks on the Caelian Hill. But it is likely that, as a member of the imperial family, Maxentius was making use of the Sessorium, the Via Labicana complex built by Septimius Severus and enlarged by Elagabalus, which, as previously mentioned, included a chariot-racing track. The Sessorium would have made for a comfortable, convenient, but discreet residence for Maxentius when he visited the city.

Revolt was fermenting in Rome, and it was the fault of Maxentius's father-in-law, Eastern emperor Galerius. Born and raised in Dacia, Galerius despised Rome, one-time seat of emperor Trajan, who had subjugated the Dacian kingdom in the second century. Galerius had rarely even visited Rome, the former capital and core of the Roman Empire, and Lactantius would claim that Galerius declared he was a Dacian before he was a Roman, and even considered changing the name of his realm from the Roman Empire to the Dacian Empire. Galerius had already engineered the removal of many powers and privileges of the Roman Senate, which, says Gibbon, "was left a venerable but useless monument of antiquity." Now, Galerius, via his Milan-based puppet, the Augustus Severus, was introducing a poll tax on all Italians, a highly unpopular move in Italy. But another move by Galerius was to prove the most misjudged of all.[56]

The Italians of the Praetorian Guard at Rome had been unhappy ever since Diocletian had eliminated their elite status by replacing them as the emperor's bodyguard. The disbandment of four of their cohorts in Gaul in 293 after they had served under the rebel Carausius had only added to Praetorian dissatisfaction. Now, in the wake of Severus's elevation to Augustus in the West, Galerius had ordered Severus to abolish the proud Praetorians altogether. There had already been riots in the streets of Rome by citizens opposed to Galerius's new tax, which the Praetorians and their colleagues of the City Guard had put down. But now, under threat of disbandment, the remaining guardsmen were themselves ready to rise up. All they needed was a leader.

The troops of Rome had first sent delegates to the retired emperor Maximian at his Lucania estate in southern Italy, asking him to return to Rome, where they would again hail him emperor in opposition to Galerius and his minion Severus—as long as Maximian agreed to put a stop to Galerius's measures. But the retired emperor was too wary of Galerius and had turned down the idea. Now, three officers came to his son Maxentius and offered to put him on the throne—two tribunes, Marcellianus and Marcellus, who commanded cohorts of the Praetorian Guard, and a third tribune, Lucianus, who commanded the cohort of the City Guard whose quarters were located beside the city's pig market.[57]

The trio offered Maxentius the throne as emperor of the West, in defiance of Galerius and Severus. To begin with, Maxentius seems to have hesitated, or even declined the offer. To accept the throne, he would put his life on the line, for his father-in-law Galerius would surely send an army to dethrone him. Yet the Praetorians vowed to put their lives on the line for Maxentius if he consented to be their emperor—they would fight his battles for him, they said, no doubt also assuring Maxentius that his father's old soldiers in Italy would flock to his standard. Unlike his brother-in-law Constantine, Maxentius had no desire for military glory, but the three tribunes would also have assured him that once in power, he could restore the glory of the city of Rome, his birthplace, and lavish grand buildings on her.

It seems to have taken another two weeks for the three tribunes to pull the conspiracy together and for Maxentius to finally agree to front the military coup they were proposing. Key to the plot was the agreement by Maxentius to pay every one of the remaining 6,000 men of the Praetorian Guard and their 5,000 citizen colleagues of the 2nd Parthica Legion at nearby Alba Longa a "donative," or bribe, to back him. This was both traditional and practical—almost every past emperor of Rome had paid the Praetorians a donative on assuming the throne. The short reign of the parsimonious first-century emperor Galba, immediate successor to Nero, had ended with his assassination for the very reason that he had refused to pay the donative.

By this stage, Rome's Praetorian prefect no longer commanded the Praetorian Guard. He had become the most senior administrator of the emperors, and the Praetorian prefect for the West was at this time serving with the emperor Severus at Milan. The tribunes of the Praetorian Guard at Rome commanded the Guard, and therefore did not have to win the prefect over to their scheme to put Maxentius on the throne. But one other prefect did have the power to foil their plot. This was the city prefect, who commanded Rome's City Guard and the Vigile Cohorts, or Night Watch, and was Rome's combined police commissioner and fire chief. Gaius Annius Anullius had been city prefect since being appointed by Severus that March, having recently returned to Rome following his first stint as governor of Africa.

So the three tribunes approached Anullius and brought him into their plot. With his help, they sounded out senators who they believed loved Rome, despised Galerius and Severus, and would support Maxentius's reign. The tribunes brought thirteen senior senators, many of them former consuls, into the scheme. Apart from Anullius, they would have included Gaius Caeionius Rufius Volusianus, Affius Insteius Tertullus, and Ruricius Pompeianus. To cement the thirteen to the plot, each was required to put up 400,000 sesterces to fund the donative that Maxentius would pay to the troops. The resulting 5.2 million sesterces, shared out among 11,000 men, would average close to 500 sesterces per soldier, approaching six months' salary for a rank-and-file soldier and in line with past imperial accession donatives.[58]

On October 28, 306, the city prefect and tribunes of the Praetorian Guard and City Guard betrayed Severus, official emperor of the West, by presenting Maxentius to their assembled troops at the Praetorian Barracks, draping the long purple cloak of an Augustus over his shoulders, and leading the troops in hailing Maxentius emperor of the West, in defiance of Severus and his patron, eastern emperor Galerius. That same day, the men of the 2nd Parthica Legion at Alba Longa would have been led by their commanding prefect in hailing Maxentius emperor, and would have received a share of the donative. According to Zosimus, just a single unnamed senior figure at Rome, apparently a senator, opposed Maxentius's elevation to the throne, and he was executed by the Praetorians for his opposition.

The newly acclaimed emperor Maxentius, aged just thirty, promised to make the city of Rome great again as he now took up residence at the vast Palatine Hill Palatium complex that included the palaces of Augustus, Livia, Tiberius, Germanicus, Caligula, and Domitian—with the latter even including its own private chariot-racing course—and established his administration. This new "usurper" emperor was to prove much more wily and formidable than Galerius and others had believed possible. Maxentius did not adopt the title Augustus at first, instead styling himself, with a flourish that has a Hollywood ring to it, the Invincible Prince.

Calling together the Senate, he abolished Galerius's taxes on Italians and promised to restore the power and glory of Rome and its Senate, immediately granting senators the honors and privileges of old. And although Maxentius was not a Christian, to enlarge his support base he put a stop to the persecution of Christians in Rome and throughout his new domain—Italy, Sicily, Corsica, Sardinia, and Africa.

Maxentius maintained Severus's city prefect Anullius in the same role, and as his Praetorian prefect and chief administrator, Maxentius appointed another member of the clique of thirteen, the senator Manlius Rusticianus. The young emperor also appointed a third member of the thirteen, Tertullus, to a twelve-month term as governor of Africa, commencing in the new year.

Maxentius would now implement a major building program. Outside the city, he immediately started work on expanding his Appian Way villa and building his hippodrome beside the villa, using state money. Called the Girulum, the new hippodrome would have the largest footprint of any circus in the Roman world after Rome's Circus Maximus. Maxentius is also known to have renovated the Caelian Hill house of his sister Fausta, the Domus Faustae, and probably likewise renovated all the imperial properties at Rome that came under his control once he assumed the throne.[59]

Then, in 307, just months after Maxentius took the throne, the Temple of Venus Felix and Roma Eterna (Lucky Venus and Eternal Rome), on Rome's Velian Hill opposite the Colosseum, was seriously damaged by fire. Erected by Hadrian in A.D. 135 where part of Nero's palace, the Golden House, had previously stood, this temple, by then the largest in Rome, represented Rome herself; Maxentius, who was styling himself *conservator urbi suae*, or Preserver of His City, quickly ordered its restoration.

If Venus and Roma had not previously been adopted by Maxentius as his patron deities, it seems they were now. Plus, spurred by the popularity the temple restoration brought him with the people of Rome, in the following year he would commence his most impressive building project of all, the Basilica of Maxentius, the largest building ever erected in the Roman Forum and the last and largest basilica, or meeting hall, built in Rome. Maxentian brick stamps indicate that, on a smaller scale, he also initiated work on new baths on the city's Quirinal Hill, which would take water from the same aqueduct that served the nearby Baths of Diocletian.

Expecting trouble from Galerius, Maxentius immediately commenced the rehabilitation of the Praetorian Guard. Giving the Guard back its status as an elite unit, he recalled many of its men who had previously been sent into retirement on Diocletian's orders, signed up new Italian recruits, and restored the higher pay, shorter service, retirement bonus, and tax-free privileges the Praetorians had previously enjoyed. To his Praetorians, too, he granted the privilege of attending the Circus Maximus, Theater of Pompey, and best imperial baths when off duty. Not only would he return the Guard to its original complement of 10,000, he enlarged it to an estimated 12,000 men. He then set his Praetorian Guard and 2nd Parthica Legion troops to work digging a deep, broad protective moat outside the new city walls that had been erected around Rome in the 270s by the emperor Aurelian.

Maxentius's new regime engendered excitement and rejoicing in Rome. For the first time in close to a century, Rome was again an emperor's seat. Rome's pride and glory had been restored, by an emperor born at Rome and who claimed Rome as his home city. It is a reputation that Maxentius would work hard to foster and live up to, and it gained him widespread popularity, at Rome and beyond. As word of his accession spread, regional and provincial leaders in central and southern Italy, on Corsica, Sardinia, and Sicily turned their backs on Severus, Galerius' chosen Augustus, and recognized the son of the admired and respected Maximian as their emperor of the West.

Resistance to Maxentius's seizure of the throne would over time grow in the province of Africa, although this would not take the form of support for Severus. Only the people of northern Italy continued to support Severus, who was based in their midst at Milan, and only then without demonstrated enthusiasm. And Constantine, Severus's new Caesar and deputy who controlled the legions of the Rhine and Britain from his headquarters at Trier, remained silent, neither committing himself for or against Maxentius.

In Nicomedia, not unexpectedly, there were fireworks. Eastern emperor Galerius, who just months before had thought he had gained total control of the empire by relegating Constantius's son Constantine to Caesar status, was enraged by the upstart Maxentius. He promptly sent orders to Severus in Milan to march on Rome with an army and deal with the young usurper. Severus acted quickly, putting together a large force from troops on the Danube and the Balkans, but Constantine declined to send troops to Severus from his Gallic command, giving the excuse that he was committed to an aggressive spring campaign against invading Franks.

As early as March 307, with the snows melting in the Apennines, Severus marched on Rome with his army. On learning this, Maxentius, knowing that he was no soldier and lacked the appeal to fighting men that his father had fostered, reached out to Maximian. Appealing to his parent to leave the quiet of his villa in southern Italy and join him in Rome, he sent him a purple Augustan cloak and the offer of shared rule alongside him. Believing he would be able to dominate his son and rule as he pleased, Maximian accepted the offer. When Maximian soon after arrived in Rome, both he and Maxentius were hailed Augustus by their assembled troops.

As Severus marched south, he soon found his army unruly and reluctant to go against Maximian and his son. Many of these troops had served under Maximian and were still loyal to him. When Severus arrived under the walls of Rome, with the city's gates closed and Maxentius's guardsmen lining the walls, Severus's troops, promised a donative by Maxentius, deserted to the father-and-son combination. In all probability, the Singularian Horse, the household cavalry, led this revolt against Severus, along with the Herculeans, who had previously served as Maximian's bodyguard.

The humiliated Severus was forced to retreat across Italy with his few remaining loyal troops and hole up on the east coast at the well-fortified naval city and one-time capital of the Roman West, Ravenna. Eusebius would later crow that Severus "shamefully retreated from the contest without a blow."[60] Maximian followed with his son's troops, and from outside Ravenna's walls he sent Severus a message offering to spare him if he surrendered. Severus, probably hoping that his old friend Galerius would shortly come with his own army and save him, accepted the offer and gave up. Taken to Rome as a captive by Maximian, Severus was subsequently consigned to house arrest at an imperial villa on the Appian Way south of Rome, outside the crossroads town of Tres Tabernae.

On the Rhine, meanwhile, Constantine's spring campaign against the Franks had achieved stunning success. The Franks had apparently heard of the upheaval in Italy. Believing the Romans would be distracted, and contrary to a solemn oath they had previously given to Constantine that they would remain his friends and allies, two Frankish kings, Ascaric and Merogais, had raided across the Rhine into Gaul. Constantine not only routed the Frankish warriors, he captured the two kings and hundreds of their fighting men, and took them to Trier in chains.

Constantine had previously kept leading German nobles as hostages to peace, but this time, in the words of one of his officials, he "rekindled the penalty of death on the captured leaders of the enemy." This was intended to be a signal from the young Roman general to all German tribal leaders east of the Rhine: if they took him on, "they are unable to hope for either victory or mercy."[61]

Trier had been burned and left devastated by an Alemanni raid in 275, and in rebuilding the city and adding features such as the largest baths complex outside Rome, Constantine's father had also renovated and improved the city's amphitheatre for the punishment of criminals and entertainment of the populous. Here, that summer, stripped to the waist and with hands tied behind their backs, the kings Ascaric and Merogais and their men were pushed up the two stone stairways that led from the lamp-lit cellars beneath the arena to the sands above.

As the Germans emerged into the sunlight, they were welcomed by the roar from the waiting Roman crowd. As twenty thousand theatergoers bayed for Frankish blood, barred iron doors in the side of the amphitheater opened, and wild animals, starved for days, were driven out—lions, tigers, or bears; we are not told which. And there, in the amphitheater that remains substantially intact to this day, Ascaric, Merogais, and their tribesmen died gory deaths in front of the delighted crowd.

In Nicomedia, Galerius had not been idle. As Severus would have hoped and expected, the emperor of the East marched on Italy that summer with a large Roman army to deal with Maxentius and Maximian and free Severus. Galerius was accompanied by his most loyal and trusted general, Valerius Licinianus Licinius, who had been born in the same Dacian town as Galerius. The pair had been close friends since childhood, becoming fellow soldiers and drinking companions.

But when Galerius entered Italy, he found every city and town closing its gates to him and treating him as a foreigner. Marching down the Flaminian Way from the east coast, Galerius encamped his army north of Rome, near the junction of the Nar and Tiber rivers. He then sent his general Licinius and his Magister Memoriae, Sicorius Probus, on ahead as his envoys, to deliver a written demand to Maxentius. The Magister Memoriae, literally the Master of Memories, was the secretary in charge of the correspondence and petitions department at Tetrarchy palatiums. Probus had served Galerius in this post for many years and had been the official who delivered surrender terms dictated by Galerius to Persia's King Narseh back in 298.

At Rome, Galerius's pair of envoys handed Maxentius a letter from Galerius in which he declared that Maxentius should humbly request the purple, not demand it by force of arms, and threatened an assault on Rome if Maxentius failed to come kowtowing to him. Maxentius and his father scoffed at the idea of begging for what they already had, and sent the envoys packing. When Licinius and Probus returned to Galerius, they reported Maxentius's haughty response, and also reported that a huge army was encamped at Rome, which, combining Maxentius' troops, Maximian's old soldiers, and the men who had previously marched for Severus, vastly outnumbered Galerius's army.

New of this would have quickly spread through Galerius's camp, and his Eastern troops, heavily outnumbered and in alien territory, lost heart. Galerius, realizing he would have to deal with Maxentius and Maximian in other ways, turned around and led his army away. To maintain the loyalty and morale of his troops, he allowed them to loot and pillage Italian farms and villages en route as they withdrew up the Flaminian Way. On November 11, once back in the East, he would appoint close friend Licinius to the post of Augustus of the West, the title appropriated by Maxentius, ignoring the reality of Maxentius's occupation of the throne at Rome with a powerful and loyal army at his back. Giving Licinius direct control of the Balkan provinces of Illyricum, Thrace, and Pannonia, Galerius based him in the Balkans.

With Maxentius firmly in charge at Rome, his father Maximian led part of their army in shadowing Galerius's retreating force until it had departed Italy. Then, in the early autumn, Maximian left most of the troops in Italy and crossed the Alps into Gaul, where he headed north to Trier to pay Constantine a visit. He arrived with his eighteen-year-old daughter Fausta, Maxentius' sister. Eutropia, mother of Fausta and Maxentius, was probably also in the party. Fired by the allure of unfettered power, Maximian came with more energy than he'd demonstrated in years, along with a pair of startling proposals.

Maximian proposed that Constantine marry Fausta, thus cementing a familial bond between their two imperial families. At the same time, Maximian would invest Constantine as one of the Augusti, putting him on an equal footing with Maxentius, Galerius, and himself. The deal was that Maxentius and his father would continue to control Italy, Sicily, Corsica, Sardinia, and Africa, while Constantine would have unrestricted control of Gaul, Britain, and Spain. In return, Constantine would guarantee to remain neutral in any conflict that continued among Galerius and Maximian and Maxentius.

In Italy, near the crossroads town of Tres Tabernae, thirty miles south of Rome, as Maximian was arriving at Trier, the life of Severus, captured emperor of the West, was terminated. This was almost certainly on Maximian's orders. Severus was either decapitated by the centurion of his guard or given the more honorable option of committing suicide. The name of the officer who supervised Severus's death is sometimes given as Herculeas, but it is likely this was not his name but a reference to his unit—he would have been a member of the Herculeans, Maximian's longtime bodyguard. Severus's remains were taken up the Appian Way and hurriedly interred some nine miles south of Rome in the mausoleum of the third-century emperor Gallienus, immediate predecessor of Claudius Gothicus.

With Severus's death, there was one less emperor, one less threat to Maxentius and Maximian. And one less threat to Constantine.

VIII

UNITED WE STAND

A ROYAL WEDDING WAS TAKING PLACE IN TRIER. It was September in the year 307, and Constantine, having almost certainly been a widower for several years by this time, was marrying Fausta, daughter of Maximian and sister of Maxentius. Constantine could see the political advantages of a union between Maximian's daughter and himself. And regaining the title of Augustus that his troops had bestowed on him at his father's passing would not have been an unattractive prospect, especially as it was backed by his own army and also by the now-enlarged army of Maximian and his son.

So Constantine had agreed to the match with the girl who, fourteen years earlier, had been the child handing him the helmet for the portrait that still adorned the wall of the Aquileian palace. Some authors have suggested that, because of that shared event during Fausta's childhood, Maximian had long intended that Constantine marry his daughter, even as far back as the time of the portrait's creation; but no proof exists of that. On the contrary, the timing of the rapid union smacks of political opportunism on the part of Maximian.

Arranged marriages were common for Roman men and women of the upper classes, but by the fourth century the girl was not forced to marry. As the noted second-century Roman lawyer Salvius Julianus put it, "Marriage could not be made by constraint, but only by consent, of the parties thereto, and the free consent of the girl was indispensable." And as it turned out, even though Constantine had only seen Fausta several times as she was growing up, he immediately took a shine to her when she came to his court as an adult. And the feeling was mutual.[62]

A surviving marble bust of Fausta shows Constantine's bride with small features, and Fausta may have been quite petite. Born at Rome, she had been raised there and in Italian palaces by her mother Eutropia while her father was frequently away on military campaigns. As the daughter of an emperor, Fausta had long borne the title *noblissima femina*, or Noble Lady, as did all the daughters of Maximian and Diocletian. Some years after this wedding of his aunt and uncle, Constantine's nephew Julian would extol Fausta's virtues to her son, the emperor Constantius II, in a public oration. Although Fausta would die before Julian was born, based on accounts passed down through the family he assured Constantius that his mother Fausta was "a beauty," with "a noble bearing and great strength of moral character." Within a few years, Fausta would demonstrate that strength of moral character with a stunning act of loyalty to her new husband.[63]

A Roman wedding ceremony was much like our own. It was always a daytime ceremony, with bride and groom coming together to pledge their troth before family and friends, who were there to witness their exchange of vows. Traditionally, the bride was accompanied by three bridesmaids and three page boys. The ceremony usually took place at the home of the bride's father or male guardian. Constantine gave Fausta her own palace at Trier, and it is possible their wedding took place there. The bride and her family members stood at the front door to welcome the groom and his family, after which all adjourned to an inner room for the ceremony, during which all parties stood.

Custom required that the bride wear a tunic without a hem, circled by a woolen girdle tied in a double knot. An elaborate wig of artificial hair adorned her head, and this was topped by a wedding wreath of woven myrtle and orange blossom. A metal collar circled her neck, a saffron-colored cloak was draped over her shoulders, and her sandals were of the same color. A veil covered her face—traditionally, an orange veil.

The bride attended the ceremony already wearing the gold wedding ring that her fiancé had placed on the third finger of her left hand at their engagement ceremony. In the case of Fausta and Constantine, only a few weeks had passed between that betrothal ceremony, when Maximian arrived at Trier with his daughter, and the wedding—just time enough for distinguished guests to make their way to Trier from throughout Constantine's provinces. The third finger of the left hand was chosen for the ring because, in earlier times, Romans had believed that a nerve ran from that finger directly to the heart. That mistaken belief had morphed into a tradition.

As with Western weddings today, during the Roman wedding ceremony the father of the bride "gave her away." This was because, under Roman law, a father was legally responsible for his daughter until she married, at which time he surrendered his guardianship as he gave her into the care of her husband, who became her new legal guardian.

Before the nuptials could be celebrated, the priest conducting the ceremony stood at an altar before the couple and some ten witnesses representing both families, and performed an animal sacrifice to Jove, to seek heavenly blessing of the union. The sacrificial animal was sometimes a ewe, more often a pig, occasionally an ox. Before the animal was killed, it was stunned by being hit on the head by a mallet wielded by an assistant to the priest—invariably, the groom. The priest, an auspex, then studied the newly dead animal's entrails for blemishes, and if it was blemish-free, he announced that the auspices were favorable for the wedded bliss of husband and wife.

The couple next proceeded to exchange their vows—the husband was expected to love, cherish, and protect his wife, the bride to love, honor, and obey her husband, and they solemnly vowed to bind themselves to one another forever. Both then applied their seals to the wedding contract, as did the witnesses. Roman law did provide for divorces. Originally, only the husband could initiate a divorce, but by Constantine's day either or both parties could do so, with the marriage settlement being a return of the wife's original dowry, which often took the form of real estate.

After the marriage contract had been sealed, the delighted guests offered their congratulations and best wishes to the newlyweds. "Felicitations! May happiness wait upon you!"[64]

Bride, groom, and guests then moved to a dining room or garden where a wedding feast lasted until the sun went down. In the case of this royal wedding, family members would have been joined for the feast by dignitaries and officials. Before the feast began, one more piece of ceremony was performed. In front of the gathered guests, Maximian, who already wore the Augustan purple, draped a new jewel-encrusted, ankle-length purple cloak of an Augustus around Constantine's shoulders.

All present would have now chorused "Hail Constantine Augustus! Hail Maximian Augustus!"

Now, for the first time in history, there were simultaneously five emperors of Rome—Constantine, Maximian, Maxentius, Licinius, and Galerius—although Galerius recognized the elevation of only one of the others. In the eyes of Galerius, and according to the rules previously set down by Diocletian, none other than Galerius and his appointee Licinius were rightful claimants to the throne. But, as Maximian and Constantine knew, in all Roman history, right was determined by might.

Speeches are always a part of weddings, and at the wedding feast that followed this illegal investiture of Constantine at least one speech was made, with its text coming down to us in its entirety. Lasting up to fifteen minutes, it was delivered by an unnamed professor of rhetoric. Some historians had thought him to be Eumenius of Augustodunum, today's city of Autun in central eastern France, then noted for its schools of rhetoric, who delivered a panegyric in Lyon in 297 or 298. But he is now believed to have been a separate figure.

The anonymous wedding orator, who would later boast that a number of his pupils had gone on to govern Roman provinces, had by this time recently joined the staff of Constantine's Palatium at Trier in a senior capacity: he was to describe himself as "a palace officer." In all probability he was the head of one of its departments. He may even have held the post of the Master of Offices, Constantine's chief of staff.[65]

It is likely that, while the audience stood, Constantine listened to the address seated, with new wife Fausta seated to his right and new father-in-law Maximian sitting to his left, with the speech indicating that Constantine and Fausta were holding hands. The orator used his speech to celebrate the marriage of Constantine and Fausta, although he never mentioned Fausta by name, as well as lauding the figurative marriage of the houses of Maximian and Constantine and the elevation of Constantine to the rank of Augustus.

"A speech is required appropriate to this marriage, which once concluded will last forever," the orator began. He turned to the happy couple. "Merely by looking at your faces we are aware that you are in such agreement, and that you have so joined not only your hands, but even your thoughts and minds, that it were possible you would wish to pass into each other's hearts.

"This is such a great blessing for the state. Indeed what more valued gift could you have bestowed, or could have received, since by this alliance of yours, on the one hand . . ." He turned to the father of the bride. ". . . you, Maximian, through your son-in-law, have regained your youth? And on the other hand . . ." He turned to Constantine. ". . . you, Constantine, through your father-in-law, have gained the title of Augustus."

He then referred to Constantine's first marriage, recalling the young man "surrendering yourself from the precise moment your boyhood ended to the laws of marriage." Now, the orator ventured to make a little joke, referring to the custom of arranged marriages. "It was," he said, "even at that time, an unheard-of wonder—a young man fond of his wife."

Although not using her name, the orator rather patronizingly now spoke of Fausta, referring to her as "so fine a woman as this," before turning to her and saying, "You indeed copy and follow the fairness and dutifulness of your father." Then telling the audience of the portrait of Constantine and little Fausta on the wall at Aquileia, which he had obviously seen, he described Fausta as being, at the time of the portrait's painting, "a young girl already worthy of respect through her divine grace."

Much of the remainder of the speech lauded Constantine, his youth and his virtues. And the professor extolled the virtues and character of Maximian, "in whom there is still such real, unimpaired strength, and who has this vigor in your whole body, this imperious fire in your eyes." He spoke of Maximian having originally taken up imperial power at the request of his brother-in-arms Diocletian, and declared that now he had taken it up again because he had been ordered to do so by his "mother" Roma, the city of Rome—ignoring the fact that Maximian had not been born in Rome and it was not his mother city.

The orator also voiced the shock that must have been shared by many around the empire when Maximian retired at the age of fifty-five, and then again when he took up the mantle of emperor for a second time: "We were amazed that you became a private citizen after wielding absolute power. It is much more amazing that you take up power again after retiring."

To the groom and his father-in-law both, he said, "May your alliance surely thrive through the everlasting roots of your affection." To the groom alone, he said, "Constantine, will our children and grandchildren ever allow you, even when you are very old, to furl the sails of the ship of state which you have filled, even as a young man, with such favorable winds?"[66]

And then, perhaps after a brief reply from Constantine on behalf of his new wife and himself, it was down to feasting and celebrating, with food and customarily watered-down Roman wine aplenty, with no expense spared. Years later, Constantine's nephew Julian would criticize his uncle for his lavish lifestyle, love of luxury, and quest for pleasure, but those days were largely still in the future at this point. One simple but traditional item on the wedding menu would have been a wedding cake, a wheat cake called the *farreus panis*, forerunner of the modern wedding cake.

After sunset, the newlyweds left the feast and retired to the groom's home, walking with attendants. In this case, the couple probably walked from one part of the palace complex to another. For the average Roman, this involved a street walk. After the bride wrung herself from the embrace of her mother, flautists led a procession playing a happy tune, followed by five torchbearers lighting the way, then the bride and groom, with the bride escorted by three page boys, all of whose parents were required to be living. One page held the ceremonial nuptial torch while the other two held the bride's hands. Guests followed, singing licentious songs. Normally, children would have lined the route, and to them nuts would have been thrown, representing the childhood playthings of the groom.

At the door to Constantine's quarters, the tall, robust young emperor bent, picked up his bride, and carried her over the threshold, which was spread with a white cloth covered by greenery. This threshold ceremony went back to the very early days of Rome, in the eighth century B.C., and the so-called Abduction, or Rape, of the Sabine Women. When the eternal city was still no more than a small town, Romulus, who had founded Rome with his brother Remus, was concerned that most of the occupants of Rome were men. In need of wives to ensure Rome's population grew, Romulus approached the surrounding tribes, but none would allow their women to marry Romans.

So Romulus had invited several tribes to a festival at Rome that involved horse racing, eating, and drinking. Most of the tribes were wary and only sent their men, but the Sabines fell into Romulus's trap by also bringing their women along. At a signal from Romulus during the feast, after much drinking, his men rose up and revealed hidden weapons. Thirty of them carried off Sabine women, one of whom was already married. As abductors carried the women over the threshold of their round huts, the other Roman men fought and drove off the Sabine men.

The final customs of the Roman marriage involved the three brides-maids following the couple into the sleeping quarters, with two carrying her spinning tools, emblems of her domestic diligence. The third and most senior bridesmaid escorted the bride to the nuptial couch, where the groom invited her to recline after removing her cloak and untying her girdle. By this time, the wedding attendants were withdrawing to allow the intimate consummation of the marriage. Ultimately, Fausta would give birth to six children by Constantine. With their first child not coming along for at least another eight years, it is possible she suffered one or more miscarriages in the meantime.

Constantine was once more both a married man and an emperor.

IX

MAXIMIAN BETRAYS ALL

M AXIMIAN, FEELING HE HAD his new son-in-law Constantine under his thumb, returned to Rome during the winter of 307–308. In January he again assumed the role of one of Rome's two "consuls ordinary" appointed by the Senate for the year, alongside his son Maxentius. With the once-dominant but now-frail Diocletian barely clinging to life in Split, Maximian now felt in a position to make a grab for broader power, at the expense of his son Maxentius. And he seems to have been encouraged in this belief by the man who had held the post of city prefect at Rome since the previous year, Attius Insteius Tertullus, commander of the City Guard and Night Watch.

At Rome in April 308, with the troops of the Rome garrison assembled before Maxentius and himself, Maximian gave a speech that shocked his son and partner in power as he stood beside him. The government of Rome had become sickly, declared Maximian, and it was all the fault of his weak son Maxentius. With that, Maximian dramatically removed the purple Augustan cloak from Maxentius's shoulders, then called on the troops to hail himself as sole Augustus.

What Maximian had not taken into account was the fact that the men of the Praetorian Guard, the unit that owed its continued existence to Maxentius, would remain loyal to the young emperor, as would Maxentius's Praetorian prefect, Rusticianus. As the troops stood silent, and Maximian's apparent ally the city prefect turned his back on him, Maximian's overconfident coup attempt crumbled to dust. Maxentius banished his father from Rome, and from Italy. A less magnanimous son would have executed his treacherous parent, but Maxentius did not have the killer instinct. Certainly, in years to come, Constantine was to show that *he* would not hesitate to punish close relatives who betrayed him.

Escorted from Italy by his son's Praetorians, no doubt with a warning from the commander of his escort that if he set foot on Italian soil again he would be arrested and executed, Maximian scurried away to Gaul with a few attendants. Arriving at Trier, he begged son-in-law Constantine, his last friend in power, for asylum. Constantine, no doubt urged by his new wife Fausta, daughter of Maximian, took in his father-in-law, even though this would alienate him from his brother-in-law Maxentius and terminate the short-lived alliance between them that Maximian had brokered just months before. The unnamed official who spoke at the wedding of Constantine and Fausta would later say, in Constantine's presence, that Constantine ordered his staff to now bend over backward to accommodate Maximian: "You ordered our services to be bestowed even more keenly on him than on you."[67]

At Rome, Maxentius quickly reestablished himself as sole emperor. Asserting his control, he overturned his father's consular appointment. In Maximian's place, Maxentius installed two new consuls for the remainder of the year—himself, and his thirteen-year-old son Valerius Romulus. This made Romulus the youngest-ever consul of imperial Rome; the previous youngest had been Marcus Aurelius's son Commodus, appointed at age fifteen.

Being replaced by a child would have infuriated Maximian, which was probably Maxentius's intent, but the appointment of the thirteen-year-old was not opposed by the Senate—of which he would sit as president—and Maxentius would reappoint young Romulus to the post again the following year. Meanwhile, made aware that his father had at one point conspired with City Prefect Tertullus, that same month of April, Maxentius removed Tertullus from his powerful post, replacing him with another member of the clique of thirteen.

To broaden his base, Maxentius now reached out to the Christian community, giving permission for the Catholic Church to again elect a Bishop of Rome and gather to conduct Christian services and burials. The bishop elected on April 18, Marcellus, would zealously attack his role, creating twenty-five Christian diocese or administrative districts within Rome, putting a priest in charge of each, and establishing a new Christian burial ground outside Rome after the church's last cemetery had been confiscated under Maximian's original rule. Bishop Marcellus also established a severe penance regime for Christians who had either handed over scriptures for burning or sacrificed to the old gods to escape persecution, and who now wished to return to the Church.

From exile at Trier with Constantine, Maximian agitated for the removal of his son from the throne at Rome and for his own official recognition alongside Constantine as emperor of the West. But while Galerius remained as emperor of the East, Constantine himself was not prepared to back Maximian. So, writing through the summer to both Galerius and his former "brother" in power, the retired Diocletian, Maximian sought the pair's intervention on his behalf.

By the autumn, Galerius, apparently succumbing to pressure from Diocletian, called a conference at which Maximian, Diocletian, and he would decide who would be officially recognized as emperor of the West. The conference was to be held in Illyricum, on the Danube at the provincial capital of Carnuntum, base of the 4th Flavia Legion and home to the rivercraft of Rome's Pannonian Fleet. Today, it is the city of Petronell-Carnuntum in Austria. To help Maximian attend this momentous meeting, Constantine provided his father-in-law with carriages and pack animals, plus, we must presume, a military escort.

As Maximian set off overland from Trier for the Danube, the sickly Diocletian left aside his favorite pastime, gardening, to make the journey from his palace at Split, and Galerius set off from the East. On November 11, 308, the trio issued a joint communiqué at Carnuntum. The will of Galerius had again prevailed—Maximian agreed to set aside his Augustan title and return to retirement. And, ignoring the claims to the throne of both Constantine and Maxentius, despite the fact that both now wore the purple and Maxentius occupied Rome and controlled Italy, the communiqué elevated Licinius, Galerius's general and old friend, to the rank of Augustus and named him emperor of the West. Maxentius was declared a usurper, and Constantine was reduced back to the rank of Caesar and made subordinate to Licinius.

Once Maxentius learned of this announcement, he refused to recognize Licinius's appointment and stubbornly held on to power at Rome, with the full backing of his large and loyal army, the Senate of Rome, and the people of Italy. Licinius, while ostensibly the new emperor of the West, would be based in Pannonia, at Sirmium, today's Serbian city of Sremska Mitrovica, on the Sava River, with an army provided by Galerius and with immediate control of the Balkans. Maximian slunk back to Trier, where Constantine allowed him to resume living, in supposed retirement, more out of love for his wife than affection for his father-in-law.

Maximian was "expelled from Rome, driven from Italy, dismissed from Illyricum," said Constantine's staff member with contempt some eighteen months later. Yet still Constantine accommodated him. "You welcomed [him] in your provinces, in the midst of your troops, and in your palace," said the official, who, speaking with hindsight, knew that Constantine's beneficence would soon rebound on him.[68]

But neither Constantine nor his counterpart, the Eastern Caesar, Daia, was happy with Galerius's handling of their claims, for Licinius had leap-frogged both to take the purple. When the two Caesars expressed their dissatisfaction with affairs, with letters flowing back and forth, Galerius offered them the title of Sons of the Augusti, a title both declined. The following year, to appease them, Galerius began referring to Constantine and Daia as Augusti. But no additional power came with the title.

Still awed by Galerius, Constantine backed down and returned his focus to fighting Germans on the Rhine. Resolved to spending more years at Trier, he commissioned a new public-baths complex, on a scale to match the best in Rome, and was building a grand new brick and marble palace complex in the center of the city, a stone's throw from Trier's forum. That palace's massive central audience hall still stands today, in use as a Protestant house of worship, the Church of the Redeemer. The complex's separate palace for Fausta was being redecorated, too—only parts of the ceiling frescoes from that palace, some featuring Fausta, survived the later building of a Christian cathedral on the site. Constantine's new palace complex would be ready for occupation by 310.

Yet, despite Galerius having declared Maxentius a usurper and enemy of the Roman people, neither the emperor of the East nor his lackey, the emperor of the West, Licinius, made a move against Maxentius. Instead, Galerius also focused on architecture, expanding and adorning a ten-acre palace and temple complex he had commenced in 298 south of the Danube at his Dacia Ripensis birthplace, as a burial place for himself and his Dacian mother Romula. Named Felix Romuliana by Galerius after his late mother, its ruins can today be found in Serbia, in the locale known as Gramzigrad.

Maxentius was left by his rival Augusti to do as he pleased at Rome and in his realms. And as it happened, he had annoying internal problems to deal with. As was the custom, he had sent portraits of himself to Africa to head processions at the opening of games at the circus and amphitheater through the year. But with the departure of Maxentius's loyal governor Tertullus in 308 and no replacement arriving from Rome, troops of Africa's resident legions had ceased to carry the portrait of Maxentius at the head of ludi parades.

Once, there had been a single legion, the 3rd Augusta, in the African province, but Diocletian had stationed seven across North Africa, from Egypt to Mauretania. Knowing that the emperor Galerius did not recognize Maxentius as their Augustus and had led a failed expedition to Italy to dethrone him, legionaries in Africa had started carrying the bust of Galerius, as a protest against the "usurper" Maxentius.

Since Tertullus's return to Rome, Africa had been run by a *vicarius*, or vicar. The *vicarii*, who were addressed as "Your Worship," were a class of Roman government deputies who ran the twelve administrative diocese or districts into which every province had been divided by the earlier reforms of Diocletian—their title literally meant "substitute," reflecting the fact they were substituting for the governor in their diocese. The vicarius now temporarily running Africa was the elderly and ineffective Lucius Domitius Alexander, who was supposed to report to Maxentius's Praetorian prefect.

When Alexander failed to discipline the locally based Roman troops for their symbolic act of defiance involving the bust of Galerius, Maxentius sent him a demand to send his son to Rome as a hostage to his loyalty. When Alexander refused, Maxentius closed the imperial mint in Carthage and withdrew its artisans to Italy, eliminating Alexander's ability to pay his troublesome soldiery.

This tactic backfired, because it incensed the soldiers in Carthage, and late in 308 they rallied around Alexander and hailed him imperator, like a victorious general of old, and declared him an Augustus, making him their emperor of Africa. This took Africa, and its dependant territory of

Sardinia, from Maxentius's grasp, and from his regime's income stream. In addition to failing to send tax monies to Rome from now on, Alexander also cut off North African grain supplies to Italy, seriously impacting bread-making capacity. As for the making of money to pay his troops, Alexander set up his own Carthage mint, and although his artisans were not as skilled as the men they replaced, and the coins they minted were rudimentary, they achieved their objective of keeping his troops paid and maintaining the circulation of currency in North Africa.[69]

In Italy, Maxentius controlled several naval fleets, and he decided that he would personally lead an amphibious expedition to Africa the following spring to put down this mutiny and remove Alexander. But when he asked the augurs to conduct a sacrifice to ensure good omens for the venture, those omens proved far from auspicious, and Maxentius cancelled the operation. For now, Africa and Sardinia would remain rebel territory and out of Maxentius's control, and Italy's existing grain stores became subject to rationing.

Another problem for Maxentius lay much closer to home. The new Bishop of Rome, Marcellus, had turned the Christian congregation at Rome into two warring camps, generating riots between Christians in the streets. Under the penance requirements imposed by Marcellus, a Christian penitent who had previously submitted to Diocletian's demands and spurned their faith would firstly be required to stand outside a church and beg other members of the congregation to pray for them. After a period dictated by the bishop, a penitent would then be permitted to enter the church for the liturgy but would have to kneel throughout while existing congregation members stood. After a further qualifying period, the penitent could stand during the liturgy. Finally, they would be able to take the sacraments. This period of penitence could last years—some penitents would die before being readmitted to the Church. As for priests who had bowed to the Edict of Diocletian, they would never be readmitted under Bishop Marcellus's rules.

The many "lapsed" Christians at Rome who had obeyed Diocletian's edict felt the penance much too strict, arguing that they had kept secret copies of the scriptures or that their sacrifices had been without conviction. While lapsed Christians called for milder terms for their return to the Church, followers of Bishop Marcellus were adamant in their calls for rigorous penance. Their differences came to blows, and bloodshed. The resulting riots were the last thing Maxentius needed, and, to end the conflict on his streets, on January 16, 309, he abruptly terminated Marcellus's bishopric and sent him into exile, where he would die. Three months later, with the Christian community again at peace with itself and law-abiding, Maxentius would permit the election of a new Bishop of Rome.

With the matter of the divisive Roman bishop seemingly dealt with, the young emperor turned his attention to more diverting affairs—chariot racing. His revamped villa and the adjacent new ten-thousand-seat circus just south of Rome were completed in early 309. The hippodrome's imperial box, from which the emperor and his family would watch racing, faced the finishing line and was connected with the Villa of Maxentius via a covered portico, allowing a casual stroll from the emperor's country house to the games.

Roman hippodromes were traditionally equipped with Egyptian stone obelisks that sat on the racecourse's central spine, and Maxentius furnished his new circus with a large Egyptian obelisk that the emperor Domitian had originally installed at the Temple of Serapis at Rome late in the first century. In 1651, known as the Agonalis Obelisk, the tall stone needle was taken from where it lay at Maxentius's abandoned circus and incorporated by the sculptor Bernini into the Fountain of the Four Rivers in Rome's Piazza Navona, where it can still be seen today.

Maxentius's adored fourteen-year-old son Romulus, who had grown into a handsome boy and was now a consul, presided over the hippodrome's dedication ceremony. Just a matter of weeks later, Romulus was dead, drowning in the Tiber, although under what circumstances we do not know. Romulus most likely died in March during the annual festival of Anna Parenna, goddess of time and the new year—on the old republican Roman calendar, the year had begun in March.

For centuries, every March 15, the famous Ides of March, Romans enjoyed the Anna Parenna public holiday, with throngs crossing the Tiber to picnic in Etruria and celebrate Anna Parenna and the coming year. Heavy drinking was part and parcel of the festival—it was said that you would live one year more for every cup of wine you drank that day. Perhaps a very drunk young Romulus fell into the Tiber returning from the festival during the evening of March 15. Another possible occasion for Romulus's death was the Tiberinalia, an obscure August 17 festival celebrating the river god Tiber. Diocletian and Maximinus Daia are on record making dedications to the Tiberinalia.

Maxentius, devastated by his son's death, held funerary games for Romulus at the new Circus of Maxentius. This was the only time since the circus's dedication that it is known to have been used for its intended purpose of chariot racing. After the funerary games, Maxentius simply walked away from his circus. Buried during Constantine's later reign, the Circus of Maxentius was only unearthed in 1960. As a consequence, it retains more architectural elements than any other surviving Roman hippodrome across the former Roman Empire.

In a mausoleum built at the villa next to the circus, Maxentius laid the remains of his dead son to rest, and at his behest the Senate declared the boy a god. The mausoleum, which would not be completed until after July that year, had the dedicatory inscription: "To the deified Romulus, man of most noble memory, consul ordinary for the second time, son of our lord Maxentius the unconquered and perpetual Augustus, grandson of the deified Maximianus senior."[70] Despite Maximian's betrayal, Maxentius still celebrated his blood connection with his father, the former emperor.

Commemorative coins subsequently issued by Maxentius show Romulus's image on one side and a small, domed building with a prominent door on the other—the round Temple of the Divus (god) Romulus, erected in Rome by a grieving Maxentius, where citizens could make offerings to the boy god. The Temple of Romulus survives today as the vestibule of the Catholic Basilica of the Saints Cosmas and Damian, Christian physicians said to have been martyred at Rome during the third century reign of the emperor Carinus. In the wake of Romulus's death, Maxentius and his wife Maximilla would soon have another child, a son. That son's name has not come down to us, although there is speculation it may have been Aurelius Valerius.

The new Christian Bishop of Rome elected with Maxentius's approval on April 18 was Eusebius of Sardinia—not to be confused with the two other bishops named Eusebius who figured prominently in the life of Constantine—his biographer Eusebius of Caesarea, and the later Bishop Eusebius of Nicomedia. Eusebius, the new Bishop of Rome, would prove just as much a hard-liner on penance as his predecessor, and by August the following year, 310, renewed Christian riots at Rome over the penance issue would also result in his removal by a frustrated Maxentius, who exiled him to Sicily, where the former bishop would end his days.

MAXENTIUS'S BROTHER-IN-LAW and rival Constantine had his own problems. In the spring of A.D. 310, he was building a bridge across the

Rhine at Cologne and planning to launch a new campaign east of the Rhine against German tribes. Meanwhile, probably at Maximian's suggestion, Constantine gave his father-in-law troops and sent him into southern Gaul to Arles on the Rhône. In 308, Constantine had transferred his treasury from Trier to Arles, so that it was well out of the reach of German insurgents. In theory, Constantius was being sent to the city with part of the army to protect the treasury and be in a position to counter any attempt by Maxentius to invade Gaul via the Cottian Alps, although there is no indication that Maxentius contemplated or threatened any such thing.

Maximian did not hurry. At each posting station along the way south to Arles, he paused to take into his column all the horses of the Cursus Publicus and to eliminate supplies of food and fodder maintained at each station, to hinder any potential pursuit. Then, in June, once he reached Arles, Maximian announced to the troops under his command that Constantine was dead. Then, reclaiming the mantle of Augustus of the West, he opened up Constantine's treasury and offered the legionaries donatives to buy their loyalty. Writing to all the *comes* who administered the provinces in Gaul and Britain, he also offered them bribes for their loyalty.

The story circulated by Constantine following these events was that, when news of this treachery reached Constantine, he turned his army around and hurried from the Rhine toward Arles to deal with Maximian. However, we now know that Constantine had advance warning of Maximian's attempted coup against him, and the indications are that Constantine had in fact waited at Trier until he heard that Maximian had laid claim to his realm, and then moved against him. As Constantine tarried to organize provisions for the march south to deal with Maximian, his troops declared they had provisions enough and set off to deal with the betrayer without him.

"It was obvious," one of his officials said to Constantine shortly after, "what great love embraced you on the part of your soldiers." It was a matter of "simple and sincere devotion," he said. "You are commended by your name, your authority—which derives from the memory of your father—the appeal of your [young] age, and finally that physique of yours. They think that they are obeying a god!"[71]

With Constantine and his cavalry riding down the banks of the Saône and then the Rhône, Constantine's infantry was ferried down the rivers on oar-powered vessels, embarking at the river port of Cabillonum, today's Chalon-sur-Saône. When the current in the Saône brought the fleet of river craft to a halt, Constantine's troops were so anxious to get to grips with Maximian that they took over the oars to speed their progress.

Constantine, riding with the cavalry, was unable to keep up, and his infantry arrived at Arles before he did, to find the city gates closed. But when Constantine's men informed the troops inside the city that Constantine was alive and would soon arrive, most of the troops under Maximian deserted him, forcing Maximian to gallop away, fleeing south to the Mediterranean coast. Taking refuge at the port of Masillia, today's Marseille, a large and ancient city then connected to the mainland by a narrow neck and protected by massive walls, Maximian ordered the city's gates closed behind him.

Marching overland, Constantine's troops gave chase. Once Constantine and his cavalry reached Marseille in late June or early July, it was to find his infantry there ahead of them and commencing an assault on the city's landward wall. The legionaries had gone against the wall with scaling ladders, only to find them too short. So, men were standing on comrades' shoulders atop the ladders to reach the parapet while others were using ropes and grappling hooks to try to scale the wall. Seeing this, Constantine ordered "Recall" sounded. He would say he was anxious to preserve Marseille from looting by his own troops, as they were entitled to do under the laws of war if they stormed the city. Reluctantly, his men obeyed, and withdrew.

From outside the city, Constantine called for Maximian to come to the top of the wall to parley, which Maximian did. As the two were talking, locals sympathetic to Constantine opened rear gates to the city, admitting Constantinian troops. Within a short time, Maximian was captured and handed over to his son-in-law. The official story that emerged was that Constantine now gave Maximian the opportunity to take the honorable way out by taking his own life, and he did so, by hanging himself.

Lactantius, who was at Trier and would have heard the news from his pupil Crispus, gave a more colorful account of the actual circumstances of Maximian's death. According to him, Constantine's young wife of three years, Fausta, had earlier gone to her husband to warn him that Maximian had approached her to participate in Constantine's murder. Fausta was asked by her father to give an assassin access to Constantine's bedchamber by opening the door to the man, after which she was to depart the scene. The assassin, a man loyal to Maximian, was to slit Constantine's throat as he slept. As there is no account of Fausta going on campaign with her husband, which the wives of Roman generals did not do, this plot had obviously been intended to play out at Trier after Maximian had departed for Arles but before Constantine had left Trier for the Rhine.

Fausta was wise enough to see that her father represented the past while her husband represented the future, and her loyalty remained with Constantine. Once Fausta had confided the murder plot to him, Constantine told her to go along with it, but on the night appointed for the murder he had a eunuch from his staff, a man of similar build to himself, sleep in his bed in his stead. The assassin duly crept in, killed the unwitting eunuch, and was then apprehended and executed. It seems that a messenger was subsequently sent speeding to Maximian to tell him the plot had been successful and that Constantine was a corpse. Once Maximian had this report, he announced at Arles that his son-on-law was dead. Constantine then set off for Arles to deal with Maximian.

Although Constantine would make it known that Maximian had suffered a "voluntary death," few would believe that he was not helped by Constantinian centurions to end it all.[72] A career soldier like Maximian would have been expected to use his sword or cut his wrists in the best classical Roman tradition. In fact, in all the annals of Roman history, hanging as a method of suicide was virtually unknown. Maximian's son Maxentius certainly did not believe that his father's death was self-inflicted. Even though Maximian had attempted to overthrow him, once news of Maximian's so-called suicide reached Rome, Maxentius had the Senate declare his father a god and issued coins memorializing Maximian.

Maxentius himself vowed to avenge his father's "murder." The unexpected ferocity of his anger with Constantine would be reported at Trier. If Maxentius and Constantine had not been enemies before this, they were now. The orator of Trier who served on Constantine's staff would express sympathy for his master over Maxentius's reaction, declaring, the following year, "The fresh agitation of that man," Constantine's brother-in-law and ally, "who above all should have supported your successes, drew attention to himself," he said.[73]

It was understandable that rumors of Maximian's murder might engender anger in his son, but that was no excuse for threats, in the opinion of Constantine's loyal official. "Individuals should nevertheless check their words, however angry they may be," he opined. The result, he said, was "deep wounds"—in the relationship between Constantine and Maxentius, and probably also between Constantine's wife Fausta and her brother.[74]

Like Maxentius, modern historians have had no doubt that Constantine was behind Maximian's death. Ironically, eight years after Maximian's demise, Constantine would reintroduce an old Roman law that had fallen into abeyance, the *poena cullei*. Under this law, "Whoever, secretly or openly, shall hasten the death of a parent, son, or other near relative," was guilty of parricide, and was to be punished by being sewn into a sack and then thrown into the sea or a river. The condemned man's life was terminated by literally being given the sack. Constantine added the rather sadistic stipulation that snakes were to be sewn into the sack with the condemned man.[75]

Shortly after Maximian's death, word reached Constantine as he was heading back to Trier from Marseille that the Germans were restive on the Rhine. Urging his troops to double the pace of their march north to counter the threat, he would have sent word ahead to Cologne that he was coming. Only a matter of weeks later, on or a little after July 25, a panegyric, or public oration, was delivered by the previously mentioned official in Constantine's capital Trier, in celebration of Constantine's July 25 *quinquennalia,* the fifth anniversary of his accession to the Tetrarchy on the death of his father Constantius.

Such milestone anniversaries were the subject of major celebrations by all members of the Tetrarchy, usually involving circus games and large public banquets. This 310 Trier oration in honor of Constantine's anniversary was most likely delivered in the Aula Palatina, or Palace of the Court, the vast basilica that served as the audience hall to Constantine's new Trier palace, which was completed that year. We know that the address was delivered in the presence of Constantine, because the orator declared, early in his speech, "It is right for me to remember with dutiful affection all the emperors, but to *celebrate* the one who is here among us."[76]

Indeed, with all the members of the Tetrarchy present at the major anniversaries of their reigns, with Constantine known to enjoy lavish ceremonials, and with the threat from the Germans on the Rhine having dissipated, as the oration reveals, there was no reason for Constantine to not be in attendance, standing at the head of dignitaries from throughout Gaul—Eusebius would later record that audiences stood for orations delivered before Constantine, and, ignoring requests to take a seat, Constantine also stood.[77]

Among this audience for the July 25 oration would have been Constantine's wife Fausta and his teenage son Crispus, the latter accompanied, quite probably, by his tutor Lactantius. Being a Christian, Lactantius must have silently fumed on hearing the orator speak of the Roman gods Jupiter and Mars, and of Constantine's veneration of two other Roman deities. It is clear from this that Lactantius had no influence over Constantine's thinking or propaganda, and he must have been horrified to hear the speaker describe a "divine" event that he said had taken place as Constantine rode north to deal with the Germans following the hanging of Maximian.

As his speech continued, the orator would mention the recent "voluntary" death of Maximian and the circumstances surrounding it—an occurrence that would have required a hasty addition to the address he had been rehearsing for months. He also gave an encapsulated life story of Constantine. And, importantly, he told of what had recently occurred on Constantine's march for the Rhine to deal with the Germans after leaving Marseille, revealing a piece of Constantinian pagan religious propaganda that would later prove both a problem and an inspiration for his Christian biographers Eusebius and Lactantius.[78]

Some authors over the years have assumed that the orator at Constantine's wedding three years earlier and the orator who delivered this quinquennalia speech in 310 were different men, but many aspects of both speeches point to them being the same figure. Both are revealed as Gallic professors of rhetoric. Certainly, the author of the second panegyric is much more familiar with Constantine, asking, at the end of the speech, for his master to look favorably on his hometown and also on the eldest of his five sons, who, he reveals, was at that time one of the *magistri privatee,* lawyers employed in managing Constantine's private estates and collecting often overdue rents from the estates' tenants—the orator obviously wanted Constantine to give his eldest an important post on his governmental staff. Yet this familiarity can be explained by the past three years in Constantine's service, during which the orator can be expected to have been in the emperor's close company.

There are two other clues that point to the two orators being the same man, in the style of the two addresses. Each speech introduces a single small, lame joke early in proceedings. In the wedding speech, this had been the jest, a misogynistic one at that, about the rarity of young men loving their wives. And both speeches, in comparing Constantine and his father Constantius, use a similar and very uncommon turn of phrase: "A great likeness of appearance has passed from him to you," he said, "as if *imprinted on your features by Nature with a stamp.*"[79]

In the July 310 quinquennalia speech, which the orator said had been "written over a long period and often rehearsed," telling us that Constantine had assigned him the task of writing and delivering the speech well in advance of the event, he began with his formulaic little joke: "There is quite a large number of people who think that my speech will be too long. . . . I shall disappoint their expectation by the brevity of my speech. I had in fact thought out more to say, but I would rather my speech were short than rejected."[80]

The orator went on to describe Constantine's march from Marseille to the Rhine in the wake of Maximian's death to deal with the massing German tribes. The day after he had doubled his army's pace to reach the Rhine as soon as possible, word arrived that "the whole commotion had subsided and that the complete calmness that you had left [on the Rhine] had returned." The Germans "suddenly collapsed, as if stupefied when they heard of your return." Now, with the urgency gone from his homeward journey and matters at Marseille satisfactorily dealt with, Constantine diverted from the highway linking Trier and Marseille.

"The successful outcome of your affairs there urged you to offer the immortal gods what you had promised." As at the beginning of every campaign by his army, Constantine would, like all Roman generals, have made sacrifices to the gods in front of his troops, promising largesse in return for heavenly support. "You had turned off to the most beautiful temple in the world," the orator continued.

Historians agree this temple was the Temple of Apollo Grannus at Andesina in northern Gaul, today's French town of Grand, southwest of Trier. Among other things, Apollo was the god of poetry and hunting, but he was also, like Sol, a god of the sun, and in this age the two gods were often interchangeable in the minds of Romans. The sanctuary of Apollo at Andesina was well known to the orator, who spoke of the god's "sacred groves" there, and the "steaming mouths of his fountains, bubbling waters, smoky with a gentle warmth."

Constantine went to this temple, said the orator, addressing Constantine directly, "and to the god who was actually present there, as you saw. For you saw, I believe, Constantine, your own Apollo, with Victoria accompanying him, offering you crowns of laurel, each one of which brings you an omen of thirty years." According to the orator, Constantine saw a vision in the sky that day, above the sun, of the two gods offering him symbols of a thirty-year reign. Lactantius, writing later, claimed that Constantine's troops also saw a strange light effect around the sun the day that Constantine saw his vision.

"But why do I say 'I believe'?" asked the orator. "You saw him and recognized yourself in the appearance of that god. You are just like him—young, full of joy, helpful, and very handsome. . . . Now, all the temples seem to call to you themselves, especially that of your own Apollo."

He went on to say that this vision was confirmation that Constantine's reign and life would last longer than that of Nestor, the wise king of Pylos in Homer's *Odyssey* who reigned for more than thirty years. In relating this vision story, the orator was not only aligning Constantine with Apollo, the sun god, but he was also saying that he had been told—quite possibly by Constantine himself, but at the very least by a senior staff member who had accompanied their chief—that Constantine claimed to have seen a heavenly vision of Apollo and Victoria, who had guaranteed him a long reign.

Some modern historians such as Michael Grant have declared that the orator simply made this up, to gain Constantine's favor for his hometown and his family. However, to tell a totally fabricated and unauthorized story about a vision experienced by his emperor was inviting punishment, not reward—in the form of exile or execution. Bear in mind that the orator was making this claim of a vision in front of Constantine and the gathered dignitaries of his realm. Earlier, the orator had mentioned that he had avoided the risk of having his speech rejected by keeping it brief. This indicates that, as would be expected for such an important occasion as the quinquennalia, the orator had run the speech by Constantine prior to delivering it, and Constantine had not rejected it, but had given it his approval. So Constantine would have known what the orator was going to say about him, including his intent to describe the vision. In fact, Constantine is likely to have directed the vision's inclusion in the speech.

This claim of a vision of gods witnessed by an emperor was powerful propaganda. We know that the mentally unstable first-century emperor Caligula had claimed to have been regularly in conversation with the moon goddess Diana, but this was not universally known until the later biography of the first emperors written by Suetonius, and was not made public in the emperor's lifetime, as Constantine's supposed vision was.

After this very public announcement of Constantine's godly vision, the story would have spread like wildfire via word of mouth, throughout Constantine's provinces and beyond. The claim of a vision of the gods had enormous power to influence the highly superstitious Roman world. This vision, the Trier orator went on, proved that Constantine was destined to rule the world, as sole ruler. One of the reasons Michael Grant doubted the authenticity of the vision story was the fact that the orator also claimed in this speech that Constantine was born to rule because he was descended from Claudius II, Roman emperor from 268 to 270. This Claudius had gained the title Gothicus for famously defeating the Goths and terminating a massive barbarian invasion at the celebrated 269 Battle of Naissus south of the Danube. Grant and other historians such as Timothy Barnes have doubted there was any genuine connection between the family of Constantine and Claudius Gothicus, considering the claim an invention of the Trier orator.[81]

However, Constantine himself would personally and very publicly claim descent from Claudius in 317, on his coinage. Several late antiquity sources would also link Constantine and Claudius Gothicus. Writing just several decades after Constantine's death, well-regarded historian Eutropius claimed that Constantine was Claudius's grandson, via his daughter, and this was repeated by twelfth-century Byzantine writer Johannes Zonaras. According to the anonymous and often inaccurate *Historia Augusta*, Constantine was Claudius's grandnephew, via Claudius's niece Claudia. And, as mentioned earlier, Valesianus, writing the *Excerpta Valesiana* around 390, stated that Constantius was descended from Claudius's brother Crispus, making Claudius the great-uncle of Constantine.

If we accept that Constantine's son Crispus was indeed named after Claudius's brother, whether this blood connection was real or not, the claim of the connection by Constantine and his family ostensibly went back as far as young Crispus's naming ceremony in 295, meaning the claim had been public for at least fifteen years by the time of the Trier oration. So, true or not, the claim of descent from Claudius Gothicus may have been well established by the time of the Trier oration, and, more importantly, Constantine himself later very publicly and indisputably endorsed his blood connection with Claudius.[82]

There is a particularly good reason to believe that Constantine actually instructed the orator to include the claimed Claudian bloodline connection in his speech. Just as Constantine or someone close to him would have told the orator about his so-called vision of Apollo and Victoria to set the groundwork for the legend that he was divinely inspired—a legend he was to push hard in the coming years—he may have promoted a family connection with Claudius Gothicus for a political motive that was important to him at the time. In 310, one man more than any other stood in Constantine's path to sole power. Constantine discounted Maxentius because of his lack of military experience, but Galerius, emperor of the East, was the military strongman of the day, enjoying the solid loyalty of his troops and pulling all the political strings. Galerius was the man preventing Constantine from expanding his realm of control beyond Gaul.

You will remember that Naissus, site of Claudius Gothicus's great and famous victory, was also Constantine's birthplace. The city was located in what had once been the Kingdom of Dardania, within Dacia. Galerius had also been born in Dardania, as he delighted in telling the world. In boasting of a connection to both Claudius Gothicus and Dardania, Constantine was telling the world that he was more than Galerius's equal. As American historian Barry Strauss has recently remarked, Constantine was "a public relations genius," and this Claudius Gothicus promotion, like the heavenly-vision story, has the stamp of that genius upon it.[83]

What the world, and Constantine, did not know at this time was that Galerius was being consumed by an insidious disease, said by Lactantius to be a form of gangrene that consumed his genitals, and which, according to Valesianus, left "inner parts of his body exposed and in a state of corruption." Modern historians think Galerius was probably suffering from bowel cancer. Within ten months of the Trier oration, the Herdsman would be dead, and the need for anti-Galerius propaganda from Constantine would die with him. The Claudius Gothicus connection would not be cited again by Constantine for another seven years, only to be brought out and dusted off when Constantine was locked in both a military conflict and a propaganda battle in 317 with his final rival for complete power, Licinius—another native of Dardania.

Interestingly, too, the orator of the Trier panegyric spoke of "your Apollo" as he addressed Constantine and revealed Constantine's Grand "vision," implying that Apollo was the favored deity of Constantine by 310. As mentioned earlier, prior to this, Constantine's only confirmed religious affiliation had been with Mars. Within three years of this reported vision of Apollo and Victoria, both gods would figure prominently and regularly on Constantine's coins and monuments, with Mars only rarely referenced.

This official connection of Constantine with the old gods would have been galling to Christians, especially to Lactantius, tutor of Constantine's son. The story of Constantine's vision of Apollo and Victoria may well have inspired Lactantius, who was then writing his book *De Morbitus Persecutorum*, or *On the Deaths of the Persecutors*, a frequently gory, mostly unsubstantiated, and, overall, a gleeful account of the painful deaths of emperors who had persecuted Christians.

When, three years after the Trier oration, Lactantius began to publish his book volume by volume, he would write that, in the immediate lead-up to the Battle of the Milvian Bridge, Constantine saw a vision above the sun, of Christ, who promised him victory. And it is this version of the vision that would find its way into Christian lore and history books. The vision that Lactantius related bore a remarkable resemblance to Constantine's claimed and previously documented vision of Apollo and Victoria, of which Lactantius made no mention.

Only one other contemporary writer would also tell of the vision of Christ reported by Lactantius—fellow Christian author Eusebius of Caesarea. Yet when Eusebius wrote his *The Church History*, in which he told, among other things, of Constantine's rise to power, he made not a solitary mention of Constantine's prebattle vision of Christ. The early volumes of *The Church History* first appeared in 313, the year after Lacantius's reported vision of Christ by Constantine supposedly occurred, and around the same time as Lactantius's *On the Deaths of the Persecutors*, with the final books being published by 325. But here is a curious thing—it was only years later, after Constantine had died and was unable to correct him, that Eusebius wrote in his new book, *The Life of Constantine*, that the emperor had seen a vision of Christ promising him victory prior to the Battle of the Milvian Bridge.

Eusebius can be expected to have had access to Lactantius's work and been aware of the claim of the Christ vision. He is likely to have been separately aware of the story of Constantine's vision of Apollo in Gaul. In his *Life*, Eusebius would recall that Constantine, in his later years, told him personally that he indeed had seen a vision of "the divinity." But to which divinity, and to which version of the vision story, had Constantine been referring? Eusebius chose to interpret it to mean it was Christ whom the emperor saw.

Like Lactantius, he made no reference to the earlier vision of Apollo and Victoria offering him victory and a long reign. But, unlike Lactantius, who placed the vision immediately prior to the Milvian Bridge battle, Eusebius wrote, after Constantine's death, that it occurred "some time" prior to the battle—and some time could be as much as two years prior, and in Gaul.

TWENTY-THREE DAYS AFTER the celebrations of Constantine's quin-quennalia at Trier, at Rome, the Christian community in Italy received a blow at the hands of Constantine's brother-in-law. On August 17, Maxentius removed Eusebius, the Sardinian-born Bishop of Rome, from his position. The bishop had proven just as dogmatic and divisive as his predecessor, and the Christian factions of Rome were again at each other's throats. Maxentius sent the bishop into exile, as he had his predecessor, and did not authorize the election of a replacement.

ON MAY 5, 311, Galerius departed the scene with his unpleasant but natural death, at the age of around fifty-three. Just days before his end, on April 30, Galerius unexpectedly issued an Edict of Toleration, in his name and in the name of the other current official members of the Tetrarchy, including Constantine but excluding Maxentius. This decree, called the Edict of Serdica by some—a copy continues to be displayed in Sofia, the ancient Serdica—was actually issued at Nicomedia. It decreed a relaxation of the persecution of Christians.

"Many were subdued by the fear of danger, many even suffered death," the decree said in part. Galerius blamed the Christians for their own persecution, stating that they "would thus make laws unto themselves . . . and collect various peoples in congregations." Despite this, Galerius, knowing that he was dying, and seeking to take out a little afterlife insurance, proclaimed, "They may again be Christians, and may hold their conventicles [secret meetings], provided they do nothing contrary to good order." He added, "They ought to pray to their god for our safety, for that of the republic and for their own, and that the republic may continue uninjured on every side, and that they may be able to live securely in their homes."[84]

Following Galerius's passing, his widow Valeria and mother-in-law Prisca were sent to live with Licinius, but, fearful of him, the pair fled to Daia in the East. Daia soon proposed marriage to Valeria. When she turned him down, he stripped her of her money and property and exiled both Valeria and her mother to a small town in the Syrian wilds, where they lived under guard. Seven months after Galerius left the stage, Diocletian would pass away in his bed at Split in December of that same year, 311, dying, it was rumored, by his own hand to end his suffering from chronic illness. By the end of 311, the old guard would be gone, and the road to the conquest of Rome and the East would open up to Constantine . . . if he chose to take it.

X

PREPARING FOR
CIVIL WAR

WITH THE DEATH of Maxentius's father Maximian, Licinius, official emperor of the West, had moved against Maxentius by sending troops from Pannonia, which he controlled, into that part of Istria that bordered northeast Italy and which came under Maxentius's control. Licinius's troops captured a coastal fort at Centur, overlooking the harbor of Parentum on the west coast of the Istrian peninsula—today's Porec in Croatia. Within weeks, Maxentius's troops recaptured the fort, only for Licinius's forces to retake and keep it in 310. To counter further provocative moves by Licinius, Maxentius dispatched troops to garrison cities and towns in northern Italy and strengthened city defenses. Perhaps because he found that Italians still strongly supported Maxentius, Licinius then backed off and made no attempt to advance his forces into Italy.[85]

With Licinius held at bay, Maxentius turned his eyes to Africa, the bleeding sore in the belly of his slice of empire, source of most of Rome's grain. By the summer of 310, encouraged by his energetic new Praetorian prefect Volusianus, who succeeded Rusticanus in the post, Maxentius dispatched a small army of crack troops under Volusianus's command to terminate the African revolt. Maxentius's African task force, roughly 5,000 strong—about the size of a full-strength legion—would have been made up of several cohorts of the revamped Praetorian Guard plus cohorts detached for the operation from other units such as the 2nd Parthica Legion and the Herculean Legion.

The 2nd Parthica had been one of three new legions formed in Italy by the emperor Septimius Severus late in the second century for his successful invasion of Parthia. Following that campaign, Severus brought the 2nd Parthica back to Rome with him, basing it just twelve miles south of the capital at Alba Longa in the Alban Hills, which made it the first imperial legion ever stationed permanently in Italy. Not entirely trusting the Praetorian Guard, Severus had let the Praetorians know that the 2nd Parthica was just a two-hour march away if the Guard proved troublesome. Always recruited in Italy thereafter, the 2nd Parthica's legionaries were granted extra privileges and were favored by successive emperors, who took the legion on campaign with them across the empire.

Septimius Severus built the legion a fine base on a sloping site at Alba Longa, with high stone and concrete walls and circular guard towers. The capacious Castra Albana, as the 2nd Parthica's base was called, grew to feature a massive baths complex and a large amphitheater for the legionaries' use. Outside its walls, a vicus, or town, quickly grew to house the legionaries' Italian wives and families. Over time, because of the location of its home base, the unit gained the nickname the Alban Legion, and its men the *Albani*. The 2nd Parthica had continued to be an elite unit until Diocletian came to the throne and removed the favored status of both it and the Praetorian Guard. Maxentius had restored the legion's elite status and gained its firm loyalty as a result.

Volusianus and his task force landed by sea at Carthage, capital of the African provinces, and quickly took the city, with the locally based troops offering little resistance. A coin issued by Domitius Alexander at Carthage that spring had depicted three military standards on its reverse: the eagle of a legion, the standard of a legionary cohort, and the standard of an auxiliary unit, suggesting that this was the extent of the military force that had enthroned him and was loyal to him. If that were the case, Alexander fielded more men, but the Maxentians were much more experienced and highly disciplined. In the face of Volusianus's fixed ranks, the locally based troops melted away.

With his men deserting him, old Alexander was forced to retreat west to the inland city of Cirta, in today's Algeria, and Volusianus followed, surrounding Cirta and then storming it. "Emperor" Alexander was taken prisoner and then garroted on Volusianus's command, suffering the Republican Roman punishment for leaders who defied Rome. At every city and town through the province, military and civil leaders who had supported the rebellion were also executed, with their property seized and added to the assets that supported Maxentius's imperial treasury at Rome.

By the autumn of 310, leaving new officers in command of the province's military and a prefect named Zenas at Carthage to govern in Maxentius's name, Volusianus was able to return to Rome with his army. He also brought large shipments of grain for the people of Italy, which ended grain rationing, and military reinforcements for Maxentius's army, among them units of nimble Numidian cavalrymen and Berber *Mauri feroces*, or ferocious Moors, light cavalry from Mauretania.

Volusianus arrived back in Rome in time for the October 28 celebration of the anniversary of Maxentius's accession to the throne. As a reward for a job well done in Africa, Volusianus was appointed Rome's city prefect by Maxentius, effective for twelve months until the following October 28. Volusianus was replaced as Praetorian prefect by Ruricius Pompeianus, a senator earnestly loyal to Maxentius.

While pro-Constantine Christian writers would later paint a picture of Maxentius always being unpopular in Rome and Italy, the dramatic increase in the grain supply as a result of Maxentius's success in Africa would have been highly popular, and the victory over Alexander by this son of Rome would have been celebrated joyously by the populace at games on his October 28 anniversary, as the Invincible Prince took their plaudits at the Circus Maximus. Some historians even suggest that, to celebrate that victory, Maxentius ordered the construction of a triumphal arch beside the Colosseum, planning to conduct a Triumphal procession through the city on its completion. If this was the case, that arch would still be incomplete two years later.

OVER 310–311, brothers-in-law Constantine and Maxentius waged a propaganda war to convince the Roman world that each was in the right. Maxentius seems to have gone to great lengths to paint himself as the wounded son of an honored if not entirely honorable Augustus, depicting Constantine as the villain for "murdering" his father. With coinage a major propaganda tool of the day, Maxentius even had coins minted at Rome over 310–311 commemorating Constantine's late father Constantius as he, Maxentius, strove to legitimize his claim to Constantius's former position as emperor of the West.

The shape of the fractured Tetrarchy remained unchanged until the death of Galerius in the late spring of 311. After that, everything changed, although slowly, like the cracked foundations of a house gradually giving way. In the East, Maximinus Daia marched into Asia Minor, Licinius's territory, and took control. Licinius called for a peace conference, and aboard a ship sitting in the Bosporus between Europe and Asia he and Daia agreed to divide the East between them. Daia took all Roman territory east of the Bosporus. Licinius claimed all the territories west of the Bosporus as far as Gaul, then went off to fight Sarmatians on the Danube.

Through this period, Maxentius remained quiet. As for Constantine, disappointing supporters who wanted him to dethrone Maxentius now that Galerius was out of the picture, he turned his back on the opportunity and set off on a tour of Gaul and Britain. But come the summer, Maxentius moved against Constantine, recruiting new troops across Italy for local defense while planning to invade the province of Raetia, to the north of Italy. This would effectively drive a wedge between the realms of Constantine and Licinius.

Constantine, becoming aware of Maxentius's plans over the winter of 311/312, apparently via agents at Rome, sent envoys to Licinius in Pannonia, informing him of Maxentius's Raetian scheme. These envoys sealed a treaty of cooperation between Constantine and Licinius, and Licinius transferred troops to defend Raetia, a move that caused Maxentius to shelve his Raetian expedition.

When Daia, in the East, learned of the new alliance between Licinius and Constantine, he sent envoys to Maxentius at Rome, and via them Daia and Maxentius secretly agreed to a treaty that made them allies. Maxentius even raised statues of Daia and himself together at Rome to honor their new alliance. Now the Roman Empire was divided into two opposing camps—Constantine and Licinius versus Maxentius and Daia.

To pay for his mobilization in Italy, Maxentius implemented local taxation. It had been Italian resentment of Galerius's new local taxes that had propelled Maxentius to the throne. Now he was doing exactly the same thing as Galerius, and it did not go down well with Italians. Constantine, meanwhile, deciding to take the war to his brother-in-law now that he was allied with Licinius, made preparations over the winter for a campaign in Italy the following spring, with Rome his ultimate goal. At the same time, he assigned warships under his control the task of blockading the west coast ports of Italy that were the destination of the Mediterranean grain fleets, thus cutting off Maxentius's grain supply for a second time during his reign. The granaries at Rome were full at the time, but as a precaution Maxentius once again introduced grain rationing, in case there was a protracted siege of Rome in the future.[86]

The physical showdown between Constantine and Maxentius, long foreshadowed, was now just months away.

XI

CONSTANTINE
INVADES ITALY

I N THE EARLY SPRING OF 312, Constantine crossed the Cottian Alps from Gaul and invaded northwest Italy with a compact and highly disciplined army, bent on defeating Maxentius, taking Rome, and taking Maxentius's crown of emperor of the West. While Galerius, emperor of the East, had been alive, Constantine had balked at taking such a momentous step and going to war with his brother-in-law. With Galerius dying in 311 and an alliance sealed with Licinius, the way had opened up for Constantine.

Some modern writers have stated that Maxentius declared war on Constantine in 311 by mobilizing his forces in Italy. Yet this had been a defensive move, not an offensive one. Maxentius made no attempt to lead his army against Constantine by invading Gaul. In fact, Lactantius claimed that the superstitious Maxentius dared not leave Rome, "because the soothsayers had foretold that if he went out of it, he would perish."[87]

So Constantine, needing an excuse to launch a civil war against Maxentius by invading Italy, let it be known that he was bent on liberating the city of Rome from "the tyrant" Maxentius. Even though, at best, Constantine had only visited Rome once before in his life, and Maxentius was a native of Rome, from now on Constantine's propaganda would paint him as the champion of Rome, "the deliverance of which" was "the motive, or rather indeed the pretence, of the civil war" that Constantine now launched, wrote Gibbon.

It is highly likely that Constantine had been encouraged to march on Rome by his mother Helena. Although she had been born in the East, of Greek background, had lived for the past six years at Trier, and is not on record having previously visited Rome, Helena was a woman of fixations, and she seems to have been fixated with the idea of making her home in Rome and living there for the rest of her life. The Italian military campaign went against the advice of Constantine's senior officers, who were probably daunted by the size of Maxentius's army, and flew in the face of ill omens when Constantine carried out the traditional sacrifices prior to launching the campaign. But Constantine was now hell-bent on pursuing it. According to the Greek historian Zosimus in his *New History* some eighty years later, Constantine had 90,000 infantry and 18,000 cavalry troops on the Rhine in 311, of which he left the majority on guard against the Franks and Alemanni in 312, taking 30,000 infantry and 8,000 cavalry with him to Italy. Being a cavalryman himself, it would be on his mounted soldiers that Constantine would rely in the coming months; and later events tell us that, before he left Gaul, he trained his cavalry in a range of dazzling maneuvers and battle tactics, to the point that, by the time they reached Italian soil, his troopers were working with the precision of a well-oiled machine.

We know little about the makeup of his army, other than the fact that his troops came from their longtime stations in Germany, Gaul, and Britain. No Spanish troops were included in Constantine's force, indicating that the Spanish provinces were still resisting his control. Constantine's infantry was made up of detachments from his legions, plus some specialist auxiliaries. Among the latter were members of units of Gallo-Belgic archers, who would later be depicted, wearing their typical ethnic caps, on the Arch of Constantine. Archers wore no armor and, apart from their bows, carried axes on their belts as secondary weapons, for close combat.

The infantryman of this time carried a long spatha, originally a cavalry sword, which had replaced the shorter gladius of earlier days. The gladius, while just two feet long, had often given Roman troops the advantage in close-quarter fighting, because it had a sharp point, handy for stabbing into the face of opponents. The spatha, while increasing the user's reach, did not have a sharp end and was only effectively used in a slashing motion. Constantine's foot soldiers also carried a long spear and a large, slightly convex oval wooden shield that had replaced the famous *scutum*, the unique curved rectangular shield carried by legionaries in Caesar's day.

Constantine's cavalrymen all rode without stirrups, as Roman cavalry had always done. Their saddle, which was like a chair, kept them in place. The mounted units riding for Constantine included less well-armored light cavalrymen with small round shields and very little armor, whose job was to dash in and launch darts at the enemy, especially at their infantry. But the cavalry arm by this time revolved around wings of cataphracts, the now standard heavy cavalry of Rome. Inspired by Sarmatian and Parthian heavy cavalry, the Roman cataphract wore fish-scale metal armor from helmeted head to metal-booted foot that made him the model for the armored knights of the Middle Ages—weapons technology, until the introduction of cannon in the twelfth century, would remain locked in a time warp for close to a millennium after Constantine's day.

The cataphract's horse was also armored, covered by fish-scale armor sewn to a leather coat protecting the flanks and neck. Metal protectors with viewing slits covered the animal's eyes. Cataphracts sometimes carried an oval wooden shield, although some cataphracts fought without shields. Their standard weapons were a thirteen-foot-long lance and a spatha. Constantine's cavalry also introduced a new weapon in this campaign, one with which Maxentius's cavalry seems not to have been equipped—the mace. This was a metal ball on the end of a long handle. Because the cataphract was so heavily armored that he was difficult to kill or disable, the mace was designed to knock opposing cataphracts from their horses. Once on the ground, the heavily armored cataphract lacked maneuverability and became easier pickings for both opposing cavalry and infantry.

Against infantry, the cataphract and his steed were like a modern-day tank: they had the capacity to simply ride over the top of, and break through, infantry lines. Within several decades, a super-heavy form of Roman cataphract unit was being deployed, the *Clibanari*. Their title roughly translates as "ovens," and these troopers looked like iron ovens on horseback. Four decades after Constantine's invasion of Italy, Roman officer Ammianus Marcellinus, who served in the bodyguard of Constantine's son the emperor Constantius II, fought in armies that fielded *Clibanari*. He would say of them: "Thin circles of iron plates, fitted to the curves of their bodies, completely covered their limbs so that whatever way they moved their limbs, their garment fitted." So completely were they encased in iron, he said, "you might have thought them statues."[88]

As for Constantine's subordinate officers, we know very little about them. King Crocus was no longer mentioned in Roman texts. He is likely to have died since leading the acclamation of Constantine as emperor at York six years prior to this, perhaps falling while fighting Picti and Scoti in northern Britain as British legends suggest. Another senior commander was now prominent in Constantine's life, a man who, within a year, would also be linked to Constantine by marriage by wedding of one of Constantine's half-sisters. A member of the Senatorial Order of Rome, he was named Bassianus.

Not only would Constantine soon make Bassianus his brother-in-law, he would attempt to elevate him to the post of his Caesar and nominated successor, indicating that Constantine held Bassianus in very high esteem and trusted him implicitly. It is probable that Bassianus was Constantine's deputy for the march on Rome, and he may have held the post of his Praetorian prefect—Maxentius, Licinius, and Daia all had Praetorian prefects as their right-hand men.

We know little about Bassianus because, within four years, Constantine would turn on him, order his execution, and issue a decree of *damnatio memoriae* against him—literally "condemnation of memory"—requiring all records, inscriptions, busts, and statues of Bassianus to be destroyed. We do not even know Bassianus's full name.

The only other Roman figure of this era with the name Bassianus that has come down to us is a Quintus Bassianus, who, according to nineteenth-century English folklore, was a Roman general who went from Gaul to aid Constantius in putting down the Carausian Revolt. According to a regional history, Quintus Bassianus was killed in the Lonsdale area in northwest England, just south of Hadrian's Wall, by rebel leader Allectus. No Roman historian offers any collaboration of this. Yet, in folklore there is sometimes a grain of truth, and perhaps this Quintus was the same Bassianus, and he was an officer of Constantius inherited by Constantine, but who, obviously, was not killed by Allectus.[89]

We do know that Constantine's Bassianus had a brother, Senecio, who held a senior post in the administration of the emperor Licinius in the East at this time. Modern scholars have speculated that both Bassianus and Senecio were members of the Anicii, a Roman family famous for growing from plebeian roots to produce many consuls. If the brothers Bassianus and Senecio were indeed members of the Anicii family, they were related to a current Roman senator, Annius Anicius Julianus, who was at Rome at this moment and was a supporter of Maxentius—almost certainly being a member of the ring of thirteen senators who'd helped Maxentius take the throne.

Once Constantine took Rome, he would execute senators who had supported Maxentius, but Anicius Julianus was not among those who perished. Just the opposite; he would, in time, be rewarded, being made a consul by Constantine in 322, shortly after being appointed city prefect for three years. This suggests that, if Bassianus and Julianus were indeed related, Bassianus would use his influence with Constantine to have Julianus spared.

So, apart from Bassianus, we are in the dark about the senior officers in Constantine's army. Of his family, his half-brothers and half-sisters were still at Toulouse, while his son Crispus, who turned seventeen this year, was back at Trier along with his stepmother Fausta and grandmother Helena.

Some Christian authors have claimed that Lactantius, Crispus's Christian tutor, was a member of Constantine's entourage for the march on Rome, serving as Constantine's religious counselor. Lactantius himself made no such claim, and would surely have been the first to boast of it had it been the case. "Lactantius certainly did not accompany Constantine to Rome in 312," says historian Timothy Barnes adamantly.[90]

In fact, there is no evidence that Lactantius was ever an adviser to Constantine himself; and when Constantine entered Italy, Lactantius would have been back at Trier with his pupil Crispus. Eusebius of Caesarea would state quite emphatically that it was not until after Constantine defeated Maxentius that he took Christians onto his staff as counselors.[91]

What is more, within a year, Lactantius would leave Crispus's employ and return to Nicomedia, to live under the emperor Licinius's rule. Lactantius did this, in the view of historians such as Barnes, to again take up his chair in rhetoric in Nicomedia once the lifting of Christian persecution was confirmed in 313. This being the case, Lactantius had no position of influence with Constantine and may have even fallen out with Crispus, or Constantine, or both, by 313.[92]

Some modern accounts declare that, on his way to attacking Rome, Constantine swept through northern Italy in a lightning campaign. The reality is very different. Through the late spring, the summer, and into the fall of 312, Constantine undertook a sometimes grueling campaign of many months against stubborn resistance from Maxentius's troops and the people of northern Italy, many of whom remained loyal to Maxentius.

Gibbon estimated that 100,000 of Maxentius's 188,000 troops stayed at Rome with the young emperor. Maxentius's remaining men were split, says Eusebius, into three divisions, and these were stationed in roughly a straight line, east to west, across northern Italy, at the cities of Turin, Brescia, and Verona. Many of these men were likely to have been north Italian levies, especially from Tuscany, which Zosimus later credited as a major source of Maxentius's troops. The troops at Rome with Maxentius were primarily Italians, Sicilians, and North Africans.[93]

After Constantine crossed the Alps, the first Italian city that his army encountered was Segusium, today's Susa in Piedmont, at the foot of the mountains and 32 miles west of Turin. Susa was large enough to sport its own amphitheater and contained a triumphal arch dedicated to the emperor Augustus. The city had been well fortified by Maxentius; as soon as word of the approach of Constantine's army reached the city, it closed its gates and lined its walls with defenders. Constantine immediately sent his foot soldiers against Susa, and under cover of their shields they set fire to its gates and scaled its walls. Susa quickly fell, but contrary to the rules of war, Constantine prevented his troops from looting the city. Ever the smart propagandist, Constantine wanted word to spread that he would treat the people of Italy leniently if they came over to him.

Constantine's army continued east, toward Turin, whose city layout was based on the grid pattern of a military camp. Today, Turin is the center of Italy's auto industry and is home to famous makes such as Fiat and Lancia—"Lancia," incidentally, means lance or spear. A large force of Maxentius's heavy cavalry came out of Turin to confront the invaders, and with the Alps to the west as a backdrop, they stood in Constantine's path. These troopers formed a well-disciplined wedge, with the point to the front. This, Roman military writer Vegetius would say several decades later, had become the standard battle formation in a cavalry-versus-cavalry battle.[94]

To counter this, and against the advice of his senior officers, who did not want their commander to expose himself to injury or death, "Bull Neck" Constantine stubbornly took personal charge of his cavalry, which outnumbered the Maxentians. He began by encircling his opponents. Then he outflanked them. Vegetius described this outflanking maneuver as the best counter for the wedge formation—it involved a reverse wedge, a deep V formation that wrapped itself along the two forward flanks of the opposing wedge, then, like a pincer, closed on the opposition.

We are told that, as Constantine and his riders bore in against their immediate neighbors, they used their maces to devastating effect, knocking surprised opponents from the backs of their horses. Constantine's infantry then dealt with the unhorsed and lumbering cavalrymen on the ground. Those Maxentian cavalrymen not butchered in this melee fled in terror back to Turin, their base, but the leaders of the city would not open its gates to readmit them. Pursuing Constantinian cavalry cornered some of these men against the city walls and butchered then. When Constantine came up, the gates were opened to him by city leaders, and he entered Turin and took its surrender.

Turin sat beside the Po River, which in the past had been the border between Italy to the south and the province of Cisalpine Gaul. Another invading general, an impetuous one, might have plunged on across the river and charged south toward Rome. Constantine was, we are told, an impetuous general, but his father had demonstrated how he himself had eliminated threats to his rear before advancing, and Constantius's example seems to have influenced Constantine. After all, tens of thousands of Maxentius's troops still remained in the north of Italy, and it would be necessary to winkle them out of their strongholds before thinking about Rome. So Constantine sent messengers to all the cities of northern Italy, calling on them to come over to his side.

In response, several cities of the north sent ambassadors to him, congratulating him on his victories to date and extending the olive branch of peace. The most important city of the north was Milan. West and a little north of Turin, this was the Tetrarchy's imperial capital for the West, and Milan was among the cities that sought peace with Constantine. He headed straight there, and at his approach the city opened its gates to him. Basing himself at Milan, occupying the palace of the emperor of the West and playing tourist, Constantine allowed his troops to rest up in camp as the summer heat began to bake the northern Italian plain.

Several times in the past, Constantine had held back from fighting his brother-in-law, perhaps to please his wife Fausta, Maxentius's sister. Now,

Constantine waited, in hopes that a daunted Maxentius might give up his throne at Rome and slink away, rather than fight him, obviating the need for further military action. From later events, we know that Constantine had agents at Rome providing him with information and fermenting unrest among the population.

Not coincidentally, a delegation of leading men at Rome now went to Maxentius, begging him to step down and prevent further bloodshed. Maxentius dismissed their pleas, refusing to abdicate. He did not physically punish the members of the delegation for their disloyalty, but he did banish them from Rome, and from Italy. As they fled to Constantine's capital Trier in Gaul, Maxentius confiscated the men's property and redistributed it among his most loyal supporters in the Senate.

Maxentius still had strong, loyal forces in the north, due west of Milan, at Brixia, today's Brescia, the first city to which he'd sent troops in 311, and, further west, at Verona. Now, he sent his Praetorian prefect, Ruricius Pompeianus, north from Rome to take command. Ruricius hurried away and took charge at Verona, boosting the morale of Maxentian forces in the north.

In the midsummer, after weeks of inactivity, and learning that Ruricius was in the north, Constantine ordered his army to prepare to march again, this time against Brescia. This small, fifteen-hundred-year-old city in Lombardy, just a few miles east of Lake Garda, site of Claudius Gothicus's defeat of the Alemanni half a century earlier, was home to several temples, a theater, and public baths, and was delivered water by an aqueduct commenced by Augustus and completed by his stepson Tiberius. Today, Brescia is home to several firearms factories, including that of the famous Beretta company.

The Arch of Constantine would depict Constantine's army leaving Milan in column of march, with armed infantry to the fore, followed by standard-bearers bunched together, then troops in marching order and carrying their loads. Cavalry are shown next, followed by a high, open, four-wheeled carriage drawn by four horses. Behind the carriage's seated driver, on a throne-like chair, is a lone passenger—Constantine.

Previously, when Rome's rulers traveled, they had been carried in litters, had ridden horses, or been conveyed in chariots. Julius Caesar had once driven a chariot from Rome to Gaul with secretaries sitting on the floor as he dictated letters and his latest book. With Constantine young and fit enough to drive a chariot or ride a horse on his army's daily marches, his unique grand imperial carriage was a reflection of his love of display, upon which both his allies and his critics were to remark.

As Constantine and his army approached Brescia, the Maxentian force based at the city came out to do battle. Again against the advice of his officers, Constantine put on his armor, mounted his favorite charger, then personally led his cavalry to the attack. His charge broke up the opposing force, and the scattered Maxentians withdrew in disorder to join the garrison at Verona. Constantine chose not to give chase, occupying Brescia instead. Within days, he was marching on Verona.

After Constantine had defeated two Maxentian armies in the field over the past few months, Ruricius Pompeianus chose not to come out of Verona, the city made famous in later times as the setting of two William Shakespeare plays, *Romeo and Juliet* and *Two Gentlemen of Verona*. Instead, Ruricius dared Constantine to take Verona by force. For this was a city perfectly situated to withstand a siege.

Colonia Verona Augusta, as it was officially known, sat on a tight bend of the Athesis River, today's Adige, so that there were only two ways to enter it—by land from the south and via two bridges over the river to the north. High defensive towers protected the bridges, and several forts guarded the land approaches to the south. A strong wall of stone and brick six feet thick and twenty feet high encircled the entire city—smaller than Rome's Aurelian Wall, which was eleven feet thick and twenty-six feet high, but nonetheless a formidable barrier to attackers.

Verona's wall had been strengthened by the emperor Gallienus in 265. With a mind to attack by barbarian hordes rather than by fellow Romans, Gallienus's refurbished defenses had incorporated the city's twenty thousand–seat amphitheater to the southeast into the wall. The gleaming pink and white limestone wall of the amphitheater was taller than that surrounding the city. Third largest in Italy, this amphitheater's arena would have now been home to the tents of many of Ruricius's tens of thousands of troops.

With Ruricius refusing to fight him in the open, Constantine was forced to make camp outside the city and commence a siege of Verona. His only route of attack was from the south, allowing the Maxentians to concentrate most of their forces on the southern part of the city wall. The forts outside the city were probably stormed by Constantine's troops early in the operation, but as the city proper held firm against attempts to climb and breach the wall, the siege stretched out for weeks. With the city able to bring in supplies and ammunition using the Adige bridges north of the city, Constantine detached a force that crossed the Adige, then marched around the west of the city to seal off the bridges. Seeing this, Ruricius led a force out from the city, over the bridges, and attacked Constantine's troops.

The battle that followed was fierce, but ultimately Constantine's troops overwhelmed the Maxentians, preventing the return to the city of survivors by sealing off the bridges in their rear. Prefect Ruricius and a few of his men galloped away, leaving Verona now completely surrounded and cut off. But rather than flee south to Rome, Ruricius rode east in search of reinforcements.

Within weeks, Ruricius returned with a large force, determined to relieve Verona. Where Ruricius secured these reinforcements we are not told, but with no more of Maxentius's troops known to be stationed in the north, it is likely that he went 140 miles due east to Aquileia on Italy's Adriatic Coast, where the Venetian Fleet, named for the province administered from Aquileia, was based during this period. Or he may have gone a similar distance southeast to Ravenna, once home to one of Rome's largest fleets of warships and thousands of Roman marines. Diocletian had allowed Rome's battle fleets to run down during his reign, and the precise size of the naval presence at Ravenna at this time is unknown.

It is likely, then, that the relief force Ruricius led back to Verona was mostly made up of marines and armed sailors, from Aquileia or Ravenna. With his new force, Ruricius launched a surprise attack on the rear of Constantine's siege lines. Constantine personally led a hastily organized counterattack, and a desperate battle ensued. Marines and sailors were traditionally freedmen, former slaves, trained to fight from ships, whereas Constantine's troops were not only Roman citizens, they were highly trained and very experienced land fighters. Plus, Constantine had the advantage of 8,000 cavalrymen, while very few of Ruricius's men would have been mounted.

These disadvantages had to tell against the Maxentians. Yet even as they were mown down by cavalry charge after cavalry charge, they stood their ground and died fighting. By the end of day, Constantine and his troops had prevailed, and the Maxentian dead lay piled over the battlefield. Constantine's men, searching through the bodies to strip them of their equipment and leave them, naked, where they had fallen, discovered the corpse of Prefect Ruricius Pompeianus. Loyal to his emperor, Maxentius, to the end, Ruricius had died fighting with his men. It is likely that Ruricius's head was severed and paraded around outside Verona's city walls by Constantine's troops, to show that he was dead and to bring the surrender of the Maxentian troops within the city. But there was no surrender. The soldiers loyal to Maxentius held out, and the siege continued.

The Arch of Constantine depicts a scene from the battle that raged at Verona's city wall, probably in the siege's late stages. To one side we see Constantine directing his troops, as his heavily armored legionaries attack one section of the wall, using their oval shields to protect themselves, with less well armored and helmetless Gallic/Belgic archers in their midst. Military historian Michael Speidel has suggested that the infantrymen were from the Cornuti, a Gallic imperial bodyguard unit. They are seen launching hand-thrown darts up at Maxentian defenders lining the wall, as the archers with them let loose arrows at the same targets.[95]

Meanwhile, we see a riderless horse, and soldiers on foot who are hurrying to join the fight with larger oval shields that those carried by their comrades closer to the wall. These soldiers appear to be dismounted *scutarii* medium cavalry, and this suggests that Constantine had ordered cavalrymen to dismount and join the infantry in storming of the wall, a tactic that had frequently been employed by the emperors Vespasian and Titus in sieges of Jewish cities during the first-century Jewish Revolt.[96]

In the same Arch of Constantine scene, some Maxentian defenders atop the wall wear similar armor and conical helmets as the attackers, and protect themselves with the same type of oval shield. Other defenders wear different armor and the old first-century-jockey style of helmet, which had a peak at the front, suggesting they were local city guards with old, outdated equipment. These defenders had run out of spears and darts, and are depicted throwing rounded stones much like oversized baseballs down at the attackers. One defender, hit by an arrow or dart, falls to his death. At a distant section of the wall, a single Constantinian attacker is shown at its base, bent low and sheltering beneath his shield as defenders above throw spears down at him.

The latter image, of the Constantinian at the base of the wall, hints at the way the siege was ultimately terminated, after a number of weeks. Constantine's troops are known to have done considerable damage to Verona's wall during the siege. This may have been by rams, but these are neither depicted on the arch nor mentioned in contemporary accounts of Constantine's Italian campaign. Rather, it seems that, under cover of shields, Constantine's men were able to undermine the wall and cause breaches at several places.

Constantine's troops poured in through these breaches, and fighting spread through the basalt-paved streets of Verona. Once the twin gates of the city's main gateway, the Porta Jovia, could be opened from within, more troops surged in, and Verona was doomed. As Constantine's troops fought their way from street to street, with residents cringing in their homes, the chief men of Verona surrendered their city to the invaders. The siege was at an end.

We are not told that Constantine spared the people of Verona as he had those at Susa. Lactantius and Eusebius, when writing of Constantine's conquest of the north, made no mention of the city's fate other than to say that it surrendered. But after months on campaign without booty, and weeks of bloody and bitter siege warfare during which Constantine's men saw comrades killed and seriously wounded around them, it is probable that Constantine's troops could not have been prevented from looting Verona, even if he had wanted to stop them. We know for a fact that Constantine punished the city as a whole by ordering that the breaches his troops had created in Verona's wall never be repaired.[97]

Surviving Maxentian troops were disarmed. Prisoners for now, they would eventually be sent to the Rhine frontier to serve as border guards. Constantine is likely to have ordered the execution of a handful of senior supporters of Maxentian among the leaders of Verona, but he spared others who had opposed him. His nephew Julian would later say that Constantine was sometimes blamed for too much clemency early in his career.

With Verona taken, the last major stumbling block on Constantine's path to Rome had been overcome. Yet, even as the summer ended, he still hesitated to turn south. Sending messengers to the remaining major cities of the north seeking their submission, he waited until Aquileia, Ravenna, and Mutina, today's city of Modena, bowed down to him, and all of northern Italy was in his hands. He made a point of marching to Aquileia to accept that city's submission, which suggests it may have been the origin of Ruricius's reinforcements. When cities in Etruria and Umbria that lay between northern Italy and Rome also sent emissaries vowing submission to Constantine, nothing stood in his path to Rome.

With the autumn, Constantine finally turned his army south, marching down the coast to Rimini, where, by early October, he joined the Via Flaminia. At last he was on the road to Rome. But, no doubt to the consternation of his officers, he moved the army south down the Via Flaminia at a dawdling pace, making numerous overnight halts after traveling only a few miles at a time, as if still hoping that Maxentius would abdicate before he reached Rome. The last thing Constantine seemed to want was a battle with his brother-in-law.

XII

MAXENTIUS PREPARES
FOR BATTLE

O N OCTOBER 12, 312, the thousand-year-old Circus Maximus, located between the Palatine and Aventine hills at Rome, was packed with tens of thousands of spectators. It was the last day of the Augustales Festival, one of the major days on the year's chariot-racing calendar.[98]

Dating back to the sixth century B.C., the massive Circus Maximus racecourse, two thousand feet long and almost four hundred wide, took the form of an elongated *U* flanked by grandstands that could seat 150,000 people. The hippodrome's two lower levels of stands were fashioned from stone, while the tiers above were made from wood. Beneath the stands were shops selling food and drink, while prostitutes and their pimps plied their trade in the darker arcades.

In the early hours of an August morning in the year A.D. 64, a fire broke out in a kitchen in one of those shops, prior to a race day. The flames quickly rose into the wooden stands above. Pushed by strong winds, the fire soon spread to nearby buildings. Lasting for days, the blaze consumed large parts of Rome. The emperor Nero, who had been participating in a singing contest at Anzio on Italy's east coast at the time, rushed back to Rome to oversee firefighting efforts. He subsequently pushed through new building regulations as he rebuilt Rome, and the Circus Maximus arose bigger and better than before, with later emperors adding various improvements over the centuries. A day at the Roman races began before dawn, with members of Rome's million-plus population and people from rural areas lined up in the dark to obtain the best seats, which were free, as a thousand troops from a Praetorian Guard cohort watched over them from their sentry posts. In the circus stands, senators mixed with plebeians, slaves, and off-duty soldiers and their families. Race days were public holidays, when the courts, the palace, and government institutions were closed and most city businesses shuttered their doors. This guaranteed big attendances, as did the fact that Romans could legally gamble on horse races, which created a thriving industry for bookmakers. A chariot race featured in the Olympic Games in Greece, but the entrepreneurial Romans had turned horseracing from a sport into a business. Four stock-issuing corporations, the Blues, Greens, Whites, and Reds, ran the races throughout the empire, entering teams in each race. Domitian increased the number of racing corporations to six, and other emperors dabbled with even more teams, but by the fourth century the teams had reverted to the original four. Their corporations bought and trained the chariot horses and their drivers, usually former slaves, ran horse farms and training facilities throughout the empire, operated their own cargo fleets to move horses around the provinces, and had first preference at horse sales, even over buyers for the army.

Chariot racing was the world's first team sport, and, like football fans today, Romans were avid supporters of one color or another, with some even mentioning the team they supported on their gravestones. Like Maxentius, some emperors, such as Caligula (a Blues fan), Nero, Domitian, and Elagabalus were such chariot-racing fanatics that they built their own private hippodromes.

For the emperor of the day, the races provided an opportunity to be seen and be applauded by his subjects, and emperors usually reserved their entrance for mid-morning, once the stands had filled and the audience had been warmed up by early events, withdrawing to the Palatium for lunch before returning for the afternoon races. The emperor reached the Circus Maximus directly from the palaces on the Palatine above, and the first the crowd saw of him was when he and his entourage appeared in the imperial box.

On October 12, young Emperor Maxentius would have arrived in the imperial box hoping for a good day's racing to take his mind off his brother-in-law Constantine. Reports had reached Maxentius about the fall of Verona, the death of his able right-hand man Ruricius, and the capitulation of cities of the north. He had banned news of this being passed on to the people of Rome, and as a result most people continued to go about their daily lives in ignorance of the fact that an invading army was slowly coming down the Flaminian Way toward Rome—although all knew that Constantine had invaded northern Italy months earlier.

Maxentius no doubt also hoped this day at the races would take the public's mind off the grain rationing he had recently implemented for a second time. Expecting Constantine to subject Rome to a lengthy siege, Maxentius was conserving the grain supply. Eusebius would later melodramatically declare that by this time, the people of Rome "were reduced to the most extreme penury and want of necessary food—a scarcity such as our contemporaries do not remember ever before to have existed at Rome." A shortage of grain had actually been a recurring theme during Maxentius's reign, starting with the African standoff with Domitius Alexander. But what Eusebius failed to tell his readers was that this latest reduction in the Roman people's food supply had been caused by Constantine's blockade of Italy's grain ports.[99]

Despite the new tax, and reduced grain supply, which would have caused grumbles in the marketplace, at taverns, and over dinner, Maxentius was still considered a Roman native by the people of the city, and Constantine was not. Everywhere Romans looked in Rome, they saw the activity that Maxentius's extensive building program generated as he glorified their city. The rebuilding of the Temple of Venus and Roma alone employed an estimated ten thousand workers. Even after initial news of Constantine's campaign in the north reached Rome, there were no riots in the streets from disgruntled Romans, and no agitation among Maxentius's troops for more money to maintain their loyalty.

Rome's Christian community was also quiet. Their acquiescence had been aided by the fact that, in July of the previous year, Maxentius had permitted the election of a new Bishop of Rome, Miltiades, a Berber from North Africa, who did not support the punishing acts of penance required of lapsed Christians by his predecessors. Maxentius had also issued a decree that returned to Christians all property in Rome confiscated under the Diocletian persecution, be they buildings or gardens inside the city or graveyards beyond the official city limits (ancient Roman law banned the interment of human remains within cities or towns).

At this point, there was no purpose-built Christian church in Rome. As had been the case in Christ's day, worshippers had generally met in private houses. The one dedicated church in Rome at this time was the Taberna Meritoria, a tavern previously converted for use as a home for fee-paying old soldiers in the Trastevere district. When the Christian community under Bishop Callixtus acquired the property around 220 and turned it into a church—Christians frequently banded together to form corporations that purchased property for communal use—local tavernkeepers had protested to the then emperor Alexander Severus. The emperor had found in favor of the Christian community, and the building duly became an authorized Christian church. Confiscated under Diocletian's Great Persecution, it was returned to Christian hands by Maxentius. In the 340s, the Basilica of St. Maria would be built on the site.

Maxentius's decree may have also included Church property in all of Italy, not just at Rome, and subsequent events suggest it did. But, as Constantine later had all record of Maxentius's decrees destroyed, there is no way of knowing for sure. We do know that Maxentius's order did not include the African provinces. Although Maxentius did not persecute the Christian community in Africa and allowed bishops to continue to rule over their flocks, those flocks were divided by another bitter internal schism that had two groups at odds with each other, with each claiming the rights to Church property: Much like the earlier Christian division in Rome, half the Christians of North Africa believed that clergymen who had yielded to the decrees of Diocletian and handed over Christian property—called traditores or surrenderers by their purist critics—were not entitled to baptize Christians or perform Church rites. Their opponents felt that any baptized clergyman should be recognized by the Church. With both sides claiming to be the legitimate Christian Church of Africa and electing competing bishops, Maxentius was not prepared to take sides.

Maxentius's toleration of the Christian Church had perhaps been spurred by Galerius's deathbed edict of toleration of Christians just months before, but he certainly also had the political motive of increasing popular support in Italy, and it gained him the collaboration, if only tacit, of Rome's Bishop Miltiades. Apart from the single delegation of pro-Constantine senators that had called on him to step down, there is no record of a widespread call for Maxentius to quit. Yet, decades later, following the death of Constantine, Eusebius of Caesarea would paint a misleadingly damning picture of Maxentius at this time.

While lauding Constantine's support of the Christian Church, Eusebius would conveniently fail to mention Maxentius's support of the Church at Rome, or the fact that his return of confiscated Christian property preceded similar action from Constantine by two years. More than that, Eusebius would claim that Maxentius was a cruel, wicked, impious man who had murdered senators and set out to rape the Christian widow of one of his prefects, who had only escaped his attentions by committing suicide, so that all Rome was in terror of his lustful predations and those of his troops.

"But the crowning glory of the tyrant's wickedness," Eusebius went on, "was his having recourse to sorcery—sometimes for magic purposes ripping up pregnant women, at other times searching into the bowels of newborn infants. He slew lions, also, and practiced certain horrid arts for evoking demons. Eusebius summarized: "In short, it is impossible to describe the manifold acts of oppression by which this tyrant of Rome enslaved his subjects."[100]

The description of Maxentius as a tyrant was one that Constantine himself would promote. But no other Roman author attributes such diabolical atrocities enacted against pregnant women and newborns to Maxentius, although, as will shortly be seen, the story of the slaying of lions was probably true. Tellingly, Eusebius's lurid description of Maxentius's supposed depraved acts was totally absent when he described Maxentius in *The Church History*, published after Maxentius's death but while Constantine was still alive. When Eusebius also wrote of Galerius, Daia, and Licinius in his later biography of Constantine, he attributed similar impiety, lust, and debauchery to them all, also adding drunkenness in their cases.

Yet, as historian Timothy Barnes pointed out, Eusebius often contradicted himself: "When Licinius was an ally of Constantine, he was a paragon of virtue and piety, but when he turned against Constantine and his divine protector, his good deeds were excised from the historical record and he became a monster of depravity and lust."[101] Twentieth-century scholar Jacob Burckhardt would be scathing in his criticism of Eusebius, accusing him of twisting and eliminating facts to achieve his own Christian propaganda ends.[102] As for Lactantius, the other chief contemporary source on Constantine and Maxentius, his view of Maxentius is far more liberal, avoiding the lurid evocations of Eusebius.

Maxentius, who was otherwise described as "effeminate" and was a man who had proven too soft to execute his own father when Maximian attempted to overthrow him, merely exiling Maximian and the later pro-Constantine delegation that approached him to abdicate, and who was demonstrably devoted to his wife and children, was perhaps not the cruel tyrant and sex fiend that Eusebius would have us believe. Certainly, with the list of horrific crimes that Eusebius attributed to him, it would seem unlikely that the "monster" Maxentius would have ventured to present himself to 150,000 of his "oppressed" and "enslaved subjects" at the games of October 12. But he did.

As he emerged from the shadows of the purple shade cloth above the imperial box, smiling and waving to the massive, buzzing Circus Maximus crowd, people rose to their feet, applauded, and cried in unison, "Hail Maxentius Augustus, the Invincible Prince!"

But Constantine's supporters in the city had been at work fermenting dissatisfaction, secretly led by senior members of Maxentius's own administration. And now, secret Constantinians turned Maxentius's self-proclaimed title of the Invincible Prince against him. A chant began in one section of the circus crowd, probably from paid agitators, and inspired by the knowledge that Constantine was intent on taking Rome: "*Constantine is invincible! Constantine is invincible!*"[103]

As the cry was taken up by others, perhaps in jest, perhaps in all seriousness, Maxentius was suddenly embarrassed and, turning, hurried from the box and back to his palace. The races that he was paying for continued without him.

WITH THE PASSING OF ANOTHER WEEK, cavalry scouts informed Maxentius that Constantine would soon reach the Tiber on his slow march down the Flaminian Way and was within days of arriving outside the walls of Rome. Urged by his advisors, Maxentius ordered the planking of all Rome's bridges across the Tiber ripped up to deny Constantine a crossing.

More than one of Maxentius's cabinet members would have known their Roman miltary history and been aware that, in December, A.D. 69, when an army loyal to future emperor Vespasian led by Marcus Antonius

Primus had advanced on Rome, forces loyal to the emperor Vitellius had left the Milvian Bridge intact and attempted to defend it. German cavalry from Primus's army had simply swum the Tiber with their horses, and, attacking from the rear, seized the bridge. This had allowed the rest of Primus's army to cross the bridge and go on to attack and break through the gates of Rome.

This removal by Maxentius of the decking of the Tiber bridges would have tipped off the population of Rome that Constantine was close. Yet there are no reports of public riots, of disunity among Maxentius's supporters, or of unrest among the Praetorian Guard that, in similar past circumstances, had seen the army assassinate their own emperor to empty the throne in favor of a usurper.

It would have occurred to Maxentius that Constantine was deliberately timing his advance to reach Rome on October 28, the sixth anniversary of Maxentius's taking power. This would have great propaganda value as far as Constantine was concerned—a bold statement to Romans that he had come to terminate the reign that Maxentius celebrated on that day.

Maxentius called a conference of his crisis cabinet, consisting of the the military tribunes and the ten remaining members of the coterie of thirteen senators who had propelled him onto the throne, now minus Ruricius, Maxentius's late firm right hand, and two senators who had died of natural causes. A clearly worried Maxentius sought advice on what he should do, no doubt reminding his companions that if he fell, they fell with him. One or more of his advisers appear to have suggested that, instead of hunkering down for a siege, Maxentius take the initiative and meet Constantine outside Rome with his larger army, on October 28, anniversary of his accession, and do battle on ground of his choosing on the river plain north of Rome, at Saxa Rubra.

In response, Maxentius would have reminded his advisers that he had never led an army in battle in his life, had never drawn a sword in anger. And his troops knew it. But his tribunes would have assured him that his accession anniversary would have great meaning to Maxentius's men, especially the Praetorians, whom he had restored to their "rightful" place of honor.

The anniversary would also have meaning to the troopers of the Singularian Horse Guard, a unit Maxentius had returned to their old forts at Rome following the defeat of Severus, making them his personal bodyguard, just as Rome's emperors since Trajan had done, giving them back the prestige that Diocletian had deprived them of. In fact, the commanders of the Singularian Horse and Praetorian Guard seem to have vowed that they and their men would fight to the death in Maxentius's name.

One participant in the meeting now made a further suggestion—that the Sibylline Books be consulted to see whether October 28 was an auspicious day for Maxentius to go into battle against his brother-in-law. The proponent of the idea would have assured his emperor that if a favorable omen could be located within these oracular books, this would embolden Maxentius's entire army.

According to legend, the original Sibylline Books had been offered for sale to Rome's last king, Tarquinus Superbus, in the time of Cyrus the Great in the sixth century B.C., by the Hellespontine Sibyl, the priestess of the Temple of Apollo at Dardanus, which gave its name to the adjacent Dardanelles. Originally, there were nine books in all, containing a treasure trove of prophetic predictions written in Greek verse. But when Tarquinus had declined to buy the books, saying they were too expensive, the Sibyl had burned three of them, then offered the remaining six books to the king, for the original price. When Tarquinus again declined to buy, the Sibyl destroyed another three books, then offered the king the last three, again at the original price. This time, Tarquinus paid up.

The three surviving books had thereafter been stored in the Temple of Jupiter Best and Greatest on Rome's Capitoline Mount, to be consulted whenever Rome was under threat. But in 83 B.C., the Temple of Jupiter had been ravaged by fire and the books were destroyed. The Senate had subsequently collected new Sibylline prophesies from around the Mediterranean. These were committed to new Sibylline Books, which were lodged in the rebuilt Temple of Jupiter until Augustus relocated them to the Temple of Apollo on the Palatine Hill, next to his palace.

Nero had been one of the emperors to consult the Sibylline Books for guidance and reassurance, in his case immediately following the Great Fire of Rome. The most recent time that the books had been consulted had been in 271, following the defeat of the Roman army led by Aurelian at Placentia by the Alemanni. The resulting prophesy, details of which are unknown, had presaged Aurelian's victory over the invaders at the Battle of Fano shortly after.

Fifteen Romans, former consuls and former praetors, were appointed for life to oversee the care and consultation of the Sibylline Books and the worship of Apollo, as part-time members of the prestigious priestly college called the *quindecimviri sacris faciundis,* or the fifteen superintendants of sacred rights. And it just so happened that Volusianus, one of the senators who had supported Maxentius since 306 and the man who had recaptured Africa for him, was one of the current quindecimvirs, making it almost certain that the suggestion to consult the books came from him. Maxentius approved of the idea, and the remaining quindecimvirs were hurriedly summoned. All were instructed to seek the answer to a simple question: If Maxentius were to lead the army against Constantine on October 28, would the gods bring him victory?

Traditionally, the quindecimvirs were supposed to only discern what sacred rites were required to secure the help of the gods in the matter under question, but over time they had tended to also interpret the books to provide a prophesy that aided decision-making. With the help of two Greek translators to ensure accuracy, by October 26, the keepers of the books had come up with sacred rite recommendations and an interpretation for Maxentius.

As previously mentioned, Eusebius wrote that Maxentius had lions sacrificed. This was to secure good omens in the lead-up to the battle and would have been at the recommendation of the quindecimvirs. Lions were considered subservient to the goddess Cybele, the Magna Mater or Great Mother, who was worshipped by Romans as the "protector of cities." Cybele was frequently depicted seated on a throne flanked by lions or riding a carriage drawn by lions. A statue of her that adorned the spine of the Circus Maximus, where the annual Megalesia festival dedicated to her culminated, showed Cybele seated on a lion.

Maxentius also had a familial connection with the lion, which would have given the sacrifice even greater significance—it was a symbol of Hercules, favored deity of Maxentius's father. In Greco-Roman mythology, after Hercules killed the Nemean lion he wore its coat, which offered protection against the elements and against almost all weapons. On a coin early in his reign, Maxentius was shown wearing a lion headdress, as he claimed the protection of his father's deity.

As for a prophesy, after consulting the Sibylline Books, Volusianus would have reported on behalf of his fellow quindecimvirs that if Maxentius went to war on October 28, "on the same day the enemy of the Romans should perish."[104] This would have invigorated Maxentius's supporters, and they persuaded their emperor to order the army to prepare to march from the city and do battle with Constantine outside Rome on the appointed day. The sacrifice of lions from the collection kept at Rome for spectacles was authorized, and planning for an October 28 battle on the river plain north of the capital began.

But Maxentius was uneasy. He is likely to have read Greek historian Herodotus in his youth. If so, he would have remembered that the fabulously rich King Croesus of Lydia had consulted Apollo's oracle at Delphi on whether he should go to war against Cyrus the Great, founder of the Persian Empire. And the response had come back that, should Croesus go to war with the Persians, "a great empire will fall." So, Croesus had invaded Persia—and sure enough, a great empire had fallen: Croesus's own Lydian Empire.[105]

Maxentius seems to have feared that he would lose the forthcoming battle, after which Constantine would turn the prophesy against him. For, on October 26, for safety's sake, Maxentius transferred his wife Maximilla and young infant son from the Palatium on the Palatine Hill to a house in the city, no doubt after a tearful parting. Clearly, Maxentius feared that, if his wife and child were to remain at the palace and he was killed in battle, Constantine's troops would rampage through the Palatium, looting it. And, just as the wife and infant daughter of Caligula had been murdered in the Palatium following Caligula's assassination, Maxentius's loved ones would also be killed.

No details of that Rome house to which Maxentius consigned his wife and son have come down to us. It may have been the Sessorium, but it may also have been the Domus Faustae, the house of Maxentius's sister Fausta, because it was right beside the newer of the Singularian Horse barracks on the southern slope of the Caelian Hill, offering protection from the Horse Guard.

Fausta's house had originally been two houses on two different levels, one on the lower part of the hill, the other set back above it, farther up the slope. Both had been confiscated from their owners at the time of the Piso Plot, an A.D. 65 assassination conspiracy against Nero. One house had been owned by the senator Gaius Calpurnius Piso, central figure of the conspiracy, the other by the conspirator Plautius Lateranus, a senator and member of the distinguished Laterani family. Along with numerous others, the pair had been executed, with their property forfeited to the state.

A century and a half later, the emperor Septimius Severus made additions to both houses and presented the House of Lateranus to a descendant of its previous owners, Titus Sextius Lateranus, a consul in 197. The Lateran house had subsequently reverted to imperial ownership, perhaps via the will of a childless Lateranus. Late in the third century, the emperor Maximian, father of Maxentius and Fausta, combined the two houses and partially buried them as he built the Domus Faustae, a new city palace for his daughter, over the top of the existing residences.

Maxentius's subsequent Domus Faustae refurbishments had included a long corridor ending in a garden portico where there was a bench for sitting and contemplating a single large statue of a god or goddess, thought to have been Roma or Venus, favored deities of Maxentius and possibly also of Fausta. In the garden of the Domus Faustae, a winding path led to the palace's private bathhouse.

Maxentius also had larger-than-life fresco portraits painted on the corridor wall, depicting male and female members of his family. Obscured but surviving to this day, the frescoes appear to include Maxentius's father and mother, as well as Fausta and himself. In sending his wife and child to this house, Maxentius would have hoped that, as it was the property of Constantine's wife, his own wife and child would be safe there from booty-seeking Constantinian troops.[106]

The following day, October 27, probably at the usual daily dawn audience between Maxentius and his clients at the Palatium, the senator Gaius Annius Anullinus, who had served as city prefect between March 306 and August 307, at first under Severus before switching his loyalty to Maxentius, sought his emperor's ear and made a proposition. Anullinus suggested that he be once again appointed to the position of city prefect, replacing Aradius Rufinus, whose term ended that day. As city prefect, Anullinus would take command of the troops staying in the city as garrison when Maxentius led the bulk of the army out to confront Constantine on the river plain. And current office holder Rufinus, who was related to Anullinus by marriage, would have supported the idea. Maxentius agreed, appointing Anullinus to the post, effective from the following day.

The battle plan that had earlier been agreed to by Maxentius for the following day contained several elements. To begin with, at dawn the army would file out of Rome and march nine miles north to Saxa Rubra, where it would form up across the plain in Constantine's path, from the Tiber to the hill where Livia's Villa was located, to offer battle. Someone also came up with a fiendish plan B, to be implemented should Constantine break through Maxentius's battle lines.

This secondary plan was predicated on the known fact that Constantine personally and impulsively led his cavalry in attack; the plan was designed to bring about his death. The originator of this scheme is unknown. Maxentius, with his interest in architecture and engineering, may have come up with it himself; but while Maxentius was known to have been angered by the death of his father in Constantine's hands, he is never on record desiring or calling for his brother-in-law's death. Later events suggest that the scheme could have originated with Volusianus, the experienced general who, as Praetorian prefect, had led the army that retook Africa for Maxentius.

The scheme involved the crossing at the Tiber. Instead of replacing the planking on existing stone bridges across the river to permit Maxentius's army to reach Saxa Ruba, a temporary floating structure would be built east of the Milvian Bridge. This type of floating temporary bridge using pontoons, still used by the military to this day, had been built by the Roman military for hundreds of years prior to this. Julius Caesar had crossed the Rhine in 56 B.C. using just such a bridge. Germanicus Caesar's armies crossed the Rhine several times early in the first century via floating bridges built by his legions. Germanicus's son Caligula crossed the Bay of Puteoli driving a chariot along a particularly large floating bridge built by his Praetorian Guard over requisitioned fishing and cargo boats.[107]

The type of floating bridge normally built by the legions was described several decades after Constantine's reign by Vegetius, who wrote that it began with "small boats hollowed out of one log and very light both by their make and the quality of their wood. The army always has a number of these boats on carriages, together with a sufficient quantity of planks and iron nails. Thus, with the help of cables to lash the boats together, a bridge is instantly constructed, which for the time has the solidity of a bridge of stone." Where time and circumstances allowed, piles were also driven into the riverbed at intervals, especially in fast-flowing waterways, to which the bridge's pontoons were lashed for added strength.[108]

It is likely that whoever conceived the scheme involving the bridge of boats had read the works of the first-century Roman authors Tacitus and Suetonius, who described a "collapsible" ship created for the emperor Nero when he decided to murder his manipulative mother Agrippina the

Younger. Created by the admiral of the naval fleet at Misenum on Italy's west coast, this vessel was built in such a way that the stern could be severed from the rest of the ship by pulling a lever, causing the ship to quickly take on water and sink. Nero had given this ship to his mother as a gift, and one night after dinner as it was rowed back to her coastal villa from his, the lever was pulled and the ship foundered. Agrippina was plucked from the water by a fishing boat, which returned her safely to shore, forcing the admiral who had come up with the idea of the sinking boat to finish her murder with a sword.

The bridge of boats conceived for October 28 contained a similar mechanism to that which had been installed on the boat created for Nero. At the pull of a lever, the bridge would part in the middle, throwing anyone crossing that section into the river. Anyone clad in heavy armor could be expected to sink like a stone. The plan was for Constantine to be lured onto the bridge, at which time the lever would be pulled, sending him to a watery death. Maxentius, fearful of defeat on the battlefield and a bloody death, agreed to the mechanism's creation, and the plan was put into effect.

That day, October 27, the Praetorians proceeded with the construction of the bridge of boats; and with Maxentius's troops throughout Rome being informed that the Sibylline Books predicted a victory the next day, each unit was briefed by their centurions on their roles in the planned battle, from the order of exit from the city to places in the battle lines. The maneuver designed to lure Constantine onto the bridge as a last resort would have been a closely held secret known only to Maxentius's inner circle.

Ammunition supplies were gathered, swords sharpened, and prayers offered at shrines in the various barracks throughout the city and the tented camps of troops not normally based in Rome—men quartered on open space on the Field of Mars in Rome's northern suburbs, in the city's amphitheaters, and on the exercise grounds of the Praetorians and Singularian Horse in the east of the city.

Word would have spread quickly from soldiers to civilians throughout the city that a battle was to be fought outside the city the next day, creating alarm and hurried preparations among the civilian population. Servants would have been dispatched to buy up supplies. In hopes of keeping the city safe, hundreds of thousands of Romans would have flocked to temples around the city to offer sacrifices and tribute to gods such as the city's protector Cybele, as well as Venus and Roma, and Jupiter. Fraught friends and relatives would have wished each other luck, remarking that the last time the city had been under threat it had been from Germans; now it was from fellow Romans. And then anxious Romans barred their doors and hunkered down to await the outcome of the coming battle.

It is likely that, knowing that the next day might be his last, Maxentius slept poorly that night, if he slept at all. Well before dawn on October 28, which would have occurred a little before 7:00 A.M., Maxentius would have attended the traditional prebattle sacrifice at a temple on the Palatine almost certainly that of Rome's protecting goddess Cybele, which over-looked the Circus Maximus. This, presumably, involved the sacrifice of lions prescribed by the Sibylline Books and described by Eusebius. Inspec-tion of the animals' entrails by the augurs provided favorable portents, after which Maxentius prepared for the fight of his life.

Throughout Rome, troops were already on the move, with the first ele-ments of Maxentius's army already departing to the north and using the completed bridge of boats to cross the Tiber and march for Saxa Rubra. In his Palatium quarters, as Maxentius was buckled into his armor by his armor-bearer and his imperial purple cloak was draped around his armored shoulders by his chamberlain, he was still not confident of victory. On his orders, in a Palatium shrine, where it was stored when not in use, his remaining imperial regalia was hurriedly packed up.

This regalia included three lances and four javelins, all with highly dec-orative bronze tips, which were carried by officials who preceded Maxentius in formal processions. There was a base for his imperial standards, which had been removed preparatory for being carried into battle by Maxentius's standard-bearers. The collection also featured a gold-and-green glass globe, and a blue globe made from the silica gemstone chalcedony.

Globes were frequently part of the iconography of the Tetrarchs and featured on the coins of both Maxentius and Constantine. Some of Constantine's later coins, such as one issued in 317, depicted Sol Invic-tus holding a globe, while a Constantinian series minted in 322–323 would show a globe sitting over an altar, and Victoria sitting on a globe as she extended a victory wreath. In Maxentius's case, he was depicted on coins, such as one from 309, enthroned and being handed a globe by Roma, goddess of Rome, proclaiming that she gives him dominion over all the world.

The globe of course represented the Earth, which most educated Romans believed to be round. Lactantius, tutor of Constantine's son Crispus, was one Roman who believed the Earth to be flat. In his book *Divine Institutions,* he derided those who believed in a round Earth. Lactantius would in turn would be ridiculed by the sixteenth-century astronomer Copernicus in his 1543 book *De Revolutionibus* for "quite childishly" mocking Greek scholars who had not only declared the Earth to be round, but had calculated its circumference—with considerable accuracy, it turned out.

The most important item in Maxentius's regalia was the emperor's scepter, symbol of his universal power, which Maxentius carried on formal occasions such as when addressing the Senate. Diocletian and Maximian had several times been depicted on coins holding identical scepters and being crowned by Victoria. Maxentius's scepter consisted of a blue-green glass globe set in a holder of bronze flower leaves, on a shaft that served as a handle.

We know all this about Maxentius's regalia because it was discovered by Italian archaeologists in 2006, carefully wrapped in linen and silk and deposited in wooden boxes. These boxes were hidden in an underground sanctuary on the lower slope of the Palatine Hill, a stone's throw from the Colosseum. Clearly, Maxentius ordered his regalia kept out of the hands of Constantine should he be defeated in the coming battle, and his Palatium staff took the boxes down from the Palatium to their hiding place, probably in the predawn darkness of October 28 so that no one would see what they were doing. They did such a good job of hiding the regalia that it would not be found again for almost seventeen hundred years. The 2006 find represents the only regalia of any Roman emperor ever to survive to the present day.

In the low early-morning sunlight, Maxentius strode from the Palatium where his horse was saddled and waiting. The emperor was armed with what a source close to Constantine would describe the following year as a "dazzling" array of equipment. The bronze cuirass covering his torso would have been decorated with gold. His father's sword with its golden eagle hilt probably sat on his left hip in a rich golden scabbard. And he would have carried a gold-decorated shield.[109]

Waiting in tense silence were his heavily armed mounted bodyguards of the Singularian Horse Guard—tall, well-built, neatly bearded Batavians, Germans, and Raetians, all wearing helmets and leather jackets covered with fish-scale armor that extended to the elbow on the arms and well below the waist. Here too were his mounted attendants—his groom, his messengers, his personal trumpeter with a buccina—a large, elegantly curved, G-shaped brass horn with a distinctive tone used exclusively to relay the orders of an army's commander-in-chief—and his standard-bearer holding one of Maxentius's personal standards.

Maxentius is believed to have had two standards bearing his personal motif. Both took the form of cloth banners hanging from cross-like frames, not dissimilar to Constantine's new standard, but minus the chi-rho. The banner of the larger standard, which, like Constantine's Labarum, would be positioned in the midst of the infantry lines in the army's battle formation, was square. The smaller standard, which would accompany the emperor everywhere, took the form of a long pennant.[110]

On the nervous young emperor's appearance, the waiting troops would have chorused, in heavily accented Latin: "Hail Maxentius Augustus, Unconquerable Prince!"

Maxentius mounted up, and then elements of the Horse Guard led the way as the emperor rode through the eerily silent, deserted streets of Rome, with the doors of every city house, shop, and tenement block closed and, presumably, barred. He trotted northwest to the Porta Flaminia, the Flaminian Gate, one of the seventeen major openings in the Aurelian Wall that led out of the city. Troops of the City Guard and Night Watch, lining the wall and manning the two cylindrical towers flanking the double gates of the Porta Flaminia, would have saluted their emperor as he passed below.

With the troops above the gate would have stood their commander, City Prefect Anullinus, smiling down at Maxentius and bidding him the luck of the gods. In Maxentius's absence, Anullinus would be in command at Rome. Once the last troops had passed through, Anullinus ordered the double gates shut and barred. Of the whereabouts at this time of Maxentius's most experienced general, Volusianus, there is no mention by contemporary sources. It is entirely possible that, claiming sudden ill health, he had taken to his bed to avoid involvement in the battle.

With cloth standards fluttering, equipment jangling, and lances pointed skyward, the 1,500 men of the Singularian Horse pounded up the Flaminian Way at the trot with their young emperor. The stone-paved, cambered highway ran straight as an arrow northwest, passing the grand monumental buildings and temples of the Field of Mars on the left and imperial gardens spreading to the right of the road, to the Tiber and the Milvian Bridge. At this point, the Tiber, which had flowed roughly from north to south on its way through central Italy after rising in the Apennine Mountains, turned sharply right to flow east-west for a distance before resuming the southerly course that would take it down the western edge of Rome on its way to the coast and its entry into the Tyrrhenian Sea at Ostia.

The floating bridge lay on this east-west stretch of the river, a little way to the east of the stone piers of the Milvian Bridge. Much of Maxentius's army had already crossed the floating bridge, and his speedier, bareheaded Mauri light cavalry would already have arrived at Saxa Rubra and taken up screening positions. Foot soldiers occupied the open-topped pontoons of the bridge, and they would have cheered as their emperor and his entourage clattered over the bridge's wooden decking. The job of these men in the pontoons, if plan B had to be implemented, would be to lie low until Constantine and his entourage had been dumped into the water, and then rain darts onto them.

Somewhere on the bridge, too, was the officer whose job it would be to pull the lever that activated the mechanism that broke the bridge. As the army's last units assigned to the battle passed over the bridge and headed up the Flaminian Way, a detachment of Maxentius's troops including trumpeters remained on the city side, positioning themselves along the river's southern bank.

A little way north of the river, the Flaminian Way came to a Y-shaped crossroads. Here, the Via Cassia branched off up into the hills, and the Flaminian Way swung to the right, to skirt the hills and trace a path over the river plain, maintaining a northeasterly course as it paralleled the Tiber. Maxentius and his guardians followed the Flaminian Way, remaining on the flat, heading for Saxa Rubra, the assembling army, and their appointment with destiny.

XIII

A DAY TO SINK OR SWIM

THE DAWN OF OCTOBER 28, A.D. 312—battle day—had brought a fine day to Rome and its vicinity. Rome experiences a humid, subtropical climate in October, and fog, rain, and even an occasional thunderstorm are known. But, typically, a maximum temperature of between 68 and 77° Fahrenheit (20 to 25° Celsius) is the norm here toward the end of the month, with a light breeze of up to ten miles per hour that sends a few puffy white clouds scudding across the azure blue sky. No account of the battle on this day mentions rain, fog, or storm, indicating that the fate of the throne of Rome was about to be decided on a pleasantly warm day.

At Porta Prima, Constantine had abandoned the impressive carriage that had carried him south. Now, in his armor, mounted on his charger, and "distinguished by the splendor of his arms," according to Gibbon, he rode south along the Flaminian Way with his purple cloak flowing behind him and his mounted bodyguard in close company, heading for the red, iron-rich cliffs that gave Saxa Rubra its name. The Battle of the Milvian Bridge was just an hour or so away.

The battle's name would be coined by later writers, but it was a misnomer. The main part of the battle would take place on the plain at Saxa Rubra, with the struggle ultimately culminating miles farther south, at the bank of the Tiber River just to the north of Rome, close to, but not actually involving, the Milvian Bridge.

Constantine's troops were still arriving when he himself reached Saxa Rubra in the mid-morning. Maxentius's army of some 80,000 men was already in place in his path, with infantry stretching across the plain from the Tiber to the red cliffs where the Villa of Livia perched, while cavalry occupied both wings. The standard battle formation for Roman armies of this time was two deep lines of infantry, with cavalry on both wings. The two infantry lines were spaced some distance apart, and the lines could each have been from 20 to 100 men deep. Archers were among the troops of the second line. A smaller reserve force of infantry and cavalry frequently stood back from the two battle lines, ready to be thrown in if and where needed.

This is the formation that would have been implemented by Maxentius's generals, the tribunes Marcellianus and Marcellus, the pair who, along with the City Guard tribune Lucianus, had engineered Maxentius's occupation of the throne. As for the standards of the units, they, along with the men assigned to their protection, were in the second infantry line—the eagles and raised hands of the legions, the animal standards of auxiliary units, the gold statuettes of victory goddess Victoria of the cohorts of the Praetorian Guard, and Maxentius's personal standard.

Marcellianus and Marcellus would have commanded on the wings, while Lucianus may have commanded the center—if not, he would have been with the City Guard back at Rome. Their emperor Maxentius was almost certainly in the central rear with the reserve, which would have been centered around the Singularian Horse.

Lactantius and Eusebius, both of them pro-Constantine, are our only contemporary sources for the battle, and Lactantius, who provided the most detail, would scoff that Maxentius's rear battle line was so badly placed that all the men at the very back had to stand in the Tiber, offering them no opportunity of retreat. In reality, only the men on the extreme right of Maxentius's army would have been even close to the river. The rest were lined up across the plain, while it was half of Maxentius's cavalry who occupied the extreme right, beside the river. Lactantius's assertion is further debunked by the height of the Tiber's bank. As confirmed on the Arch of Constantine, the bank was too high to permit men or horses to physically stand in the water.

The location for the battle, as chosen by Maxentius's advisers, was actually a wise one. With the river on one side and cliffs rising to wooded hills on the other, the opposition could not outflank Maxentius's army. If Constantine wanted to reach Rome, he would have to go through Maxentius's forces, not around them. Secondly, forced to face south by the positioning of Maxentius's battle lines, Constantine's troops would have the sun in their eyes by mid-morning, when battle could be expected to begin.

Facing Maxentius's army, perhaps a thousand paces away, Constantine matched Maxentius's battle formation with two lines of infantry of his own, with cavalry similarly stationed on his wings. But with only half as many men as Maxentius to call on, Constantine's battle lines, while as long as those of his opponent, were only half as deep. Constantine had personally dictated the disposition of his units in the battle lines. His new standard, the Labarum, would have been located in the second row at the middle of his infantry line, with its fifty-man protection squad.

Constantine himself took up a position on one wing, at the head of his cavalry and accompanied by his mounted bodyguards of the *Scholae Palatini*—literally the Palace Schools. Constantine's successors to Diocletian's Divine Comatensis bodyguard units, each schola was made up of the finest-looking young Roman citizens from good families, in training as officers. Initially comprising just one wing of 500 men, Constantine's scholae would eventually number five, encompassing 2,500 officer cadets in white.

Lactantius wrote that Constantine went to the most dangerous part of the line, which, traditionally, was the right wing. Attacking Roman generals always put their best troops on their right wing, because Roman troops always carried their shields on their left arms, leaving their right sides exposed. According to Vegetius, a wise commander always took his position on the right. In this era, he said, the second-in-command positioned himself in the middle with the infantry, and the third-in-command on the left wing. If Bassianus was Constantine's second-in-command as believed, he would have been in the center, with the infantry.

The troops of both sides, all being part of the Roman army, looked basically the same. By this era, the rank and file infantry wore a conical helmet with cheek flaps and rear neck protector, breeches, leather boots, and a loose, long-sleeved, knee-length tunic. In earlier centuries, legionary tunics had been short-sleeved and red, but the color by Constantine's day was not identified, although it was unlikely to have been white, the color of the tunics of their tribunes.

Roman legionaries of the past had worn segmented body armor, but this had disappeared by the fourth century, with the field infantryman primarily relying on his large oval shield for protection. Whether he wore an armored leather jacket with iron mail sewn on, beneath his tunic, is unknown, but the extra protection that legionaries of old had worn on their shins in the form of metal grieves curving around their legs had been dispensed with. Most infantrymen were now armed with a single *lancia,* a spear of about five feet in length that had metal tips at both ends, and, on their left hip, a long spatha-style sword.

As demonstrated by the Arch of Constantine, there was one striking visual difference between Constantine's helmeted troops and Maxentius's helmeted troops as they faced each other this day—Constantine's infantry and cavalry marched to battle wearing plumes on their helmets. Up until the first century, Rome's legionaries and officers had always gone into battle wearing helmet plumes made from horsehair. Hollywood has often depicted those plumes as red, but the only historical example ever found intact was yellow. From the second half of the first century, plumes had become detachable and were only worn for parades and ceremonials. Constantine's troops had not worn their helmet plumes during the siege of Verona, but on October 28 they wore plumes.

Constantine, we know, had a love of display, and his army's order of the day, passed out along with the day's password, would have been "don plumes," as if Constantine expected to do battle that day—which he probably did, knowing in advance that Maxentius was coming out to fight on October 28. So, as his troops put on their equipment before leaving camp at Prima Porta that morning, they had taken the plumes from their baggage and fixed them in place.

Within months of this battle, one of Constantine's officials would boast that the outcome of the struggle this day was accomplished by treachery in Maxentius's camp. Constantine almost certainly had accomplices among Maxentius's senior advisers. These secret turncoats had not only persuaded Maxentius to fight at Saxa Rubra on October 28, but it also appears they had covertly sent a message to Constantine alerting him to when and where Maxentius would make his stand.

As for Constantine's order of battle for the contest, almost nothing is known about his individual units or their placement. We know most about his cavalry, which was dominated by large numbers of heavily armored cataphracts. There were also his Schola Palatini mounted bodyguards, plus the lighter, less heavily armored *scutarii* cavalry seen at Verona, and, as seems likely from subsequent events, *equitatae*, specialist units that combined infantry and cavalry. The Arch of Constantine shows archers, foot soldiers, and light cavalry delivering the coup de grâce for Constantine beside the Tiber at battle's end, and it is almost certain that the foot soldiers and cavalrymen depicted there were from *cohors equitatae*.

Vegetius said that by his day it had become common for Roman generals to include a number of equitata cohorts in his cavalry formations. Developed in the first century, these independent auxiliary units combined cavalry and infantry of the same nationality, frequently German or Batavian. *Milliaria* equitata cohorts comprised 240 cavalrymen and 800 infantry. Smaller *quingenaria* equitata cohorts were made up 120 cavalrymen and 480 foot soldiers. Riders and foot soldiers cooperated closely in battle, with infantrymen hitching a ride with horsemen to the hottest part of a fight.

It is highly likely that Constantine possessed a number of Rhine-based equitata cohorts, and this would explain how, with horsemen able to travel much more quickly than infantry, the mounted men and foot soldiers shown on the Arch of Constantine reached the Tiber together as they pursued Maxentian troops.

We know much more about Maxentius's army in this battle. Having lost most of his heavy cavalry to Constantine in northern Italy, Maxentius was primarily reliant on light and medium cavalry, with his sole heavy cavalry being the 1,500-member Singularian Horse Guard. Maxentius's strength lay in his infantry, made up almost entirely of Italian soldiers. The 12,000 men of the Praetorian Guard were "the firmest defense of his throne," in Gibbon's opinion, and they would have occupied the prestigious but dangerous right wing of their emperor's infantry line. Before they left their Rome barracks, known as the Castra Praetoria, the Praetorians' tribunes would have led them in swearing an oath not to give an inch of ground to the enemy, and to fight to the death for the emperor who had given them back their honor and their pride.

The men of Maxentius's next best unit, the Albani of the 2nd Parthica Legion, were probably situated on the left wing, the second most important battle disposition for a Roman general. The more inferior, less experienced, and less committed infantry units that Maxentius had inherited from Severus filled the lines between the Guard and the Albani. One of these units would have been the Herculean Legion, marching with shields bearing the lion emblem of Hercules. Created by Diocletian to serve Maximian as his bodyguard in place of the Praetorian Guard, the unit had gone on to march for Severus before switching allegiance to Maxentius.

Of Maxentius's men, probably only Praetorians and Albani, and perhaps some Herculeans, would have seen recent action, in the African campaign led by Volusianus. Constantine's men, meanwhile, had all regularly seen action on the Rhine and more recently through the spring and summer in northern Italy. After the series of victories over Maxentius's forces north of the Po, Constantinian morale would have been buoyant, despite the fact Constantine's troops were outnumbered here two to one.

As the two armies faced off, with the men of the front rank of each front line standing shield to shield and those of the second awaiting the order to close up, silence would have fallen over the battlefield, broken by the occasional whinny of nervous horses that had picked up the tension on the air, and the flap of cloth banners on their staffs in the morning breeze.

Constantine, at the head of his cavalry on his right wing, close to the tree-lined hills, launched the battle. Ordering his personal trumpeter to sound "Charge," he spurred his horse into action. As the general's buccina sounded, its call was echoed by the trumpets of the cavalry units, with the mounted cornu players charging forward with their comrades.

As heavy cavalry on Constantine's right wing followed him in charging across the plain toward the Maxentian cavalry facing them, the trumpets on Constantine's left wing also sounded "Charge," and cavalrymen there spurred their horses into action. All the while, the infantry lines on both sides stood motionless. Light and medium cavalry on Maxentius's wings received the charge. Men on both sides let out war cries as they came together, and soon a melee of murderous action was taking place in front of the watching foot soldiers.

Maxentius's thousands of light cavalry from North Africa did not lack for courage. Unarmored, bareheaded, with small round shields, they were trained to dash in against enemy infantry, launching darts with deadly accuracy before galloping away. But, up against Constantine's heavy cavalry in close, congested fighting where there was little room to maneuver or use their steeds' speed, they were at a distinct disadvantage. As their darts glanced off cataphract armor, the maces of Constantinian horsemen knocked Africans flying.

Maxentius's medium cavalry fared little better, and it did not take long for Constantine's mounted units to break up opposing cavalry formations on both wings. Soon, surviving Maxentian riders were heading for the cover of the trees in the hills to the west, intent on escaping the one-sided battle, deserting Maxentius and his Italian infantry.

As Constantine and his riders dealt with remaining opposition cavalrymen who attempted to stand and fight, the trumpets and cornets of Constantine's infantry now also sounded "Charge." In the middle of the battlefield, Constantine's front line swept forward at the run, heading for the middle of Maxentius's line. The charge avoided Maxentius's crack troops on the right and left, the Praetorians and the Albani, and instead aimed for his weaker units in the center. As the front line surged forward, archers in Constantine's stationary second line sent wave after wave of arrows looping overhead, to land on the opposition's front line.

In the civil war of Julius Caesar's day, the Roman troops of the opposing front lines usually ran at each other, to collide in the middle of the battlefield with a clash of shields. But at the 48 B.C. Battle of Pharsalus in Greece, the senatorial forces had stood to receive the charge of Caesar's infantry, after his cavalry had seen off theirs. Maxentius's front line did the same, standing their ground. With the cornets of their legions sounding "Close up," the second line troops, who had been standing six feet apart, stepped forward, to also stand shoulder to shoulder.

With the men of the very front line locking their shields together in front of them, those behind them raised their shields over their heads and the heads of the men in front, to protect against the hail of arrows, and waited, most with their lances projecting forward over the shoulder of the man in front. In earlier times, legionaries in the battle line launched several javelins each at the enemy running toward them, then drew their short swords for close combat. In this era when the infantry held on to their double-ended spears for close combat, and with no report of archers in Maxentius's ranks, it seems that the dart-equipped Herculeans would have been the only ones to return missile fire, with each man launching his five darts and then drawing his sword as the opposition rushed up onto them.

Vegetius said that the troops of each side only let out their war cry as they came together. Josephus, writing a little over two centuries earlier about the first-century Judean War, described the ferocious Roman infantry war cry as "a terrible shout."[111] With that resounding, deep-throated, animalistic roar and a tumultuous thud of wood on wood, laminated, hide-covered shields crashed together. Maxentius's stationary first line held firm, bringing the Constantinian charge to a standstill. Now, men in the front ranks of both sides began jabbing and hacking at each other.

Gradually, after as long as an hour of stalemate, men in Maxentius's center began to give ground. Perhaps it was the Herculeans, armed now only with swords, who gave way to the spear thrusts of the opposition. But slowly, step by slow step, the Maxentian center began to fall back, still maintaining good order but giving ground. The men of the 2nd Parthica on the left wing would have resisted this, but they risked being outflanked if they stayed where they were, so their centurions also ordered a slow retreat, step by orderly step. On the right wing, however, the proud men of the Praetorian Guard had not taken a backward step.

We do not know the timeframe involved, but, as the fighting continued, the slow withdrawal of Maxentius's center and left wings while the Praetorian Guard stubbornly held its ground, resulted in the Praetorians being left behind and isolated en masse. This allowed Constantine's second line to come up and, with the aid of cavalry, surround the Praetorians, as the remainder of Maxentius's army pulled back down the plain, still under frontal attack. As the situation deteriorated, Maxentius and the Singularian Horse Guard turned and galloped back to the Tiber. Seeing this and losing heart, some of his infantry began to surrender.

At the Tiber, the Singularian Horse reformed in battle lines, with the river at their backs. Maxentius and his attendants positioned themselves to the cavalry's rear, close to the floating bridge. Along the length of the bridge, the infantrymen in the pontoons hunkered down and waited for Plan B to be signaled. Now, with his heart racing, Maxentius waited. With the Praetorians surrounded at Saxa Rubra, a series of skirmishes had ensued across the river plain to their rear. Other units were trying to hold out here and there, but, as thousands of Constantinian cavalrymen swept down on them, unopposed by Maxentian cavalry, Maxentius's hard-pressed infantry surrendered in droves.

This freed up some Constantinian forces to push on down the Flaminian Way in pursuit of Maxentius, among them cavalry, infantry, and archers. Walking fast, it would have taken soldiers on foot a little over an hour to cover the distance between Saxa Rubra and the area of the Milvian Bridge. So it is possible that the archers in their ranks were mounted. Among these pursuing troops was Constantine himself, riding hard, accompanied by cataphracts. From a distance, Maxentius would have identified his brother-in-law from his golden helmet and armor, flowing purple cape, and glittering standard. As Constantine led his cavalry in engaging the waiting Singularians, Maxentius gave an order to his buccina player, who sounded "Withdraw!" On the far bank of the Tiber, waiting Maxentian cornu players repeated the call.

Maxentius turned his horse and, followed by mounted attendants and Singularian bodyguards, he rode onto the floating bridge. With the thunder of hooves on wood, he, and the men following, commenced crossing the river. On the plain, Singularian units parted, to allow Constantine to pass through them and continue the pursuit onto the bridge, as per the plan to entrap him. Constantine took the bait, spurring his horse to chase down Maxentius.

Prior to the Battle of Pharsalus, Julius Caesar had disseminated the order that he wanted the Senate's commanding general Pompey the Great, his father-in-law, spared if cornered. Constantine issued no such order regarding his brother-in-law prior to the Battle of the Milvian Bridge. Infuriated that Maxentius had dared go into battle against him, Constantine wanted his brother-in-law dead. But in his haste, he was playing right into Maxentius's hands.

Now Fate, or a betrayer in Maxentius's ranks, turned the tables in Constantine's favor. As Maxentius reached the middle of the floating bridge, it suddenly parted beneath him. The lever that operated the bridge's self-destruct mechanism had been pulled, too soon, either in error or quite deliberately, and Maxentius became the victim of his own trap. As the bridge separated, his horse tumbled into the Tiber, taking the young emperor with him. Behind Maxentius, mounted attendants, his standard, and cavalry bodyguards also cascaded into the water, as the bridge broke up. Troops who had been skulking in the pontoons also found themselves in the river, and they joined a confusion of floundering horses, soldiers, and pieces of timber being carried away by the Tiber's flow.

Somehow, Maxentius, apparently a good horseman, managed to remain in the saddle. Clinging to his charger's neck, he urged the horse to swim for the southern bank and safety. The horse reached the river's edge, as his men there ran to help their emperor. The terrified horse attempted to climb the bank with Maxentius on his back, but it was too high, too steep, too slippery. With flailing legs, the horse fell back into the water, tipping Maxentius from his back. Dragged down by his heavy armor, Maxentius sank out of sight, and never resurfaced. Eusebius, writing of Maxentius's fate, would liken Constantine to Moses, and Maxentius and his drowned Singularians to Pharaoh's chariot force perishing in the Red Sea.[112]

The Singularians were skilled in swimming rivers with their horses, and many of those cavalrymen who had gone into the river stayed with their steeds, with a number attempting to go to the aid of their emperor. The northern bank of the river was now quickly lined by Constantinian troops—mounted cavalrymen, infantrymen, and archers—who let fly with arrows and darts at the Maxentian troops in the water. Some Singularians hung on to their horses, others tried to float away with the help of their wooden shields. Most made easy targets for the Constantinians on the bank. Even those who reached the southern bank were cut down by arrow and dart as they tried to clamber up the steep bank to escape the river of death.

The bulk of the men of the Singularian Horse, stranded on the Tiber's north bank, disorganized and dismayed, turned, stood, and fought. But with their emperor gone from sight and those Maxentian troops who had been on the south bank now streaming back down the Flaminian Way to the walls of Rome, they knew that the battle was lost, and soon some of the Singularians stranded north of the river were throwing down their weapons and capitulating.

By the time that the sun set at a little after 5:00 p.m. that evening, the fighting, the yelling, the cursing, and the slaying had come to an end. The Battle of the Milvian Bridge was over. At Saxa Rubra, the surrounded Praetorian Guard kept its vow and never took a backward step. As a consequence, Praetorians had died in their thousands, with their bodies heaped where they had fallen. Their end may have taken hours, but, as will be seen a little later, Constantine would credit his cavalry with ultimately destroying the Praetorian Guard. Few Praetorians survived to be taken prisoner, but among them, it would later appear, were their leaders, the tribunes Marcellianus and Marcellus.

The demise of the emperor's best troops would be emulated almost fifteen hundred years later, when France's Emperor Napoleon lost the 1815 Battle of Waterloo and his Imperial Guard similarly refused to either surrender or retreat and were massacred where they stood.

Up and down the length of the river plain, thousands of other Maxentian troops from the 2nd Parthica Legion, the Herculean Legion, the Maurii, the Singularian Horse Guard, and other units, surrendered. Stripped of their arms and equipment, as were the Maxentian dead, the downcast captives were herded together under guard. Constantine probably returned to his camp at Prima Porta for the night, as, across the river, despite Maxentius's disappearance and the capitulation of his army, the gates of Rome remained closed.

XIV

CONSTANTINE
THE VICTOR

A s October 29 dawned, Constantine's troops were busy laying
new wooden decking over the stone bridges that crossed the Tiber,
including the Milvian Bridge. Constantine also had men looking for the
body of Maxentius in the Tiber. Divers found the emperor's armor-clad
body on the river's muddy floor. Ropes were attached, and the corpse was
hauled to the surface, then dragged onto the bank, as curious Constantinian soldiers crowded around to gape at the white-faced cadaver. On
Constantine's orders, Maxentius's head was cut off with the blow of a centurion's sword, then placed on the end of a spear for public display.

Soon, a message was delivered to Constantine from City Prefect Anullinus in Rome. Congratulating Constantine on his victory over Maxentius,
hailing him Augustus, and vowing his own allegiance and that of the City
Guard and Night Watch, Anullinus advised that he was ordering the gates
of Rome to be thrown open, that he was looking forward to personally
greeting Constantine in the suburbs. No doubt replying by addressing the
city prefect as "most esteemed Anullinus," as he would continue to do
over the next few years, Constantine advised that he intended making a
triumphal entry into Rome that same day, following the same route as the
parades of Triumphs of old, before putting in a lengthy stay at Rome—he

would end up spending six weeks enjoying his victory and putting his stamp on the Eternal City.

It is clear that City Prefect Anullinus, rather than suddenly changing his colors once Maxentius was dead, had sided with Constantine for some time before this, and had betrayed Maxentius in the same way he had betrayed the emperor Severus six years earlier to side with Maxentius. An orator in Trier the following year, delivering a panegyric in front of Constantine that lauded him for his victories over Maxentius, would state that Constantine had already known before he crossed into Italy that he would defeat his brother-in-law. The speaker would declare that this was because Constantine had received "divine inspiration," referencing both a "superior divinity" and "lesser gods."[113]

It is also likely that as early as 311, as Maxentius was beefing up his defenses in Italy, Anullinus had begun sending Constantine secret messages, vowing to help him overthrow Maxentius if and when Constantine invaded Italy and did battle with Maxentius's troops. And Anullinus was not alone. As events were soon to show, Volusianus, another member of Maxentius's inner circle, had been in league with Anullinus in the betrayal of the emperor they had helped create.

It is likely that on the previous day, possibly even before the sun had set on Maxentius's defeat, Anullinus, as city prefect, had ordered the City Guard to arrest a number of the members of the clique of thirteen senators that had elevated Maxentius to the throne, and to locate and arrest Maxentius's wife and son. We hear nothing more of the City Guard tribune Lucianus; if he had not died in the fighting outside the city and had remained inside Rome, he may well have been put to death on the orders of City Prefect Anullinus.

Later on the day following the battle, October 29, Constantine made his triumphal entry into Rome behind a procession of his troops. The Arch of Constantine shows him making his entrance sitting on an open, single-seat, four-wheeled carriage. This is a smaller carriage than that shown at Verona, and identical to the one on which the goddess Cybele, protector of cities, was frequently depicted. Cybele was celebrated every March during Holy Week, and then, on April 10 during the Megalesia Festival when her seated statue was transferred in a procession from her Palatine Temple to the Circus Maximus for a day of races in her honor. A highly decorated, four-wheeled golden carriage would have been kept for this annual procession. Because of Cybele's close connection with Apollo, Constantine is likely to have ordered Anullinus to send out the carriage of Cybele for his procession through Rome.

Anullinus himself came to meet Constantine in the suburbs, beyond the Flaminian Gate, accompanied by fellow senators—apart from those who had been arrested and were now awaiting Constantine's pleasure. All bowed down to their new emperor, then led the way into the city at the head of his triumphal procession. The Arch of Constantine shows Constantine's infantry at the head of the army, marching with shields on their left arms, spears resting on their right shoulders, swords on their hips, and plumes still on their helmets. Cavalry followed, equally well armed.

The Arch also shows two bareheaded, unarmed men being pushed along by armed troops, with one of the pair looking fearfully back toward Constantine, as if hoping for mercy. This pair appears to be prisoners, senior officers of Maxentius—in all likelihood the tribunes Marcellianus and Marcellus. This reflects the age-old practice of leading captured enemy commanders through Rome's streets in triumphal parades. The two prisoners would no doubt subsequently join the arrested senators in the Carcer, the city prison.

More cavalry follows in the procession depicted on the Arch, and then Constantine himself, driving his carriage seated on a low-backed throne and wearing lengthy robes. What the Arch of Constantine does not show is the head of Maxentius being paraded on a spear. However, we know from a number of sources, including Zosimus, Valesianus, and the 313 Trier panegyric, that it was indeed carried through Rome to demonstrate to the people that Maxentius was truly dead, and to demonstrate that resistance was futile.

According to his propagandist Eusebius, Constantine's triumphal route was lined with the population of Rome, "their countenances expressive of the gladness of their hearts," and who "received him with acclamations of abounding joy."[114] Quite how much genuine rejoicing there was as the people of Rome watched an army of fully armed foreigners march in conquest through their streets is open to speculation. For one thing, the Triumph was being celebrated by Constantine for a victory over fellow Romans, contrary to the tradition stipulating that Triumphs only be celebrated for victories against foreigners.

To many people of Rome and Italy, it would have seemed that Constantine the outsider was treating them as foreigners, and conquered foreigners at that. At best, the Roman public would have shuddered at the sight of the head of local son Maxentius on a stick and smiled apprehensively and waved anxiously when their new ruler passed by on his godly carriage, as they worried that Constantine might unleash his foreign troops on them and their city unless they appeared welcoming and submissive.

Constantine's procession took him from the Field of Mars in through the Triumphal Gate in the old Severan Walls, through the Circus Maximus, around the Palatine Hill, and by the Colosseum to the foot of the Capitoline Mount. At the Triumphal Gate, Constantine alighted from his carriage. Apparently to project an air of humility, he walked the rest of the route.

Yet even this would not have impressed his harsher critics in the crowd, for an ancient law of Rome required that troops entering and stationed within the pomerium, the old sacred boundary of the city that, according to legend, had been drawn personally by Romulus, founder of Rome, only be "half armed" at all times—that is, with sword, but without spear and shield. The city had long since outgrown the pomerium, but the old boundary was still respected, and in all past triumphal processions participating half-armed troops had been bareheaded and had worn white robes, not their helmets and bloodstained tunics and armor as now. But who would dare tell the conqueror of Rome that he was breaking Roman law?

Outside the Colosseum, Constantine's procession passed a giant bronze statue of a nude male figure. Some one hundred feet tall, it was almost the same height as today's Statue of Liberty in New York. The statue had been commissioned by Nero, who had the head modeled on his own. It initially stood in the vestibule of his fabulous palace, the Golden House. To make way for the Temple of Venus and Rome, Hadrian moved the statue to its present location beside the Colosseum using twenty-four elephants, replacing Nero's head with another representing sun god Sol Invictus, complete with a radiant crown. In his right hand, Sol held a ship's rudder to a globe representing the Earth, a symbolic statement that the course of world affairs was in his hands.

After passing Sol's statue, Constantine and his procession moved along the Sacred Way. En route to the Forum Romanum and the Capitoline Mount, they walked through the victory arches of Titus and Septimius Severus. At the foot of the steps that led up to the Temple of Jupiter Best and Greatest on Capitol Hill, Constantine's procession halted. But

Constantine refrained from emulating the practice of triumphant generals of the past, who had climbed the steps to the Temple of Jupiter on their knees before making sacrifices to Jupiter in thanks for their victories. Instead, Constantine turned away and walked to the Curia Julia, the Senate House, in the Forum.

There in the Curia, the Senate had quickly assembled to hail their new emperor, heap praise on him, and vote him the title Augustus Maximus, or the Greatest Augustus. By unanimous vote, the senators declared that from this day forward, Constantine would be named first in all official state documents, ahead of the emperors Licinius and Maximinus Daia. Until much later in life, Constantine would ignore the title voted to him by the Senate of Rome. From the day he defeated Maxentius and took Rome, he styled himself Victor Constantine Augustus.

In a short, modest address to the senators, Constantine, describing himself as the liberator of Rome, promised to recognize the status and privileges that the Senate had enjoyed in the past, promised not to punish the city or its people for following Maxentius, and decreed the recall of the members of the delegation exiled by Maxentius and the return of their confiscated property. Invalidating the decrees of Maxentius from the past six years, Constantine would also issue a decree of *damnatio memoriae*, requiring all records, inscriptions, statues, and busts of Maxentius to be destroyed, wiping the short-lived emperor's official memory from the face of the Earth. This ensured that no positive information about Maxentius would reach future generations, and also ensured that the anti-Maxentius propaganda issuing from the pens of the likes of Eusebius and Lactantius became accepted as historical fact.

During his October 29 visit to the Senate, Constantine ordered the release of men imprisoned during the reign of Maxentius, but he also invalidated all honors granted by Maxentius to members of the Senate and ordered the immediate execution of the officers and senators who had put Maxentius on the throne and kept him there. It appears that, in addition to the tribunes who had enthroned Maxentius, six senators from the clique of thirteen were put to death. These would have included Tertullus, city prefect under Maxentius for twelve months between 307 and 308, and another of Maxentius's city prefects, Statius Rufinus. Maxentius's prefect over 309–310, Aurelius Hermogenianus, a leading law codifier under Diocletian who had probably advised the young emperor in 306 that his claim to the throne was valid as he was the son and heir of Maximian, had died in 311.

Of the other senators who had been behind Maxentius, Ruricius had been killed in the fighting in northern Italy, and Neratius Junius Flavianus had apparently died in office while city prefect that February. Julianus, the likely relative of Constantine's deputy Bassianus, was spared. Turncoat City Prefect Anullinus was also spared. But more than that, Constantine confirmed Anullinus's appointment as city prefect until December 8 of that year, gave him the new title of Patricius, which ranked him between a Praetorian prefect and a Caesar, and appointed him his governor of Africa for 313.

To replace Anullinus as Rome's city prefect in 313, Constantine would reappoint Aradius Rufinus, another Maxentius supporter, but more impor-tantly a relative of Anullinus, which no dount influenced his appointment. Immediately prior to Anullius taking the post, Rufinus had served as Max-entius's city prefect from February to October that year. Another spared member of the clique of thirteen, Rufinus would serve as Constantine's city prefect until December 313. Thereafter, he would receive no further posts under Constantine.

In the new year, when Anullinus traveled across the Mediterranean to again take up the governorship of Africa, he would take Maxentius's rot-ting head with him, for display to Prefect Zenas and Maxentius's other officers and supporters in the North African provinces, as proof that he was dead and to ensure a bloodless transition of power to Constantine. "Most Esteemed" Anullinus would return to Rome in 314, after which he received no more appointments and disappeared from the record, possi-bly exiled by Constantine and subject to damnatio memoriae—his monu-ments in Africa were defaced following his last governorship.

Volusianus was another member of Maxentius's inner circle who was both spared and rewarded by Constantine for apparently covertly work-ing against Maxentius in the lead up to the Battle of the Milvian Bridge. His reward may have been for inventing the mechanism that parted the floating bridge, and for ensuring that it broke when Maxentius rode across it. Constantine elevated Volusianus to the prestigious position of Com-panion of the Augustus, made him City Prefect of Rome from 313 to 315, appointed him a consul in 314, and gave him special authority to rule in legal cases in his name.

Eager to show his loyalty and thanks, in 314 Volusianus would erect a statue of Constantine in Rome's Forum of Trajan, at his own expense. But in 315 he would fall afoul of the emperor, as Volusianus's rivals in the Senate apparently convinced Constantine that he could not be trusted. Fickle Volusianus became too big for his boots and too fond of power; or so Constantine came to think. Removed from his post as city prefect by Constantine in August 315, Volusianus would shortly after be exiled from Italy, with all his property forfeited. He would die in exile some fifteen years later.

Volusianus, Rufinus, and Anullinus appear to have acted in concert as a traitorous cabal, covertly working behind Maxentius's back to collaborate with Constantine and bring down the emperor they had sworn to serve. As it turned out, their rewards would be fleeting, as Constantine decided that men who could betray one emperor—in Anullinus's case, it was three emperors he had betrayed in short order, Severus, Maximian, and Maxentius—could just as easily betray him, and he removed these duplicitous players from the game.

For the six other senators who had backed Maxentius and remained true to him, a swift death was their reward. According to the hyperbole of the pro-Constantine panegyric at Trier in 313, Maxentius had been a "monster" who had handed the treasures of Rome to the senatorial clique who had backed him. "Granting to these butchers of their own country other men's wives, and the lives and goods of innocent people," said the orator of Maxentius, "he bound them to himself to the death."[115] That death would be via decapitation at the hands of a Constantinian executioner.

The condemned men would have been taken from the city prison below the Capitoline Mount and marched from Rome in chains to be executed outside the city. The countryside beside the Appian Way had proven popular over the centuries as the location for summary executions, among the tombs that lined the highway. Here, the prefects, tribunes, and centurions responsible for the assassination of Caligula had been dispatched. According to Christian tradition, the Apostle Paul was also beheaded in a similar spot beside the Appian Way. It is likely that Constantine ordered the condemned men executed on the site of Maxentius's Appian Way villa. Forced to kneel and project their necks as a centurion stood over them with sword raised, they would have lost their heads in quick succession.

To reveal the whereabouts of Maxentius's wife Maximilla and two-year-old son, Constantine would have had the freedmen and slaves on the staff of Maxentius's Palatium interrogated. But just as they never revealed the location of their late emperor's hidden regalia, they would not have revealed the city hiding place of his loved ones. At some point, mother and child were discovered by Constantine's searching troops. The child, we know, was promptly put to the sword.

The fate of Maximilla, wife of Maxentius and daughter of Galerius, is not recorded; she disappears from history. The consensus among historians is that Constantine also had Maxentius's widow executed, to remove any threat to his power—while she lived, she could remarry and produce a grandson of the legitimate emperor Galerius who could become the focus of a bid for the throne. Gibbon wrote that Constantine "extirpated his [Maxentius's] whole race."

Gibbon went on to note that Constantine would have expected Maxentius to have eradicated Constantine's family had he won the contest between the pair, although, despite Eusebius's rhetoric, it is likely that just a single opponent of Maxentius was killed during his reign, the senator executed at its commencement. In other cases, Maxentius had exiled opponents, including his traitorous father, who was allowed to live and continue to pose a threat.

Maximilla and her child were probably protected by a detachment from Maxentius's Singularian Horse Guard, and there may have been a short, bloody battle as Constantine's troops fought their way into the house and the guardsmen expended their last breath striving to protect their charges. The House of Fausta shows evidence of being damaged by a fire in Late Antiquity—there is also evidence that Constantine subsequently had the building refurbished—and this may have been caused during this struggle.

As punishment for serving his brother-in-law, Constantine would send most of Maxentius's surrendered military units out of Italy to the empire's loneliest frontiers, to act as border guards. But two units were victims of a special vindictiveness—the Praetorian Guard and the Singularian Horse Guard. Constantine abolished both and ordered their survivors to raze to the ground their quarters in the east of the city, the massive Castra Praetoria and the Singularians' two Caelian Hill bases, known as Old Fort and New Fort. But not before his own troops looted the buildings of their contents, including the banked savings of the previous occupants. The Praetorians had put Maxentius on the throne, so their punishment is not surprising. The Singularians were perhaps punished for serving Maxentius too well, and to the last.

Work on destruction of the horse guard forts began almost immediately, on November 9.[116] So intent was Constantine on destroying all memory of the Singularians that he also ordered the destruction of every marble horse guard tombstone in the unit's graveyard adjacent to the forts. He would in time give the land on which the forts and graveyard had stood to the Christian Church at Rome, but the graveyard site would lie abandoned for more than eighty years, until, late in the fourth century, a Christian church was erected on the site, fronting the Via Merculana—the Church of St. Marcellinus and Peter, celebrating two Christian martyrs reputedly beheaded in 304 on the orders of a Roman magistrate serving under Constantine's father the emperor Constantius during the Great Persecution.

With Constantine soon departing Rome, the troops doing the job of wrecking the graveyard and forts would not follow his orders to the letter once his back was turned. The rubble of the destroyed New Fort would cover the still-intact underground shrine of the Singularians, a vaulted room where their standards and the gold the troops had put away as savings had been kept for centuries. The gold would have been looted by Constantine's troops before they set the guardsmen to work destroying their headquarters. That shrine room survives to this day, beneath the nave of the Church of St. John Lateran, which would be built over the top of the site of the fort and dedicated in 324.

Meanwhile, the finely engraved tombstones of 609 Singularian horsemen who had served the emperors over the centuries would be preserved intact beneath the Basilica of Saints Marcellinus and Peter. Clearly, in Constantine's absence someone in charge defied his order to obliterate the guardsmen's tombstones, apparently seeing it as a sacrilege. The largest collection of Roman cavalry headstones ever unearthed, when they were discovered in modern times, the find was to prove a treasure trove for archaeologists and historians.

As inscriptions with Maxentius's name on them and every official bust and statue of Maxentius were sought out and destroyed, Maxentius's villa and circus beside the Appian Way were abandoned. However, the mausoleum's inscription to Romulus from his father Maxentius would survive, apparently because someone again disobeyed Constantine's orders. The Egyptian obelisk in the center of the racetrack was toppled and left where it fell, and the circus buried—this was why it would be uncovered in such good condition in later times. And Constantine ordered that the seating capacity of the Circus Maximus at Rome be increased to twenty-five times that of Maxentius' circus—250,000.

Constantine abandoned work on Maxentius's new baths on the Quirinal—they would later be completed by Constantine's son Constans then restored and rededicated after a fire by another of his sons, Constantius II. As for the Temple of Venus and Roma that Maxentius had rebuilt, Constantine ordered it rededicated in his own name. He even ordered that the Temple of Romulus, built by Maxentius to honor his dead son, also be rededicated in his name. Then there was the massive white marble-clad Basilica of Maxentius with its soaring vaulted concrete ceiling domes—it was within weeks of opening by the time of the Milvian Bridge battle, and Constantine now ordered the basilica's prompt completion, specifying that it be officially dedicated to him and renamed the Basilica of Constantine. In addition to also renovating the House of Fausta, possible site of the executions of Maxentius's wife and child, Constantine also modified the Villa of Livia at Saxa Rubra, the opening point of the battle that had ended with the death of Maxentius.

Constantine also specified that a huge statue of himself be lodged in the apse at the western end of the new basilica, from where it would dominate the interior of the building. Forty feet high, it would depict Constantine seated on a throne. Some historians believe that this statue was already under construction at the time and had been intended to depict Maxentius. The final statue, the Colossus of Constantine as it was to become known, would be in place by 314, when Eusebius completed *The Church History*, which mentions it, and ready for Constantine's return to Rome in 315. The statue's head and limbs were sculpted from white marble. Its torso is believed to have been constructed using bricks and timber covered by a massive brass cuirass—which would have been looted and melted down when Rome was sacked by Goths a century after this. The ten-foot-high marble head has survived to this day along with sections of various limbs, including, inexplicably, two right hands—in both cases, the index finger of the right hand points to the heavens.

Eusebius would contend that this statue of Constantine held a Christian cross in its left hand. Eusebius, who is believed to have never visited Rome and so never saw the statue for himself, based this assertion on the inscription on the base of the statue: "Through this sign of salvation, which is the true symbol of goodness, I rescued your city and freed it from the tyrant's yoke, and through my act of liberation I restored the Senate and the people of Rome to their ancient renown and splendor."[117]

However, modern historians believe that the statue in fact held a representation of Constantine's imperial scepter of state in its left hand. This is supported by the *Regionaries*, a detailed official survey of Rome's monuments and buildings conducted for Constantine from late 312 and completed by 315, in time for the emperor's return to Rome. This survey makes no mention of any Christian monument in the city at that time, seeming to rule out the supposed cross in Constantine's hand, a very obvious symbol that would certainly have made it a Christian monument in the eyes of Christians and non-Christians alike.[118]

On coins he issued from 313, Constantine would regularly be shown with the scepter of state which it is believed was held in the statue's left hand. Constantine would have inherited the scepter from his father Constantius, and it appears identical to that of Maxentius discovered in 2006—a globe set in leaves on a staff. But not once during his long reign was Constantine depicted holding a cross on any coin he issued. And while his coins were produced at different mints around his realm, Constantine would have personally authorized the images and messages his coinage portrayed to the Roman world.

So, if not a cross, what was the statue's "true symbol of goodness"? The answer is provided by a silver commemorative medallion produced by Constantine in 315, the year the Colossus of Constantine was dedicated by him at Rome. This medallion was made at the Italian imperial mint at Ticinum, today's Pavia, twenty-two miles south of Milan. This same mint, transferred to Pavia from Milan in 275, produced the A.D. 313 gold medallion featuring Constantine and Sol Invictus discussed shortly.

Everything about the 315 medallion's imagery points to its being produced to reflect the 315 dedication of the Colossus of Constantine in the Basilica of Constantine, and it seems to depict Constantine as he appears in the statue. On the obverse side, the medallion shows Constantine from the chest up. He wears a cuirass and holds a shield decorated with the wolf and twins, the traditional symbol of Rome that harked back to the myth that a she-wolf had suckled city founders Romulus and Remus. An imperial scepter identical to that of Maxentius's scepter is also shown on the medallion, and a horse's head. The meaning of the horse's head is made clear when you turn over the medallion.

On the medallion's reverse, Constantine is shown on a dais address-ing dismounted cavalrymen. Two vexillas shown behind him were either Maxentius's two captured standards or perhaps the standards of two Con-stantinian mounted units that had excelled in the Milvian Bridge battle. Roma, goddess of Rome, stands beside Constantine, who wears a cuirass and in his left hand holds a standard bearing a statuette of Victoria—the standard of the Praetorian Guard. This image very clearly announces that Constantine was praising his cavalry for destroying the Praetorian Guard and capturing its standards, allowing him to become the savior of Rome. In this image, too, echoing the two surviving right hands of the Colossus, the index finger of Constantine's right hand points to the heavens, to indi-cate that he believed he had obtained his victory over Maxentius by divine providence.

Returning our attention to the face side of the coin, we see that Con-stantine wears a headpiece that some have described as a helmet, and others a crown. From his conquest of Rome forward, Constantine habitually wore a diadem in public—a crown, richly decorated with gold and jewels. This crown appears to be what Constantine wears on the 315 medallion, with several additional elements. The top of the crown is covered with a number of rosettes, symbol of war goddess Bellona, plus a single but prominent chi-rho emblem. The chi-rho, which, as has been pointed out earlier, was traditionally associated with good, appears to be the "true symbol of good-ness" referred to in the statue's inscription.

It is likely that, in addition to the metal cuirass worn by the Colos-sus, a larger-than-life version of the crown depicted on the coin sat on the Colossus's marble head—until it was looted in a later sack of Rome. Almost certainly then, the image on the medallion of 315 mirrors how the Colossus of Constantine appeared—diadem with chi-rho and all. On a 317 coin, which would be issued following a key battle, Constantine would be depicted wearing a genuine battle helmet that bore a large chi-rho.

Another image that would frequently appear on Constantine's medal-lions and coins from 313 would be that of sun god Sol Invictus, and this gives us a clue to where Constantine stayed during his fifty-four-day sojourn in Rome. He appears to have resided at the Sessorium, the imperial palace complex in the east of the city, totally eschewing the Palatium complex on the Palatine, home to the rambling palaces of Roman emperors of old. This would have been intended to signal that he was denying the Palatium, and

Rome in general, any further legitimacy as the seat of emperors. It may also have been influenced by fact that the Sessorium contained a temple dedicated to Sol Invictus, who was featuring prominently in Constantine's thinking at this point.

In 313, Constantine would produce the previously mentioned limited edition gold medallion in which he was depicted with Sol Invictus. God and emperor are shown as companions, equals, although with Constantine at the fore. Constantine carries a shield, on which is depicted Sol driving his chariot, with his four horses trampling a hapless victim—Maxentius. The message on the medallion reads "Sol Invictus, Companion" of Constantine. Sol, and this same message, would appear on coins of Constantine for the next decade.

Within days of entering Rome, Constantine summoned the leading men of the city to the Forum Romanum with their male children, to hear him give an address. There, on the western side of the Forum, Constantine took pride of place on the Rostra of Augustus in front of the Five Columns Monument, which had been erected here to celebrate the 303 decannalia of the Tetrarchs and vicennalia of Diocletian. Behind Constantine rose the monument's columns, topped by larger-than-life statues of Diocletian, Maximian, Galerius, and Constantine's father Constantius, all flanking a statue of Jupiter.

Selection of the Five Columns Monument location for Constantine's speech was obviously intended to link him to the previous tetrarchs and give legitimacy to his seizure of the throne—for, just like Maxentius, Constantine was a usurper who had taken the throne at Rome by force. If Constantine had indeed accompanied Diocletian to that 303 ceremony, when, on this spot, the Tetrarchs had renewed their vows to serve the Roman people, Constantine would have been in the official procession to the Rostra as a tribune of the guard, in white robes and with sword on his hip, together with the standard-bearers of legions with eagle standards, and Praetorian Guard standard-bearers with their standards of Victoria. They can all be seen today on a surviving *in situ* relief of the monument that records that 303 ceremony.

For his 312 address to the men of Rome in the Forum, surrounded by soldiers, and supporters in togas, Constantine also wore a toga, and probably a jeweled crown. Someone close to Constantine with knowledge of Rome's laws, probably City Prefect Anullinus, must have informed him of the ancient law he had broken on October 29 when he sent his men marching fully armed through the older part of the city, no doubt also relaying the alarm that this act had generated among citizens and senators alike. For the Arch of Constantine reveals that, as the emperor delivered his speech from the Rostra, his soldiers below him around the Rostra were bareheaded, wore simple robes, and were half armed, with just a sword on the left hip, as the law required.

In his speech, with the turncoats Anullinus, Volusianus, and Rufinus no doubt among the supporters seen standing behind him on the Rostra, Constantine promised to continue to recognize Rome as the capital of the Roman world, as Maxentius had, and to honor its Senate, as Maxentius had. When some in the crowd called for the punishment of all of Maxentius's cronies, in particular the senators who had only recently changed sides, Constantine replied that enough punishment had been dealt out already. In doing so, he protected the turncoats, men who would be useful to him, for now. More than that, he discouraged informants from coming forward to tell him things he did not want to know about the past deeds of senators who were now his loyal lackeys.

To bribe his way into the hearts of his new subjects, he also promised to reward the citizens of Rome financially with a donative, as earlier emperors had done on taking the throne. Sure enough, Constantine invited the citizenry to a *liberalitas*, a money-giving ceremony. The exact location for this ceremony is not recorded, but the Arch of Constantine shows Constantine sitting on a high throne for the event, seemingly in the apse of a building which, left and right of him, appears to have a multi-vaulted ceiling. This was almost certainly the new Basilica of Constantine.

Clad in a toga, the new emperor doled out money from his throne as men in togas passed below him with right hands extended to accept his largesse—money taken from Maxentius's treasury at Rome. If the liberalitas did indeed take place in the new basilica, this would explain why Constantine subsequently chose to place the enthroned statue of himself in the basilica's apse—to continually remind the people of Rome of the day he had been so generous to them on this very spot.

Now, too, Constantine decreed public feasts, and chariot races at the Circus Maximus, to celebrate his victory and to win over the populace at large. While Constantine was engaged in conciliating the Senate and people of Rome, attempting to convince them of his good intentions and stamping his name on the city in place of Maxentius's, his clerks were sifting through Maxentius's letters and records at the Palatium. Among the many things of interest that they discovered were the letters that had sealed the secret treaty between Daia and Maxentius. Lactantius, who reveals this, says that Constantine had already seen the statues depicting Maxentius and Daia in friendship pose at Rome, statues that would have been swiftly torn down and destroyed as part of Constantine's damnatio memoriae against Maxentius.

In December, while Constantine was still in Rome, word reached him from Trier that the Franks were causing trouble on the upper Rhine. It is likely that this news arrived with his mother Helena, for she is believed to have begun residing at Rome that December, after which she would call Rome home for the rest of her life. Constantine presented his mother with the Sessorium complex, and she moved into the garden villa on the site. _Plus, before departing the city, Constantine ordered the construction of new imperial quarters at the Sessorium to permit him to use the complex when in Rome. These quarters would be erected in the Varian Gardens, close to, and supplied by, the aqueduct that ran along the northern edge of the gardens. Constantine also provided the funds for his mother to restore the complex's run-down baths, which came to be called the Terme Eleni-ane, or the Baths of Helena.

Leaving his mother and much of his invasion army at Rome, Constan-tine departed the city on December 22 and hurried from Italy to the Rhine to deal with the Franks. The urgency of his departure is indicated by the fact that this was the second-last day of the Saturnalia Festival and three days before the annual celebrations dedicated to Sol Invictus, which took place every December 25.

He left the Palatine Hill palaces abandoned and probably looted of their furniture, decoration and fittings. He also left Maxentius's conquered troops at Rome for the moment, continuing the destruction of the Praeto-rian and Singularian barracks. Most of these former troops of Maxentius would, in the spring, be sent north to the Rhine and Danube frontiers. The majority remained in their existing units, but the humiliated survivors of the disbanded Praetorian Guard and Singularian Horse Guard would be distributed among other units.

Come July 313, an official at Constantine's capital Trier would refer to these defeated troops of Maxentius in gloating terms: "Stripped of their wicked weapons and rearmed against foreign enemies, they have forgotten the delights of the Circus Maximus, of Pompey's Theater, and of the baths of the noblemen. They patrol the Rhine and the Danube, watching out for robbers."[119]

Constantine chose to punish one Italian unit that had loyally served Maxentius, the 2nd Parthica Legion, in what appears to be a particularly sadistic fashion. Two hundred years earlier, the unit had been raised in Italy to fight in Parthia. Constantine decided to send them back to the Parthia region with a permanent posting to a hot, lonely Mesopotamian base, far from their loved ones in Italy. But as Maximinus Daia controlled that part of the Roman world, Constantine had to seek Daia's approval for the transfer. It seems that, prior to leaving Rome, he wrote to Daia, telling him of his overthrow of Maxentius and suggesting the legion's relocation to Daia's realm—perhaps as a means of winning the support of the eastern Tetrarch, who, he knew, had been secretly allied to Maxentius. Until Daia agreed, the disarmed Albani would have to cool their heels at their Albana base, watched over by Constantine's troops. As it happened, changing events would delay the legion's transfer until late 313.

To reach the Rhine with the snows of early winter by this time blocking his passage of the Alps, Constantine is likely to have taken a warship from Ostia, the port of Rome, to southern Gaul, before traveling overland through Trier. Despite his promises to the Senate and people of Rome that he would honor both, he would not only fail to keep his word now that he had conquered Rome, he would punish the Senate and city. From now on, Constantine required the wealthiest Romans of the senatorial class who chose to sit in the Senate to pay him a fee of eight pounds of gold a year. Less wealthy senators were required to pay seven pounds of gold. Constantine also closed the imperial mint at Rome, depriving the Senate of the ability to make money and propaganda. Plus all the powers of the Senate, and the past privileges and honors involved with membership of the Senatorial Order restored by Maxentius, were summarily abolished.

In this way, the Senate was reduced by Constantine to nothing more than an expensive gentlemen's club. If Roman noblemen wished to attend the Senate and debate affairs of state over which they no longer had any say or control, they would have to pay for the privilege, and pay heftily, watched over by foreign troops and answering to an emperor far away.

As he turned his back on Rome, Constantine ensured that the Eternal City would never again be the seat of a Roman emperor as it had been under Maxentius and the vast majority of his predecessors, and it would never again be the capital of the Roman Empire. In the wake of Rome's demotion, not even Milan, being an Italian city, would receive Constantine's favor. For the time being, Trier would remain Constantine's capital, and Arles his favored retreat, as he increasingly gave thought to creating a new capital for himself in the East.

XV

AND THEN
THERE WERE TWO

ONCE CONSTANTINE REACHED THE RHINE in January 313, he
quickly dealt with the Frankish problem, punishing two kings
of the Franks. The indications are that the kings were being kept as
hostages to their people's good behavior, and their tribes became restive after hearing that Constantine was campaigning in Italy. It would
appear that Constantine had the two kings executed, and, under threat
of more punishment of hostages, the tribes quieted. Now, Constantine
began planning a major spring and summer offensive that would push
through Germany east of the Rhine all the way to the Elbe River. Not
since Drusus Caesar early in the first century A.D. had a campaigning
Roman army set eyes on the Elbe. This would be a history-making
enterprise.

But then a message reached Constantine from Licinius, Augustus of
the East. No doubt in response to a letter from Constantine advising
that he had killed Maxentius, "liberated" Rome, and taken the mantle of Augustus of the West for himself, Licinius's letter proposed a formal alliance between himself and Constantine, an alliance that would
be cemented by a marriage between Licinius and Constantine's eldest
half-sister Flavia Julia Constantia, who was aged eighteen or nineteen

at this point. Constantine agreed to the alliance and the marriage, suggesting that the two emperors meet in the vicinity of Milan in February.

The meeting duly took place outside Milan. There at the meeting place, probably in a tented imperial pavilion located between the sprawling camps of the two emperors, the marriage of young Constantia and the fifty-year-old, double-chinned, beetle-browed Licinius was duly celebrated. Two years later, Constantia, who is believed to have been a committed Christian, would give her husband a son and heir, Valerius Licinianus Licinius, who would become known as Licinius II.

Constantine was fond of Constantia, and later events that show her powers of persuasion suggest that it was via her Christian influence that, at this February meeting outside Milan, Constantine and Licinius sealed a joint imperial decree, to become known as the Edict of Milan. Issued in both their names—assuredly with the name of Licinius, the more senior of the two Augusti, coming first—the document decreed freedom of religion for Christians and followers of all other gods. "No one whatsoever should be denied the opportunity to give his heart to the Christian cult or that cult which he should think best for himself, so that the supreme deity, to whose worship we freely yield our hearts, may show in all things his usual favor and benevolence."[120]

Licinius was not a Christian. Like Diocletian and Galerius before him, his supreme deity was Jove, as shown by the images and dedications on the coinage of his reign. As for Constantine, many historians and theologians today believe that, as his coins and the soon-to-be-erected Arch of Constantine were to vividly show, it is most likely that at this time his supreme deity was still the sun god, Apollo/Sol.

The edict of Licinius and Constantine went on to require the return of previously confiscated Church property, including buildings, gardens, and graveyards to Christian communities throughout the provinces controlled by both Constantine and Licinius, as Maxentius had already done in Italy. "The same shall be restored to the Christians without payment or any claim of recompense," said the decree. Anyone who had purchased confiscated Church property or been given such property as a gift by local administrators, and who wished for compensation, was required by the edict to apply to their district's vicarius for consideration of a payment from the imperial treasury.[121]

The Edict of Milan became known as a turning point in the history of the Christian Church, and via it Constantine has frequently been credited with ending the persecution of Christians in the Roman Empire. In fact, Galerius had been the first Roman emperor to officially terminate Christian persecution with his decree of 311, and Maxentius had been the first emperor to return Church property to Christians, that same year. Constantine and Licinius were merely formalizing and broadening the already two-year-old initiatives of Galerius and Maxentius.

When Eusebius wrote of the Edict of Milan in his hagiographic *The Life of Constantine*, he made no mention of Licinius's role in its creation, erasing him from the narrative and giving his hero Constantine sole credit. Likewise, Eusebius failed to mention that Maxentius had led the way in the return of Church property. When Lactantius reported the Edict of Milan, he did so not only in its original Greek but in its entirety, inclusive of the fact that it was a joint communiqué issued by both Licinius and Constantine. Yet over succeeding centuries, Christian apologists would set Eusebius's version of events in concrete, to eliminate Licinius and make Constantine the Church's hero.

Later that same year, Constantine would write to "most esteemed" Anullius, the betrayer of Maxentius now governing the North African provinces for Constantine, instructing him to liaise with a member of his Palatium staff in the matter of the return of property of the Christian Church in Africa to its original owners. There are no similar letters on record from Constantine requiring the return of Christian property in Italy, seeming to confirm that Maxentius's decree of 311 extended beyond Rome to all of Italy.

In his letter to Anullius, Constantine named the member of his staff with whom Anullius was to liaise in this matter as Hosius, who, according to the letter, in turn answered to Constantine's Arles-based treasurer Heracleides. Christian writers have since assumed that this mid-ranking official was the same Hosius who had been Bishop of Córdoba in western Spain since 295. Bishop Hosius would certainly be used by Constantine in 324 to carry a letter to the Bishop of Alexandria from his then-capital of Sofia, and to mediate a Church dispute, as Constantine began to assert his control over the Eastern Church. This has led to the assumption that the two men named Hosius were one and the same, and that the bishop was on Constantine's staff and advising him on Christian matters at least since 313.

However, Bishop Hosius, whose name was also variously written Osius and Ossius, is believed to have served uninterrupted in his post at Córdoba for more than forty years, and his only recorded movements outside Spain date from 324. So it is highly unlikely that a Bishop of Córdoba would have briefly served as a middle manager on Constantine's staff in Gaul in 313. The Hosius in question here was most likely a different man, with the same or similar name as the Spanish bishop. There were, after all, three men named Eusebius who figured in the life of Constantine, and a fourth Eusebius would serve in a senior post on the staff of his son Constantius II.

Constantine and his new brother-in-law Licinius seem to have spent some time celebrating their new familial and political alliance outside Milan, but by early March word arrived from the East that Maximinus Daia had invaded Licinius's territory, leading a Roman army of 70,000 troops from his capital of Antioch in Syria and arriving in Bithynia en route to the Bosporus.

According to Lactantius, Daia had been infuriated by the news that Constantine had killed his secret ally Maxentius, taken Rome, and made himself emperor of the West. Perhaps Daia was determined to fulfill the obligation of his treaty with Maxentius, but it is more likely that the news made him determined to overthrow the emperor of the East and don his mantle while Licinius's back was turned. Whatever Daia's motivation, his swift march into Bithynia had taken Licinius completely by surprise. Now, Licinius hurried out of Italy to counter Daia, and Constantine returned to Trier.

MAXIMINUS DAIA, the forty-two-year-old son of a sister of emperor and powerbroker Galerius, was handsome, clean-shaven in the new fashion, and a demonstrably successful military commander who had in the past protected the empire's eastern borders with an iron fist. Daia had even assumed the title of pharaoh in Egypt, which he controlled from Syria: he would be the last to use the title. His record was that of a harsh, arrogant bully.

Daia had more actively persecuted Christians in his realm than had other Tetrarchs in theirs, and this earned him the enmity of Eusebius of Caesarea, who accused him of executing Christians via decapitation, crucifixion, and beasts of the arena, and of gouging out the eyes of others. According to Eusebius, too, Daia emulated his uncle Galerius with heavy drinking. He also attributed to Daia the same unproven predilection for moral depravity of which he accused Maxentius: "He could not pass through a city without continually corrupting women and ravishing virgins."[122]

Tactically, Daia's invasion of Licinius's territory during the early spring of 313 was bold, but it was not without its risks. To catch Licinius off guard, he had marched his 70,000 infantry and cavalry through Anatolian mountain passes clogged with snow. Not only had he been forced to abandon much of his heavy equipment along the way, some of his men had perished in the cold. Still, by the second week of April he had succeeded in reaching the relatively narrow Bosporus strait, where he secured shipping and transferred his army across this waterway that Persia's King Xerxes had temporarily crossed with a bridge of boats eight hundred years earlier.

On landing on the European side of the strait, Daia's army cut off the key Bosporus port city of Byzantium. As Byzantium closed its gates to him, Daia mounted a siege. Eleven days later, the city submitted. But the delay had given Licinius time to assemble an army of 30,000 men in the Balkans, with which he was marching rapidly east into Thrace to counter the invader. With Byzantium in his hands, Daia advanced fifty-five miles due west along the Bosporus coast to the harbor town and important crossroads of Heraclea Perinthus, which he also put under siege. Eight days later, Heraclea, too, surrendered.

Learning that Licinius's army was approaching from the west, Daia marched eighteen miles inland to the location of the first Cursus Publicus way station on the highway from Thrace to the Balkans. When he arrived there, he learned that Licinius was encamped at the next Cursus station, a further eighteen miles west at Tzirallum, which became the modern Turkish town of Corlu. Envoys from each camp met to discuss a possible settlement, but when both sides were found to be acting duplicitously, negotiations were abruptly broken off, with combat seen as the only recourse.

That night as Licinius slept, according to Lactantius, who painted a picture of Licinius as a devout Christian, the emperor dreamed that an angel of God came to him and dictated a prayer to him. When Licinius awoke, he summoned a secretary and dictated the prayer to him. That prayer was read to all Licinius's troops when they assembled the next morning, prior to taking up their battle positions.

The two armies met that same day, April 30, on a flat area close to Licinius's camp that was ironically called Campus Serenus, or Cheerful Field. No details of what became known as the Battle of Tzirallum have come down to us. We only know that Licinius's outnumbered 30,000 men completely outclassed Daia's 70,000 border troops from the Eastern frontier. Daia's men broke and ran. Daia himself had come prepared with an escape plan; swapping his armor, golden general's girdle, and purple Augustan cloak for the cheap tunic of a slave, he fled with his bodyguards to the Bosporus coast and a waiting ship.

Crossing back to Asia, Daia retreated to Nicomedia, from where he attempted to put together a new army. As Licinius gave pursuit, he issued an order for Daia's arrest and execution. In June, finding no local support, Daia commenced a retreat across today's central Turkey. By July he had reached Tarsus, within several days' ride of his home city of Antioch in Syria. Tarsus, capital of the province of Cilicia and twelve miles inland from the Mediterranean coast on the Tarsus River, was renowned as the first meeting place of Antony and Cleopatra, and as the birthplace of the apostle Paul. In Daia's wake, Licinius entered Nicomedia, where, according to Lactantius, he gave thanks to God for his victory. There, on June 13, Licinius ordered that the Edict of Milan be posted on the city's public notice board.

By August 313, Daia was running out of friends—and hope. First issuing his own edict of toleration of the Christians, he then took his own life, using poison. Once Licinius learned of the death of Daia, he assumed full control of the East and conducted a purge of all who had been close to Daia. Executing the dead emperor's son and daughter, he also put to the sword the daughter's fiancé Candidianus—a son of Galerius from his first marriage, who was later adopted by Galerius's second wife Valeria. A son of the short-lived Western emperor Severus II who lived in Daia's realm was also put to death on Licinius's orders. Daia's unnamed wife was arrested at the imperial palace at Antioch, which sat on an island in the middle of the Orontes River, from where she was flung into the river to drown.

As for the wife and daughter of Diocletian, Prisca and Valeria, who had been living under house arrest in rural Syria on Daia's orders, they were also on Licinius's execution list, because they posed a threat to his reign via their familial connection to Diocletian and Galerius. But, in their Syrian exile, Prisca and Valeria learned of their death sentence and succeeded in escaping from the remote town where they were being kept, apparently with the aid of their sentinels. Dressing as plebeian women, mother and daughter went on the run.

Still at large fifteen months later, the pair was recognized in Thessaloniki, today's Thessalonica in northeastern Greece, and handed over to the authorities. Licinius's troops wasted no time in dragging the pair into Thessalonica's forum, pressing them to their knees, and publicly beheading them. The headless bodies of the two unfortunate women were subsequently thrown into the Mediterranean. Much later, both would be made saints by the Catholic Church as Christian martyrs, even though both were clearly executed for political motives, not their faith.

With the deaths of Maxentius and then of Maximinus Daia, the Roman Empire's ruling structure had been pruned to just two emperors—Licinius in the East, based in Illyricum, and Constantine in the West, based in Gaul. In writing to congratulate Licinius on his victory, Constantine would have offered him the 2nd Parthica Legion, as he had offered them to Daia, on the condition that they be posted to remotest Mesopotamia. Licinius obliged, and the Italians of the 2nd Parthica tramped away from Albana, leaving behind their comfortable, purpose-built base in the Alban Hills.

The families of the Albani seem to have traveled with the legion, or trailed behind it, as it walked all the way to its new base in Mesopotamia, the hill town of Bezabde, near today's Cizre in southeastern Turkey, beside the Tigris River. The legion would be wiped out in 360 when a Persian army overran Bezabde, but it was apparently re-formed. The legion's original base and civilian town at Albana would lie abandoned for years until 326, when Constantine gifted both to the Catholic Church. The basilica dedicated to John the Baptist that initially rose there later became today's Cathedral of St. Pancras.

Despite Constantine's gift of a legion, and even though Licinius had married Constantine's sister, Licinius did not trust Constantine. The feeling was mutual, and it was inevitable that the two emperors would come to blows, sooner or later.

XVI

CONSOLIDATING POWER

CONSTANTINE SPENT THE REST OF THE YEAR 313 consolidating power. In Trier that summer, he presided over the marriage of another of his half-sisters. This was seventeen-year-old Anastasia, second-eldest of his three sisters. As the name Anastasia had Jewish origins and was adopted by some Christians, later historians suggested that the name given to Constantine's sister indicated the secret adherence to Christianity of their father Constantius. It could just as easily have indicated the adherence to Christianity of Anastasia's influential mother Theodora.

Anastasia's groom was Constantine's trusted deputy Bassianus. By making Bassianus his brother-in-law, Constantine was bringing him into his family and setting him up to become his Caesar and successor. Meanwhile, with his mother Helena now living in Rome and no longer looking over his shoulder, Constantine brought other children of Theodora and Constantius from Toulouse to his court at Trier, among them his eldest half-brother Julius, who now joined the emperor's inner circle along with Constantine's son Crispus.

An oration given before Constantine at court this year was probably delivered at Trier on the July 25 anniversary of his accession. The overly poetic and jingoistic style suggests the orator was not the same man who had delivered the address on the occasion of Constantine's anniversary in 310. This speaker lauded Constantine for his deeds over the past year and congratulated him for his defeat of Maxentius, his conquest of Rome, and the elimination of Maxentius's family and most intimate and loyal supporters. With the damnatio memoriae in place, the orator did not speak of Maxentius by name; he merely called him "the tyrant" as he gleefully described the young emperor's drowning.

"Gulping down the wrongdoers, the Tiber swallowed the tyrant, too, as he vainly tried with his steed and dazzling weapons to get away over the steep bank on the other side. . . . Rome has a new and lasting foundation. All who might ruin her are done for, root and branch."[123]

Although Maxentius's name disappeared from records, writings, and conversations during the rest of Constantine's lifetime, after Constantine's death Maxentius was again mentioned by Roman writers and historians from time to time, although never favorably. One of the stories to emerge from the pro-Constantine camp would be repeated in 398 by an otherwise anonymous historian known as Valesianus. Writing about Maxentius's legitimacy, he would claim that Maxentius had not been the son of the emperor Maximian at all. "When his mother was questioned about his parentage, she admitted that he was the son of a Syrian," he claimed.[124]

This Syrian father of Maxentius was said to be Afranius Hannibalianus, city prefect of Rome in 297–298, who was supposedly divorced by Eutropia in 287 so she could marry Maximian, some twelve years after the birth of Maxentius. This would have made Maxentius the stepson of Maximian. That being the case, for Maxentius to have been Maximian's heir and successor, Maximian would have had to formally adopt him. There is no record of that, and he would have taken Maximian's name if he had become his adopted son, so modern historians dismiss this claim.

What is more, it has to be wondered whether Eutropia really would have admitted that Maxentius was not the son of Maximian. Eutropia would live well into old age, as a committed Christian; and despite all that would happen in the family in the coming years, she would continue to have influence over her son-in-law Constantine. While touring Palestine late in life, she would write to Constantine to complain that an altar to Roman gods had been built outside Hebron at the entrance to the Cave of the Patriarchs, burial place of the biblical figure Abraham and members of his family. Constantine would bow to his mother-in-law's wishes and order the altar removed. Perhaps trashing Maxentius's legitimacy was the price for retaining Constantine's favor—or, as is more likely, the story that Maxentius was not Maximian's son was baseless gossip.

WHEN CONSTANTINE DEFEATED MAXENTIUS and claimed the Western throne, he inherited the title and role of Pontifex Maximus, high priest of Rome. During the Roman Republic, this ancient post was an elected but essentially honorary one, without any real power, but its prestige had made it sought after among senators. Julius Caesar had been Pontifex Maximus before he became dictator of Rome. Prior to his dictatorship, he used the Regia, the comparatively small official residence of the Pontifex Maximus adjacent to the Temple of Vesta in the Forum Romanum one of the duties associated with the role was acting as guardian to the priestesses of Vesta, the Vestal Virgins.

Augustus and every emperor who succeeded him kept the title and role of Pontifex Maximus for themselves. After Constantine's death, the post would be held by the non-Christian brother-in-law of Constantine's brother Julius, until that pontiff's death in 358. For two years, the post would remain vacant, until, in 360, the pious Christian emperor Gratian, who did not feel himself equal to the task, would grant the title to the Bishop of Rome, Pope Damasus I, and all Bishops of Rome retained it thereafter. Today, the leader of the Catholic Church is still known as the Pontiff in recognition of that original grant of title.

Ever since Licinius became emperor of the East, Pontifex Maximus had been among his roles and titles. Maxentius had taken the title Pontifex Maximus in the West, as revealed by a statue of him unearthed at Ostia, where Maxentius wears the regalia of the Pontifex Maximus. Similarly, Constantine, once he took Rome, was entitled to the title in the West, but he used only it occasionally, as in 326 when calling a council of Christian bishops at Nicaea. In later life he was to demonstrate that he increasingly took the role of Pontifex Maximus very seriously, certainly more seriously than some predecessors.

Pontifex Maximus literally means "the greatest bridge builder." It was the role of the Pontifex Maximus to act as the bridge between the gods and mortals, and Constantine seems to have taken to himself the role of acting as a bridge between the thrones of heaven and earth, overseeing the affairs of this Christian "cult"—as he would describe Christianity over the next few years, as well as governing the other cults of Rome as the Pontifex Maximus had previously done. He did not abolish any of the existing cults or limit their rights or their rites. However, from 313, Constantine actively involved himself in the administrative affairs of the Christian Church. As Aurelius Victor described it, Constantine employed himself in "regulatory religious practices."[125]

One of the complaints of earlier members of the Tetrarchy had been that the Christian Church had set itself up as a separate authority, challenging the authority of the emperors by establishing their own laws and customs so that the Church became, in effect, a state within a state. Maximinus Daia had recognized this, and while he was alive he had attempted to counter the organizational strength of the Christian sect by establishing a system whereby the priests of all other deities in his Eastern provinces were required to wear a white robe and answer to a senior pontiff who reported to the emperor.

Now, rather than resisting and fighting that separate authority from without, as Diocletian, Galerius, and Daia had done, Constantine asserted his control over the Church as he endeavored to regulate it from within, insinuating himself over the existing Church hierarchy. He began by communicating regularly with bishops in his Western Empire on matters of church administration, focusing most attention on those bishops who were the most senior in their provinces and who wielded the most power in the Christian community.

Constantine informed Church leaders that, while they were bishops of spiritual matters, he was the bishop of all other matters on earth. Addressing them as "brothers," he referred to the Christian bishopric as a "brotherhood." This put the Christian bishops in the same basket as existing elected colleges of senior priests such as the Brothers of the Wolf, who supervised Rome's annual Lupercalia festival, and the Arval Brothers, or the Brothers of the Fields, who supervised the celebration of rites that sought to ensure good harvests.[126]

Constantine permitted Miltiades to remain Bishop of Rome, even though Miltiades had been elected during Maxentius's reign and with Maxentius's approval, but he established no official connection with the bishop. There is no record of his even meeting Miltiades while at Rome. When a controversy erupted in the Christian community in Africa in 313, competing Christian bishops there wrote to Constantine at Trier, asking him to intervene by appointing a panel of three bishops of Gaul to investigate and rule on the matter. Constantine took advantage of this request to involve himself in Church affairs for the first time by writing to Miltiades, instructing him to chair a meeting at Rome of three Gallic bishops, including Trier's longtime bishop Maternus and the Bishop of Arles, to decide the African issue.

Miltiades, obeying the emperor's command but determined not to yield entirely to Constantine's power, took it on himself to expand the emperor's brief by summoning the three Gallic bishops nominated by Constantine plus a further fifteen bishops from Gaul, Italy, and Germany. In a first for the Christian Church, the nineteen bishops would preside at sittings of this synod in Rome that September, with both sides invited to come from Africa to put their cases before the assembled bishops.

To serve as the location of the synod, Constantine loaned Bishop Miltiades the Domus Faustae, the Rome palace of his wife Fausta, which sat right next door to the Singularian Horse Guard's leveled New Fort and graveyard on the Caelian Hill. Some years after this, Constantine would hand over the horse-guard land and the Domus Faustae to the Church, together with the income from imperial properties in Italy, Gaul, and Africa to permit construction of the St. John in Lateran basilica in 224. It has been assumed by many historians that the Domus Faustae, which became the official home of the Bishops of Rome in the 220s, was also gifted by Constantine to the Church in 224; but, as will later be explained, this was more likely to have occurred in 226.

The synod of bishops chaired by Bishop Miltiades commenced in the Domus Faustae on September 2, 313, and was expected to run for many days. The matter considered by the panel of bishops was the same one that had caused a schism between the two factions of the Christian Church in Africa during the reign of Maxentius. The Bishop of Carthage since 311, Caecilanus, was not only a surrenderer who had given up the holy books of his see during the Great Persecution, but he had been consecrated by another surrenderer, Bishop Felix of Aptunga (Abthugni).

In opposition to Caecilanus, Christians in Carthage—who felt that surrenderers should only have the power to baptize or administer the sacraments after themselves being baptized again and re-ordained—had elected Donatus Magnus as their own "pure" Bishop of Carthage and Primate of North Africa, with the supporters of Donatus becoming known as the

Donatists. It was the task of the synod to determine which of the two men was the valid bishop of Carthage. In doing so, they would determine whether the purist view of the Donatists should prevail across the Western Church, a determination that would exclude surrenderers from positions of power in the Church.

Bishop Miltiades was clearly a pragmatic man, one who wanted the Church to be as inclusive as possible to increase the size of the congregation; so, sitting as chief judge, he made the synod as difficult as possible for the Donatists by treating the hearing like a court case, enforcing strict rules of evidence and argument. This annoyed the Donatists so much that they stormed out of the House of Fausta without presenting their case. On the synod's third day, Miltiades and his panel of bishops declared in favor of Bishop Caecilanus and the surrenderers, and against the Donatists.

This allowed Constantine to instruct his governor in Africa, "most esteemed" Anullinus, to now distribute Church property in his provinces to Bishop Caecilanus's faction. When Donatus and his followers appealed to Constantine for a new, fairer hearing, the emperor instructed the Bishop of Rome to convene a second synod, this time at Arles in Gaul, the following year. Miltiades would not live to sit at the Arles synod, dying in office in January 314. His successor, Sylvester I, convened the Council of Arles, as it became known, which sat in August 314 and was attended by representatives of forty-three Christian bishoprics.

Sylvester proved just as pragmatic as Miltiades. Not only did the council headed by him find against the Donatists, it found their teachings to be heretical and excommunicated Donatus himself. To ensure that nobody such as Donatus could again be elected to a bishopric, this synod decreed that future ordinations of new bishops would require the involvement of three existing bishops. The council also decreed the excommunication of any Christian who participated in chariot racing or gladiatorial fights, or acted on the stage.

The Donatists did not take their exclusion lying down. They again appealed to Constantine, who referred them back to Sylvester. The breakaway Donatist faction of the Christian Church would continue to exist in North Africa until the Middle Ages, finally dying out under Islam, even though Constantine backed Sylvester and the faction that officially became known from 380 as the Catholic or Universal Church.

Until 314, Constantine kept the Church at arm's length but under his watchful eye. From 314, he became increasingly involved in its administration, writing letters of guidance to senior bishops around his realm for the rest of his life. In all his letters, Constantine would refer to "the great divinity," without specifying that divinity. In just a single recorded letter of 314 he referred to "Christ the savior." This was so at variance with the terminology used in Constantine's other letters that many modern authorities agree that this single reference was an interpolation by another writer.

Such an interpolation was made easy by Constantine's poor grip on the Greek language. Greek was the language of the administration of the Roman Empire and of the Church; but Eusebius tells us that, because Constantine was not confident in his Greek language skills, he dictated all his letters in Latin to secretaries who translated them into Greek for transmission. This gave ample opportunity for a Christian secretary to change Constantine's usual terminology of "the great divinity" to "the savior Jesus Christ" on one occasion, and to make other insertions.

It is to be remembered that Eusebius collected Constantine's letters and appended a number of them to his *Life of Constantine*, so he himself had the opportunity to make alterations and insertions. And we know that he quite deliberately failed to include a number of Constantine's letters in which the emperor expressed sentiments that conflicted with Eusebius's theological views; these letters are extant via other sources. So Eusebius, or the editor who completed and pulled together Eusebius's *Life of Constantine* and its appended letters and works for publication after his death—quite possibly Constantine's official Greek translator Strategius Musonianus, who was a Christian—had the opportunity to heavily edit, alter, and propagandize the material.

Another work attributed to Constantine and published together with Eusebius's biography of Constantine, *Oration to the Saints,* is believed by some experts to have been heavily interpolated by another author, while in the view of the historian Timothy Barnes it was wholly rewritten by Constantine's Greek translator. Irish bishop and Church historian Richard Hanson felt the entire work an outright fabrication. Certainly the oration's language and its knowledge of Greek philosophy appear well beyond Constantine's scope, as demonstrated by his letters, which are often confused and lacking in theological knowledge.[127]

IN JULY 315, Constantine returned to Rome for the first time since his defeat of Maxentius and his departure from the city in December 312. He timed his return to coincide with his decannalia, the tenth anniversary of his reluctant claiming of the purple in Britain following the death of his father. To celebrate the occasion, Constantine would hold games at the Circus Maximus. Julius Caesar had maintained his own gladiatorial school, but while Constantine was no fan of gladiatorial contests he had no complaint with chariot racing—unlike the Christian Church. But while in Rome, Constantine, the lover of spectacle and display, was most interested in seeing and dedicating two grand new landmarks with his name on them.

The first of these was the Colossus of Constantine, erected within the Basilica of Constantine, built by Maxentius but appropriated by the man who had vanquished him. The other was the triple-arched triumphal Arch of Constantine, erected beside the Colosseum, where it still stands. Rome's thirty-five existing triumphal arches had been erected to celebrate Roman defeats of foreign foes, whereas, as one of the inscriptions on Constantine's arch proclaimed, this new monument was designed to celebrate Constantine as "liberator of the city and founder of peace," which was an artful way of getting around the fact that his victory had been not over foreigners but over fellow Roman citizens.

To this day, historians have disagreed over the origins of Constantine's arch, and one or two have argued that it should not even be called the Arch of Constantine. Some think the arch went all the way back to the emperor Hadrian in the second century, and had been, like the Basilica of Maxentius, appropriated by Constantine. Archaeological studies of the arch's foundations lend some weight to this second-century dating of the arch's origin but do not confirm it. No source during or following the life of Hadrian ever mentioned the existence of a Hadrianic arch beside the Colosseum, although that does not preclude its transfer from another site on Constantine's orders. Other historians suggest that, like Maxentius's basilica, the arch was commenced by Maxentius, for his victory over Domitius Alexander and his African supporters. Others still feel it was an entirely new construction, commenced immediately after Constantine's 312 departure from Rome by the compliant Senate.

Whatever its origins, the Arch of Constantine was finished in a rush, to be ready in time for the emperor's 315 decannalia. The basic construction of the massive monument is without fault. Its triple-arch design was not new—a triple arch dedicated to Germanicus Caesar had been built in Rome early in the first century A.D. The surviving Arch of Septimius

Severus erected early in the third century also used the triple-arch design. It is the Arch of Constantine's decoration that evidences the bid to save time and money by the Senate, which organized it—probably, as mentioned earlier, led by the turncoat Volusianus, who was again serving as city prefect when Constantine returned to Rome for the arch's July 315 dedication.

Most of the arch's carved relief panels were stolen from earlier monuments to the emperors Trajan, Hadrian, and Marcus Aurelius, with the heads of those emperors chiseled off and replaced by that of Constantine. At least one scene, showing Roman cavalrymen overrunning opponents, is likely to have been saved from the demolished barracks of the Singularian Horse Guard. Another anachronism takes the form of eight large, full-length figures of captive Dacians who stand atop eight marble columns on the front and rear of the arch. All were taken from an earlier second-century monument to Trajan which most likely decorated the Forum of Trajan. Like Parthian prisoners shown elsewhere on the arch, these Dacians bear absolutely no relation to Constantine, unless they were intended as a subtle message to Licinius, who had been born in Dacia.

Just five of the arch's scenes, on the frieze, depict events from 312. And these are relatively small, compared to the older panels. The new panels were fashioned by a sculptor or sculptors with skills inferior to those of the artisans who had created the arch's earlier lifelike scenes. The heads of the fourth-century figures are over-large, their legs pudgy, the attempts at creating perspective amateur. The same workshop that produced these newer panels appears to have fashioned surviving porphyry sarcophagi during this period, including one likely to have been destined for Constantine himself. To modern eyes, and compared to the older images on the arch, the figures in these fourth-century images look more like cartoon figures than real people.

As a monument, with its stolen sculptures and the heads of earlier leaders replaced by that of the conqueror of the city, the Arch of Constantine is the type of edifice one would expect from a tinpot dictator of the modern era. As a work of art, the column has offended the eye of artists and historians for centuries. It is, said Edward Gibbon, "melancholy proof of the decline of the arts, and a singular testimony of the meanest vanity."[128]

As an historical record, the five panels depicting Constantine's conquest of Italy and defeat of Maxentius are the most valuable images, but they are propaganda and should be viewed as indicative rather than definitive. The scene at the Milvian Bridge, for example, shows Singularians and their horses floundering in the Tiber as spearmen and archers menace them from the north bank, with one Singularian still astride his horse and another staying afloat by clinging to his wooden shield. More Constantinian infantrymen are seen running up, with victory goddess Victoria flying above them and looking like Superman in flight. Maxentius's trumpeters are shown on the south bank, sounding "Withdraw."

Maxentius is not shown in this Tiber scene, and, unlike the other four new panels, neither is Constantine. Meanwhile, on the scene depicting Constantine's triumphal entry into Rome, the head of Maxentius on a spear that we know to have been part of the procession is nowhere to be seen. This editing out of Maxentius from his own death scene was clearly a conscious effort by the Senate, which commissioned the panels, not to rub Romans' noses in the demise of their emperor at the hands of their conqueror.

As a guide to Constantine's religious affiliations in 315, the arch leaves Christian theologians disappointed: there is a total lack of any reference to Christ or Christianity. Not a single Christian symbol appears on the arch—no cross, no chi-rho symbol, no depiction of Constantine's new Labarum standard. Instead, the structure is covered with representations of Rome's traditional gods. Constantine is actually shown sacrificing to the sun god Sol, while in another scene Sol is depicted driving his chariot. Other sacrificial scenes decorating the arch show the deities Hercules, Silvanus, and Diana, as well as several river gods, while the goddess Victoria appears multiple times.

Eusebius was to claim that a reference to "divine inspiration" on the arch's dedicatory inscription, appearing in large letters on both the north and south sides of the arch and unveiled in front of Constantine in July 315, referenced the Christian God. But this is more likely to have referred to Sol Invictus, the god to whom Constantine is shown sacrificing. The arch's main inscription reads, in full: "To imperator Caesar Flavius Constantine, the greatest, pious, blessed Augustus, by divine inspiration and greatness of mind, from a tyrant on the one side and every faction on the other side at once, with his army avenged the republic with just arms, the Senate and people of Rome dedicated this arch as an emblem of his triumphs."

Zosimus tells us that Constantine, later in his reign, tore down new buildings that did not meet his exacting standards. Yet, while Eusebius claimed Constantine became increasingly Christianized during his reign, never over the remaining twenty-two years of his life did Constantine have his triumphal arch at Rome altered to either remove the old gods, to add Christian symbols, or to update the inscription.

There is another curious thing about the arch, one that is starkly evident today. In the newest panels, in which Constantine was depicted in Italy and at Rome, while all the other figures around him still have their heads, Constantine's head is conspicuously absent—not worn away by weathering, but neatly and precisely chiseled off. This was the work of the Italian nobleman Lorenzino de' Medici in the sixteenth century. Whether he had a particular dislike of Constantine is uncertain; he also decapitated all eight of the Dacian prisoners on the arch. For his vandalism, de' Medici was exiled from Rome.

For two hundred years the damaged figures would remain as de' Medici had left them. In the 1730s, Italian sculptor Pietro Bracci was commissioned to carve new heads for seven of the eight Dacian prisoners, and a complete new figure for the eighth Dacian, as well as new heads for Constantine and other figures on the reliefs between the Dacian prisoners. Yet, for reasons that have not come down to us, Bracci did not give Constantine back his head on the four damaged fourth-century frieze reliefs. Over the centuries, was there a lingering dislike among Romans of Constantine, this man who had taken the city's last homegrown emperor along with Rome's status and dignity in 312? Certainly, to this day, the Maxentian basilica appropriated by Constantine continues to be called the Basilica of Maxentius by Romans, or, at best, the Basilica of Maxentius and Constantine, not, as Constantine decreed, the Basilica of Constantine.

Following the July 25 dedication of his triumphal arch, Constantine is believed to have spent several weeks in Rome, no doubt staying at the Sessorium. Before his return to Trier, he may have presided over annual festivals dedicated to Sol and Victoria that fell in August. In August, too, he terminated the tenure of the duplicitous Volusianus in the post of city prefect, leaving the Senate to send the man into exile the following month.

Turning his back on this city that he neither loved nor felt comfortable in, Constantine returned to Trier. He would not visit Rome again for another eleven years. From now on, his focus would be on Licinius.

XVII

DEALING WITH LICINIUS

B Y THE END OF 315, Constantine had decided to push forward with his plan to make his deputy and new brother-in-law Bassianus his Caesar and designated successor. This was even though Constantine had an adult son, Crispus, by his first wife, and even though in February 316, at Arles, the very same place where Crispus had been born to Constantine's first wife, Fausta delivered their second child and Constantine's second son, whom they named Constantine. Fausta had given birth to the couple's first child, a girl, Constantina, in 314 or 315.

Why Constantine chose to elevate Bassianus over his own adult son we do not know. It might be surmised that, just as Constantine's mother Helena had previously caused him to send his half-brothers and half-sisters away from his court, she was now opposed to the son of his (German) first wife becoming his Caesar, although Helena appears to have become fond of Crispus once he matured.

With letters to Licinius proving far from productive, come the spring of 316, Constantine gave his twenty-four-year-old half-brother Julius the task of going to Licinius at his capital Sirmium (Sremska Mitrovica) in the Balkans and putting the case for Bassianus's elevation to the rank of Constantine's Caesar. Constantine's plan was for Bassianus to base himself in Italy once he was Caesar to Constantine, probably at Milan, "to stand as a buffer between Constantine and Licinius," in the words of Valesianus.

It was logical to think that, being brother to Licinius's influential wife Constantia, Julius would have a better chance than most envoys of winning Licinius's approval for the elevation of Bassianus. But when Julius arrived at Licinius's court, the irascible Licinius dismissed the idea out of hand. What was more, as Julius returned to Constantine with the bad news, Licinius initiated a plot to overthrow Constantine from within. Calling in Senecio, brother of Bassianus, who served on his own staff, Licinius instructed him to secretly communicate with Bassianus at Trier and urge him to take up arms against Constantine.

The details of what followed are sketchy. According to Eusebius, Constantine had more than a thousand prophetic dreams in his lifetime, and he now dreamed that Bassianus was plotting his assassination. When Constantine awoke, he ordered the immediate arrest and summary execution of Bassianus. It is more likely that the plot was revealed when a courier carrying a letter from Senecio to Bassianus was intercepted. There is no proof that Bassianus had any intention of betraying Constantine or had taken any steps to do so. In fact, it may have been Licinius's cunning plan to implicate an innocent Bassianus in a concocted scheme, thus removing an able deputy from Constantine's side. If that were the case, Licinius's plan worked to perfection.

With Bassianus's execution, his wife Anastasia, sister of Constantine, disappears from the record. Constantine was seemingly paranoid about a threat to his life, and likely fearful that Anastasia was involved in the plot with her husband, so she was probably executed or exiled. Her brother Julius, who had returned from his mission to Licinius empty-handed, was somehow implicated in the plot and was sent into exile at this time—he would not be heard of again for two decades. His wife Galla, daughter of the late Maxentian supporter Neratius Junius Flavianus, bore Julius a son, Gallus, in 325 or 326, and the birth took place at a remote village in Tuscany, north of Rome, suggesting that rural Italy was Julius's initial place of exile. Later, he was known to be in exile at Corinth in Greece.

Perhaps Julian stood up for his sister and brother-in-law when the Senecio plot was uncovered, and this earned him Constantine's ire and banishment. Only much later, when Constantine's mother Helena was off the scene, would Constantine bring Julius back to his court. Having lost faith in most of those around him, Constantine failed to appoint a replacement for Bassianus and brought his son Crispus, now aged twenty-one, closer.

Infuriated by the Senecio plot, Constantine wrote to Licinius demanding that Senecio be handed over to him for punishment, seemingly absolving Licinius from involvement in the affair. Not only did Licinius refuse to hand over Senecio, but Constantine received a report that Licinius's troops had entered Emona, a one-time legion base and later a colony for retired legionaries on the Ljubijanica River in today's Slovenia, twenty-two miles from Aquileia. There, Licinius's men toppled statues of Constantine that decorated the town's forum. Archaeologists proved in 2008 that the town stood at the eastern border of Constantine's territory, supporting the belief of historian Anthony Barnes that the town had been ceded to Italy from Pannonia as early as 280.

To cheekily pull down Constantine's statues, Licinius's troops had deliberately invaded Constantine's territory. Incensed, Constantine mobilized for war. Putting together an elite force of 20,000 of his best cavalry and infantry, he marched toward Licinius's half of the empire. That October, he crossed the border into Pannonia Secunda, invading Licinius's territory. Subsequent events suggest that Constantine's son Crispus was one of his officers for the campaign, for within eighteen months Crispus would be commanding one of Constantine's armies.

To counter Constantine, Licinius quickly assembled a force of 35,000 men and marched from Sremska Mitrovica. Two hundred miles into Pannonia, at Cibalae, today's Vinkovki in Croatia, Constantine's army camped within striking distance of Licinius's larger force.

On October 8, the emperor of the West fought the emperor of the East at the Battle of Cibalae, as it became known. Hydatius, fifth-century Bishop of Aquae Flaviae in the province of Gallaecia, in today's Portugal, noted the date of the battle as October 8, 314, but historians are in agreement that it actually took place two years later. We know very little about the battle. Eusebius later wrote that, during the struggle, Constantine ordered his new Labarum emblem to be moved to that section of the battlefield where his troops were faring worst, to lift morale.

According to Eusebius, Constantine told him that, in this battle, the standard-bearer carrying the Labarum lost his courage as opposition troops closed in and men around him began to panic, and he decided to flee. With the standards usually in the army's second line, this indicates that elements of Licinius's army, perhaps his cavalry, had broken through Constantine's frontline infantry, causing the panic.[129]

The bearer of the Labarum, thrusting his emperor's standard into the hands of another member of the Labarum Guard, then turned and ran for it. But the deserter had barely handed the standard to another and taken a few steps away when he was struck in the belly by an enemy dart, which killed him. The new standard-bearer and the Labarum both subsequently survived the battle without a scratch, even as a shower of enemy darts came their way, with the closest coming within a spear's length of the new standard-bearer.

With the emperor's standard seen to stand firm, Constantine's infantry regained their composure, and Constantine led his cavalry in a charge that broke through Licinius's front line. Many of Licinius's infantrymen threw away their arms and prostrated themselves before Constantine, begging for mercy, which Constantine granted. But the bulk of Licinius's troops held firm, so Constantine ordered his infantry to charge.

The struggle lasted until sunset, with fortunes waxing and waning all day. By nightfall, Constantine's cavalry had won the day and 20,000 of Licinius's infantrymen lay dead on the field. We are not told of Constantine's casualty numbers, but his army was left substantially intact. Meanwhile, in the darkness, Licinius withdrew with most of his cavalry. Constantine ordered his cavalry to follow, but not too closely, purposely allowing Licinius to escape. At this stage, Constantine held hopes that his brother-in-law, in realization of "the desperate state of his affairs," would "return to sounder reason" and seek surrender terms that would preserve his life.[130]

Licinius returned to Sremska Mitrovica. There, he gathered up his wife Constantia and young son Licinius and fled to Dacia. But he had no intention of giving up the fight. As Constantine's army advanced toward Thrace in the following days, Licinius sent word to his *dux limitis*, or frontier commander, Aurelius Valerius Valens, that he was appointing him his Caesar and deputy. At the same time, he commanded Valens to assemble a fresh army in Constantine's path at Adrianopolis in eastern Thrace, today's Turkish city of Edirne, where Licinius would join him.

Constantine, following the Via Militaris that ran between Singidunum, modern Belgrade, through today's Serbia, Bulgaria, and Turkey to Byzantium at the Bosporus, reached Philippi in Thrace. This town was famous as the site of the final battle between the Liberators, as the first-century B.C. assassins of Julius Caesar were called, and Octavian and Mark Antony.

While encamped at Philippi, Constantine was approached by envoys from Licinius seeking a peace settlement. Furious to learn that Licinius had unilaterally appointed a Caesar while he himself had been expected to beg Licinius's permission to do the same, and emboldened by the outcome at Cibalae, Constantine sent the envoys back without a reply to Licinius's peace overtures, leaving them without a doubt that he was fighting mad. In response, Licinius, equally angry, invested Valens with the purple as a full Augustus, and prepared for battle. Valens, seeing the opportunity to become emperor of the West should he and Licinius defeat Constantine, enthusiastically participated in all that followed.

It was in late December or early January when the forces of Constantine and Licinius once again confronted each other, this time astride the Via Militaris on the plain of Mardia in Thrace—in the vicinity of today's town of Harmanli in northeast Bulgaria, 140 miles from Sofia. Prior to battle, as had been the custom for hundreds of years, the commander's standard was kept in its own tent, which was treated as a shrine. But Constantine now required that his Labarum be installed in a tent erected outside the protection of his camp.

There in this tent, which Eusebius called a tabernacle, echoing Moses, to whom he frequently compared Constantine, the emperor spent hours alone with the standard, attended only by his most devoted bodyguards. According to Eusebius, Constantine spent these hours offering prayers to a heavenly deity, which Eusebius claimed was the God of the Christians, and the emperor was "honored after a little time with a manifestation of his presence"—Constantine claimed that a god appeared to him. Then, unexpectedly, Constantine rushed from the tent, "suddenly [giving] orders to his army to move at once without delay, and on the instant to draw their swords . . . and immediately commence the attack."[131]

The Battle of Mardia was "a long and indecisive struggle," according to Valesianus. As nightfall approached, Licinius's army withdrew, escaping in the darkness. With their mounted forces intact, Licinius and his deputy Valens met in the night and agreed that Constantine would expect them to retreat to Byzantium. So they turned aside from the highway and headed for Beroea, today's Veria in central Macedonia, southwest of Thessalonica, with the aim of getting behind Constantine and cutting off his line of supply. Their assumption proved correct, for Constantine was "eagerly pushing on," driving his army up the Via Martialis in the darkness in the belief that he was on Licinius's heels.[132]

Licinius's cavalry circled behind Constantine's marching army, overran his baggage train, and captured his servants. When news of this reached Constantine on the highway, he realized he had been outwitted and out-maneuvered. Licinius now used this tactical success to send one of his officers, Mestrianus, to Constantine in the hope of securing armistice terms, promising to do whatever Constantine required of him to bring a cessation of hostilities. With his men "worn out from fighting and from marching," Constantine decided against continuing the military offensive, and, drawing up tough terms, sent them back to Licinius in the hands of Mestrianus.[133]

Licinius agreed to surrender all his territories west of Thrace while retaining control of Thrace, Asia Minor, Syria, and Egypt. This brought Pannonia, Dalmatia, Dacia, Macedonia, and Greece under Constantine's control. Licinius also agreed to remove the purple from the shoulders of Valens, demoting him to his original post of frontier commander. Constantine also required that he be allowed two Caesars, with Licinius appointing a single Caesar approved by him, specifying that the official investiture of the new Caesars take place in Sofia on the first day of March that year, anniversary of the ascension to the purple of Constantine's father Constantius.

The investiture ceremony duly took place in Sofia on March 1, 317, with Constantine's son Crispus appointed his first Caesar and his one-year-old son by Fausta, Constantine II, the other. Crispus was also granted a special title by his father, Prince of Youth, the same title that Nero had long ago sported before he became emperor. As his lone Caesar, the humiliated Licinius appointed his infant son and Constantine's nephew Licinius II, who was not yet two years of age. That same day, Licinius had his former imperial associate Valens executed; whether this was required by Constantine or was on Licinius's initiative alone, we do not know.

Licinius withdrew to Nicomedia following the humiliating investiture, where, according to Valesianus, he "was stirred by sudden madness and ordered that all the Christians be driven from the palace." Whether this meant that all Christians were removed from the Palatium staff, and whether Licinius blamed Christians for his losses to Constantine, is unclear. Licinius's wife Constantia remained a devout Christian, and many historians believe that Licinius himself was either a Christian or had become well disposed toward Christianity via the influence of his wife. Certainly the Bishop Eusebius, who had been appointed Bishop of Nicomedia under Licinius, after previously serving as Bishop of Beirut, retained his post, as did the deacons and priests who served under him.

Constantine, meanwhile, took up residence in Sofia, to be closer, he said, to the Danube frontier, but especially to defend his newly won territories from any insurgency by Licinius's troops. To command Gaul and Britain, he dispatched Crispus, his son and new Caesar, to Trier. Constantine himself is not on record as ever again returning to Trier. Instead, over the next few years he moved between the Danubian border and imperial palaces in Sofia, Thessalonica, and Sremska Mitrovica. At the latter, on August 7 that year, Fausta bore him another son, Constantius II.

To act as Crispus's able deputy and guiding hand, Constantine appointed the wealthy senator Junius Annius Bassus to the post of Praetorian prefect for Gaul. A member of the noted Annii family, Bassus would go on to ably and loyally serve Constantine for a dozen years. Later, using his own money, he would build the Basilica of Junius Bassus on Rome's Esquiline Hill, which would become a church in the fifth century; a Catholic seminary today occupies the site. Junius's son Junius would become Rome's city prefect in the 350s.[134]

Now, to celebrate his dynasty, Constantine issued a series of commemorative coins linking himself with three former emperors: Claudius Gothicus, from whose line he claimed descent; his own father Constantius; and, no doubt to the surprise of many, his late duplicitous father-in-law Maximian. Following Maximian's "suicide," Constantine had banned all official mention of him, but now the emperor of the West was very visibly claiming a familial link with the father of his defeated brother-in-law Maxentius.

Constantine may have included Maximian in this coin set in part to honor his wife Fausta, Maximian's daughter, for, in 317, he also issued coins celebrating her. With Fausta's profile on one side and on the other an eight-star symbol and victory wreath representing Venus, goddess of love, fertility, and victory, these coins described Fausta by her then-official title, Noble Lady. Constantine's dominant motive for issuing the coins commemorating the three past emperors would have been to give his sons and successors a solid blood link with legitimate emperors—as if he was troubled by the accusation that Licinius would have been leveling at him for the past five years, that he was a usurper who had taken the crown of the Western Empire by force.

Once Crispus settled in the palace at Trier, he began minting coins of his own in Gaul and Britain, and they would often depict a young man who had apparently inherited his father's fine physique and the good looks of his mother Minervina. Crispus's coins invariably employed military images to celebrate his campaign successes as he led Constantinian forces in countering Germanic insurgency along the Rhine. They frequently depicted the goddess Victoria and showed Crispus's shield decorated with the head of Medusa, an image that had adorned the shields and breast-plates of Rome's emperors and generals for hundreds of years past.

Early on, too, Jupiter frequently appeared on Crispus's coins, while the inscriptions described him as "Noble Caesar" and "Our Caesar," plus, with the image of a fortress, "Foresight of the Caesars," imparting the message that via the young Caesars the emperors were preparing the future protec-tion of the state.

No other gods, including Sol, appeared on Crispus's coins. But neither did any Christian symbols. Even though the chi-rho had been depicted on some of his father's coins since 313, it would not be until some years later that we find Crispus's coins depicting the chi-rho, along with an altar and a globe. Prior to this, the coins of Crispus would several times depict the young Caesar's personal military standard. And perhaps surprisingly, unlike his father's Labarum, Crispus's princely standard did not include the chi-rho.

On the Rhine, Crispus proved an effective military commander, despite his youth, and was adored by his father's troops. In a panegyric delivered at Trier in 317, the Gallic orator Nazarius lauded the young Caesar for his victories over the Franks that year. In 318, 321, and 324, Crispus led the legions of the Rhine on major campaigns that kept the Franks and the Ale-manni in check. Three times during this period, his father rewarded him with the consulship for the year, and Crispus's coinage and Eusebius's *The Church History* indicate that at least once his troops hailed Crispus imper-ator for his military success, echoing his father's achievement at a similar age. Eusebius wrote that Crispus was "an imperator most dear to God, and in all regards comparable to his father."

In January 322, the twenty-six-year-old Crispus married a young woman by the name of Helena. We know nothing about the bride, although she was likely to have been a relative, and his father would have approved her choice and presided over the couple's wedding at one of his capitals. Helena quickly fell pregnant, and in October 322 gave birth to Crispus's son and heir. The child's name has not come down to us, for reasons that will become apparent in a later chapter. Eusebius reported in *The Church History* that Constantine was delighted to become a grandfather.

Crispus's successes on the German frontier freed up his father to campaign against the numerous and aggressive Sarmatians, who sought every opportunity to cross the Danube into Roman territory to plunder Roman provinces. Licinius, too, had his hands full with Sarmatians in his Eastern part of the empire, and for a time an uneasy peace held between the emperor of the West and his brother-in-law the emperor of the East as they focused on external enemies. But the ego and ambition of the pair could only be kept in check for so long.

XVIII

THE FINAL SHOWDOWN

IN 321, AFTER CONSTANTINE PURSUED plundering Sarmatian forces into Thrace and sent them reeling back across the Danube, Licinius complained that his brother-in-law had entered his territory without his permission. But Licinius took no further action over the incursion when Constantine returned to his own territory. To bolster his forces, Licinius allied with a king of the Thüringen Goths named Rausimod, whose people hailed from the forested lands north of the Dniester River in today's Ukraine.

Two years later, on April 28, 323, as Rausimod's men increasingly crossed the Danube to penetrate his territory, Constantine issued a decree threatening any Roman who collaborated with the Goths with death by fire, and commenced a military campaign to drive them out. The now forty-six-year-old Constantine went into battle wearing an armored cuirass bearing the image of the head of Medusa,the mythological snake-haired Gorgon, the same image as that carried on the shield of his son Crispus. In Greco-Roman mythology, the sight of Medusa's horrific head was said to terrify the enemy, with her gaze turning opponents to stone. Roman emperors since Augustus had sported Medusa's head on their armor.[135]

Not only did Constantine pursue the Goths into Thrace, he pushed them back across the Danube and then cornered Rausimod in barbarian territory and massacred his force. Rausimod himself died fighting beside his men. News of this incensed Licinius. Not only had Constantine killed his ally, but his brother-in-law had again entered Licinius's territory without permission.

By 324, Licinius had formed a new Gothic alliance, this time with the Thüringen prince Alica. Bringing together an army of 165,000 men at Adrianople in the interior of Thrace, he prepared to confront his brother-in-law. Constantine, meantime, had been planning for this day for several years. As he marched east that summer from Thessalonica with 130,000 men—the largest army he had ever assembled—a fleet of 230 warships he had been building up on the Adriatic sailed to the Aegean under the command of his son Crispus.

This fleet had a twofold purpose. First, it was to force its way through the Dardanelles Strait, cross the Sea of Marmara, and take the Bosporus Strait, which separated Thrace and Bithynia, today's Anatolia, thus preventing Licinius from escaping from Thrace. Secondly, the fleet was to protect Constantine's own supply lines from Licinius's Eastern Empire fleet of three hundred ships. Constantine had demonstrated his keen appreciation of the need to protect his lines of communication as far back as 312, when he had resisted the temptation to march on Rome before he eliminated the Maxentian forces in northern Italy, forces that would have threatened his rear had he bypassed them.

Adrianople, originally Hadrianople, had been founded by Hadrian in the second century on the site of an earlier Thracian settlement. The city sat beside the Meric River, the Roman Hebrus, with its lower course forming much of the border between modern Turkey and Greece. Licinius camped his vast army on the eastern side of the Hebrus, outside Adrianople, and established a defensive line that ran for twenty-three miles between the river and a height overlooking the city.

At the beginning of July, Constantine gave the impression that he was preparing to build a bridge across the Hebrus River at one heavily forested point, drawing defenders to the bank opposite. On July 3, his main force in fact forded the Hebrus at another place some distance away, taking the defenders facing them completely by surprise and annihilating them. With Constantine's army now over the Hebrus and threatening to outflank and surround him, Licinius withdrew his forces and massed them on the higher ground outside Adrianople.

As the battle of Adrianople unfolded, Constantine personally led his troops in a slow, blow-by-blow slog up the slope outside the city. "Constantine's army had great difficulty in scaling the heights," said Valesianus, but "at last his good fortune and the discipline of his army prevailed, and he defeated the confused and disorganized army of Licinius." In this fighting, Constantine was wounded in the thigh, although not seriously. This was enough for him to break off the engagement, permitting Licinius to escape yet again. Licinius went east to the port city of Byzantium on the Bosporus Strait, with the survivors from his army straggling after him.

Closing the city's gates, Licinius established a strong garrison at Byzantium. But because the city was vastly overcrowded with civilians and troops, he used his naval fleet to ferry many of his troops across the Bosporus to the Asiatic side, tasking them with defending against a landing there by Constantinian forces. Confident that Byzantium's sea-facing walls were impregnable to attack from the water, Licinius prepared to defend against a landward siege by Constantine.

As Constantine's army took up positions outside the walls of the city and commenced to lay siege, Constantine ordered the construction of a fleet of light Liburnian ships on the Dardanelles shore, and instructed Crispus and his admirals to secure the narrow Bosporus Strait east of Byzantium with their fleet and so cut off Licinius from Asia. As Crispus's ships sailed from Piraeus, the port of Athens in Greece, and anchored off Macedonia, Licinius's admiral Abantus—called Amandus by some sources—crammed many of the ships of his fleet into the narrow Dardanelles to protect his emperor. With two hundred opposition warships crowding the strait off the town of Callipolis, today's Gallipoli on the Dardanelles's European shore, where the narrow strait meets the broader waters of the Sea of Marmara, Crispus recognized the foolishness of trying to match Abantus's numbers in such confined waters. Selecting eighty triaconters—small, light, and fast warships with just thirty oars—and leaving his larger vessels awaiting orders, he led his squadron to the attack.

After Crispus's ships were able to dive in and out against Abantus's bottled-up fleet of large, unwieldy biremes and triremes, sinking several opposition ships, Abantus withdrew his fleet to where the strait joined the Sea of Marmara. Crispus put in to the Thracian port of Eleus and sent for the rest of his fleet. When these ships joined him the following day, Crispus led his entire fleet against Abantus, who held off from engaging. At midday, the north wind abated and a strong southerly suddenly sprang up, driving many of Abantus's ships onto the rocky Asian shore as Crispus watched.

Abantus himself escaped with four ships and succeeded in reaching the Asian shore, where he fled with the aid of waiting land forces, leaving young Crispus the victor. Over the two days, Abantus had lost 130 ships destroyed or captured, and 5,000 sailors and marines. More importantly, Licinius had lost control of the straits.

Meanwhile, Licinius himself had departed Byzantium by water, probably by night, taking his treasury with him. Crossing the strait to Bithynia, he landed at the town of Chalcedon on the Asiatic coast. Today the eastern Istanbul suburb of Kadikoy, and easily reached by road via the modern Avrasya Tunnel, Chalcedon then sat isolated on a small peninsula jutting into the Sea of Marmara, close to the mouth of the Bosporus. And, mirroring his actions with the ill-fated Valens several years before, Licinius appointed one of his senior officers to the purple, making him a fellow Augustus and giving him the throne of the West—which Constantine happened to be occupying at the time.

The officer promoted by Licinius was Sextus Marcius Martinianus, or Martinian as later historians came to call him. Up to this point, Martinian had been serving as Licinius's Master of Offices. In receiving the purple, Martinian was elevated above Licinius's Praetorian prefect, Julianus, who had loyally and efficiently served his emperor for the past nine years. The new Augustus was put in command of half of Licinius's army and sent to the town of Lampsacus on the eastern shore of the Dardanelles, opposite Gallipoli, with orders to prevent Constantine's forces from making a successful amphibious landing in that vicinity.

With Licinius's departure, the gates of Byzantium were opened to Constantine, and he entered the city as its liberator. He was surprised to be joined there by his son Crispus, who landed from the strait fresh from his swift and overwhelming naval victory. Both sides now regrouped, with Constantine making his headquarters at Byzantium and Licinius basing himself across the Bosporus at Chalcedon. At the same time, Licinius added the Gothic auxiliaries of Prince Alica to his army.

Through the remainder of July and August, and into September, Constantine waited for the fleet of Liburnians to be constructed on the Dardanelles so he could deliver all his troops to the Asian side of the straits in one fell swoop. Licinius, meanwhile, never having won a single battle against his brother-in-law in seven years of conflict, prepared to make his last stand.

In the third week of September, using the ships of his battle fleet as transports, Constantine landed to the north of Chalcedon with tens of thousands of troops. He then marched south, toward the town of Chrysopolis, today known as both Uskudar and Scutari, on the road to Chalcedon. As soon as Licinius learned of the landing, he sent word south for Martinian to hurry to join him with his troops from Lampsacus, then personally set off with his army in an attempt to reach Chrysopolis before his opponent.

Constantine won the race to Chrysopolis and occupied the town as Licinius approached with his army. It is believed that Constantine had 100,000 troops marching for him at this point, with part of his army assigned to the Liburnians being built on the Dardanelles. Licinius still commanded 120,000 men, 30,000 of whom were at his capital, Nicomedia, a little to the east, while roughly half the remainder would have been with Martinian at the Dardanelles. This means that, as the two main armies now came together at Chrysopolis, Constantine's troops outnumbered those being personally led by Licinius.

It was September 18 when both sides lined up, confronting each other on the plain beside the waterway that divided Europe and Asia. It was Constantine who, as usual, initiated combat. But instead of his frequent tactic of leading his cavalry to the attack on the wings, Constantine led a full-frontal charge of cavalry and infantry that overwhelmed Licinius's outnumbered army. According to Valesianus, in the fighting that followed, Licinius lost 25,000 men. The remainder turned and fled down the shore of the Sea of Marmara. Now the Liburnians carrying Crispus and Constantine's reserve arrived on the scene, and this caused Licinius's survivors to throw down their arms and surrender. This same day, Martinian was captured by Constantine's forces. As for the Gothic prince Alica, if he was personally leading the Gothic auxiliaries in Licinius's army, he appears to have escaped.

Licinius again fled, this time sixty miles southeast to his capital, Nicomedia, reuniting with wife Constantia and son Licinius II and surrounding himself with his last 30,000 fighting men. Constantine marched his army to Nicomedia, making camp outside the city walls and preparing to deal a final blow to his brother-in-law. The day after his arrival, his sister Constantia came to him, leading a delegation that included Bishop Eusebius of Nicomedia, Bishop Theoginus of Nicaea, and a party of Christian deacons and priests.

Constantia came to beg her brother to spare her husband, but Constantine was distrustful of her Christian companions—in particular Bishop Eusebius. "At the moment when the clash of the opposing armies was at hand, he underhandedly sent 'eyes' to spy on me," Constantine angrily complained of Eusebius the following year, "and stopped just short of contributing armed assistance to the tyrant [Licinius]." Because Constantia vouched for Eusebius and his colleague Theoginus, whom Constantine referred to as "his accomplice in folly," Constantine tolerated them. But he was less lenient with their entourage: "I publicly arrested the priests and deacons who came with Eusebius," he declared in late 325.[136]

Nonetheless, Constantia was able to soothe her brother's temper and negotiate surrender terms that she took back to Licinius inside Nicomedia. Licinius accepted those terms, and both he and Martinian abdicated the purple at once, returning to the roles of private citizens. That night, Constantine hosted a genial victory banquet at which Licinius and Maximian were guests of honor. Following the banquet, the now sixty-year-old Licinius was sent to live in comfortable exile at the imperial palace in Thessalonica, apparently accompanied by his wife and infant son. Martinian was sent into exile in mountainous Cappadocia in central Asia Minor—possibly at the castle on the imperial estate of Macellum where the future emperor Julian would later be exiled between the ages of twelve and eighteen along with his elder brother Gallus.

Now, at last, Constantine reigned supreme. Styling himself Victor Constantinus Augustus Magnus—Victorious Augustus Constantine the Great—he combined Licinius's armies and navy with his own and combined the thrones of East and West to become the first emperor since the early part of Diocletian's reign to rule as sole sovereign of the Roman Empire.

XIX

TAKING CONTROL OF
THE EASTERN CHURCH

W ITH THE DEFEAT and departure of Licinius, Constantine took up residence at Nicomedia and brought the administration of the Eastern Empire under his control. This administration had been handled efficiently for close to a decade by Licinius's Praetorian prefect, Julius Julianus. The prefect was related to Bishop Eusebius of Nicomedia, and this might account for his life being spared by Constantine. But not only did Constantine do nothing to punish Julianus for serving Licinius so loyally for so long, he even praised him and made him a consul for the coming year.

Julianus would remain close to the imperial family, and some years later the emperor's half-brother Julius would marry Julianus's devoutly Christian daughter Basilina, who would bear him a son, the future emperor Julian. Constantine's treatment of Prefect Julianus suggests, that, like Volusianus and Anullius under Maxentius, Julianus may have been Constantine's secret agent and informant at Licinius's court.

As far as we know, Constantine's son Crispus, who had been instrumental in the defeat of Licinius, now returned to his capital, Trier, without any apparent new honors. But now that Constantine was the sole Augustus, he did spread honors around, bestowing the title of Augusta on both his mother and his wife—since the reign of Augustus, the title of Augusta had traditionally been given to the empress and sometimes also to the mother of the emperor. Coins issued by Constantine to celebrate the elevation of the two most important women in his life show both in identical poses, with crimped hair tied back in a bun, wearing pearl necklaces. Helena's coins linked her with Salus, goddess of safety and welfare, with the inscription describing her as the "Safety of the Republic." Fausta's coins linked her with Spes, goddess of hope, and described her as the "Hope of the Republic."

With the defeat of Licinius, old Helena, who was now in her seventies, remained at Rome, but the thirty-five-year-old Fausta would have transferred from Sofia to Nicomedia to join her husband. Constantine had kept Fausta close over the past decade, just as he had kept her almost continuously pregnant. In addition to Constantine II and Constantius II, she gave birth to another son, Constans, in 320, and a total of three daughters, Constantina, Fausta, and Helena, making Constantine the father of seven children. The couple's youngest daughter, Helena, would marry her substantially younger cousin Julian just days after he was declared Caesar to Constantius II in 355.

The indications are that Constantine genuinely loved Fausta, but his motivation for filling her with children may have been prompted by the same sentiment as that voiced by the emperor Titus in the first century: "Legions and fleets are not such sure bulwarks of imperial power as a numerous family."[137]

Constantine had for some time been thinking about creating a new imperial capital to eclipse Rome, at one point considering Thessalonica, and at another Sofia, as the site. But with the conquest of Licinius's realms, a new candidate emerged: Byzantium, a well-fortified city ideally located on the border of Europe and Asia. He would give the city his own name, renaming it Constantinopolis, or Constantinople as we know it.

To increase the city's population—the number of residents of Byzantium was much less than that of Rome—he issued orders for new settlers to be moved to Byzantium from throughout the empire, depopulating entire villages and towns, and also called for the construction of new public buildings worthy of his capital. But while his domineering mother still lived—and still resided at Rome—he chose to do this discreetly and, apparently, behind Helena's back.

Helena considered Rome the center of the Roman world, and she was determined to make it the center of the Christian world. In 320, having moved into the newly constructed imperial quarters at the Sessorium, leaving empty the Varian Gardens villa that she had previously occupied, she converted the villa's high-roofed atrium into a Christian chapel for her private use. She followed this with the creation of a mausoleum where she intended that both she and her son would lie in perpetuity, even commissioning an elaborate porphyry sarcophagus for Constantine, with the casket's exterior decorated with scenes from his victorious battles. Clearly, Constantine had not communicated to his mother the fact that Rome was the last place he wanted his bones to lie.

More importantly, Helena had also championed the construction of a basilica over the site of the demolished Singularian Horse's New Fort, next door to the House of Fausta. At his mother's behest, Constantine provided both the site and the funds for this basilica, which was dedicated in 324 by Bishop Sylvester I as the Basilica of Christ the Savior. Today, much refurbished over the centuries, this is the Archbasilica of St. John Lateran, the oldest surviving church in Rome and considered the Mother Church of Catholicism and the seat of the Pope, ranking it higher than the Vatican's St. Peter's.

All seemed well with Constantine's world, and, as he turned to dealing with the threat to his northern borders from Goths, Sarmatians, and Vandals, he commanded the Christian Bishops of the East and West to meet in council late the following spring under his aegis at Nicaea, not far from Nicomedia, where he intended to cement his control over the church. And then, when the spring of 325 arrived, a mood swing overtook him, and he ordered the immediate execution of Licinius at Thessalonica and Martinian in Cappadocia, with a damnatio memoriae issued for the erasure of every inscription, statue, and recorded act of the pair.

The official story was that Constantine had learned that Licinius was plotting with the Goths to regain his throne, and this led to his being executed on Constantine's orders. However, Valesianus was to claim that it was merely the fear that Licinius would emulate Constantine's father-in-law Maximian by betraying him, together with demands from his troops for Licinius's removal, that led to Licinius being preemptively hanged—the exact same fate as that suffered by Maximian.

Valesianus, apparently a Christian, had no sympathy for Licinius, declaring that he deserved his fate for participating in the Great Persecution initiated by

Diocletian, and noting that all the other members of the Tetrarchy who had led the persecution were already dead. Constantia, Licinius's widow and Constantine's sister, was brought to Constantine along with her son. She would remain at Constantine's court for the rest of her life, a veritable prisoner, with her brother preventing her from ever marrying again.

Just as he had following the death of Maxentius, Constantine now issued a coin that depicted him stabbing a serpent to death with a lance. According to Eusebius, Constantine described Licinius as "a twisting snake" and "a dragon driven out of the public administration through the providence of the supreme god and by our service."[138] Eusebius failed to remind his readers of the Greco-Roman legend in which Apollo stabbed the serpent Python at the Delphic sanctuary. Constantine was in fact linking himself with the sun god, as any Roman versed in Greco-Roman mythology would have perceived.

In the spring of 325, too, the meeting of Christian bishops called by Constantine was convened at Nicaea. The First Council of Nicaea as it became known opened on May 21 in the imperial palace at Nicaea, which the emperor loaned to the Church for the occasion, involving more than three hundred bishops—almost all from the East. Some writers have suggested that Constantine had extended invitations to all eight hundred Western bishops; but it is hard to imagine, with Constantine offering to pay the travel and accommodation costs of all attending bishops and two companions each, that the bishops of the West would have en masse ignored an invitation from their emperor.

The attendance of just five bishops from the West, one from each of Gaul, Spain, Africa, the Danubian provinces, and Italy, was purely token, as would have been Constantine's intent. What is more, the Italian bishop who attended came not from Rome, but from Calabria. The fact that the Bishop of Rome, considered the leader of the Church in the West, did not attend, tallies with Constantine's dislike of, even disdain for, Rome. It seems he deliberately failed to invite Rome's Bishop Sylvester, even though the bishop would have been close to the emperor's mother.

Constantine already controlled the Church in the West, and, in the guise of guiding the Church as a whole, he intended to bring the Eastern bishops, who had spent the last few decades under Licinius's rule, under his power. Constantine in fact considered this meeting in Nicaea so important to his administration of the empire that he postponed for a year his scheduled vicennalia—the celebration of his twenty years as emperor—which was due to take place at Rome on July 25 that year in the tradition established by Diocletian.

Constantine did not sit as president of the Council of Nicaea, but formally opened it, appearing in jewel-encrusted purple cloak and golden crown. He thereafter sat as an interested observer, allowing the bishops to conduct proceedings before him. The council lasted many weeks, not terminating until August, but breaking on July 25 to allow the bishops to attend the emperor's local vicennalia celebrations. By the time attendees departed, they had agreed on twenty major church laws, or canons, including matters regulating religious observance at Easter.

The most important council decision involved the creation of what became known as the Nicene Creed. Arian, a presbyter from Carthage, had long been preaching that Christ and God were two separate though linked entities, and had gained many followers of his ideology, which became known as Arianism. But this idea of two gods, a father and a son like Jove and Apollo, went against the Judeo-Christian concept of a single deity. Opposing Arian's theology, the bulk of the bishops attending the Nicaean council professed the belief that Christ and God had to be one.

When the competing ideologies were put to the vote, Arian only had two supporters among the bishops, and all three men were promptly excommunicated from the Church by the council. Constantine, to add the weight of his authority to the council decision and assert his control over the Eastern Church, promptly exiled the three excommunicated clergymen.

Only toward the end of the fourth century would Church leaders adapt the Nicene Creed to incorporate the concept of the Trinity—Father, Son, and Holy Ghost, three entities, but indivisible and therefore one. Incidentally, the Trinity was actually a pagan concept first promulgated in the fourth century B.C. by the Greek philosophers Plato and Aristotle, and went back even earlier to the mathematician Pythagoras (570–495 B.C.), who taught that all things are three. "We make further use of the number three in the worship of the gods," said Aristotle, referring to the Greek gods.[139]

Both Eusebius of Caesarea and Eusebius of Nicomedia attended the Council of Nicaea. The Nicomedian bishop firmly believed in Arian's philosophy of two Gods, but when push came to shove, knowing that Constantine had long been suspicious of him as a sycophant of Licinius, he signed the council declaration that made Arianism a heresy. But within several months, he proved unable to live with his conscience and recanted, publicly stating his support for Arian and his ideology. When Constantine learned of this, he was furious. Taking Eusebius's action as a personal slight, he sent him into exile, along with Theoginus and Arian.

The bishop would continue in exile for three years. But he was an eloquent and persuasive man, and Constantine loved praise and popularity, said Zosimus, and fell victim to flattery. From exile, Eusebius of Nicomedia won the emperor's confidence via letter, convincing him that Arianism was not at odds with the Nicene Creed, and in 329 Constantine returned him to Nicomedia and his bishopric.

XX

KILLING HIS WIFE
AND SON

B Y THE SPRING OF 326, as Constantine was preparing to travel to Rome to attend his delayed vicennalia celebrations there that summer, something very odd occurred. Ever since the abdication of Licinius, there had been no official mention of Crispus, the emperor's popular, heroic son and Caesar, although he was clearly back in Trier and keeping the Rhine frontier under close watch, as his coins, minted in the earlier part of 326, indicate. But then, sometime between mid-May and mid-June, Crispus turned up in the Adriatic city of Pola, today's Pula in Croatia, facing intense questioning from a local magistrate.

Why the young Caesar was out of Gaul, in a small coastal city in his father's immediate domain, and suffering the indignity of questioning by a minor official, has never been explained. What followed is also shrouded in mystery. Crispus was condemned to death by the magistrate. Almost immediately after, Crispus was dead, having taken, or been administered, poison. Meanwhile, his half-brother and fellow Caesar, the ten-year-old Constantine II, had been dispatched by their father to Trier to take Crispus's place, as nominal commander in Gaul.

Initially, Crispus's punishment may not have been intended by Constantine to be death. It is possible that he initially sentenced him to exile, as evidenced by the fact that Crispus was in Pola at the time of his death. The historian David Woods suggests that Crispus was on his way to exile on the Adriatic islands off Pola. Exile of family members was a form of punishment employed by Constantine—he exiled his brother Julius for decades after he displeased him, for example. And we know that the islands off Pola were used as places of banishment for the Roman elite during this era—a senior member of Constantius II's cabinet would be exiled there. Constantius II himself had Gallus, elder brother of future emperor Julian, executed in Pola.[140]

Why the Pola magistrate subsequently delivered Crispus a death sentence is open to question, but this may have been on Constantine's orders after more damning evidence reached his ears. Perhaps poison was passed to Crispus so that he could take own life—an honorable way out, in Roman eyes. Certainly, Constantine was disgusted with his son, for he immediately issued a decree of damnatio memoriae, erasing all official record of Crispus's life. Now, too, Crispus's wife Helena and their unnamed infant son, Constantine's first grandchild, disappeared. Both are believed to have also been executed. Crispus's damnatio memoriae meant that all references to the lives and fate of both were similarly eliminated.

In July, as if nothing had happened, and apparently joined by his wife Fausta and their six children, including Constantine II, now his surviving Caesar, Constantine arrived in Rome from the East. No doubt with much pomp, ceremony, and his usual love of display, he celebrated his vicennalia on July 25. Within days, the empress Fausta was also dead, murdered on Constantine's orders, followed by a damnatio memoriae decree to remove all official record of her existence. Fausta was aged no more than thirty-seven at the time of her death.

Fausta's place of death was later revealed to be a bathhouse, in which she was locked on Constantine's orders. Historians have assumed this to have been at Rome, and the involvement in Fausta's death of Constantine's mother Helena, who was resident in Rome, lends credence to this assumption. In which case, the site of Fausta's demise may have been the baths at the Sessorium, but more likely the small bathhouse at Fausta's own palace at Rome, the Domus Faustae.

The method of Fausta's death has also been the subject of much debate. Some historians have assumed that she was drowned in a bath. Others have speculated that the heat in the bathhouse was deliberately increased to an intolerable, fatal level. However, it is to be remembered that Roman bathhouses contained three baths—hot, cold, and lukewarm—plus changing facilities. So, to make the entire interior of a large bathhouse, such as that at the Sessorium, unbearably hot by stoking up the fires beneath the heated baths would have been difficult, if not impossible. In a small, private bathhouse such as that identified at the Domus Faustae by archaeologists, it may have been possible.

Yet another hypothesis has been offered by David Woods, who suggests that a very hot bath was used as a form of abortion by Roman women, and Fausta was trying to rid herself of an unwanted pregnancy when she died. This is because Fausta's death was linked by Roman and Byzantine historians with that of her stepson Crispus. If one historical account is to be believed, Fausta had a romantic affair with Crispus, and, Woods suggests, she was pregnant with Crispus's child by July 326.[141]

Considering the fact Fausta and Crispus lived on different continents at the time, modern historians have queried where and when the pair would have had the opportunity for a sexual encounter. For Fausta to be obviously pregnant in July, it would have been necessary for her to have been impregnated in the late winter of 325/326 or the spring of 326. It is not impossible that Crispus traveled to join his father's Nicomedian court for some ceremonial event during this period—perhaps his father celebrated the March 1 anniversary of Crispus's elevation to Caesar, for example.

A further historical version of the story of the untimely deaths of the pair has Fausta in love with Crispus, but when he rejected her advances, she told Constantine that Crispus had raped her, which resulted in Crispus's punishment. Another variant on the story has Constantine learning that Crispus and Fausta were jointly plotting against him, without necessarily being romantically linked, and this resulted in the deaths of both— although why they were executed at least a month apart is not explained under this scenario.

One consistent factor in several historical accounts is the involvement of Constantine's mother. Helena was said to have adored Crispus by this stage, and to have been horrified by his death. Blaming Fausta for Crispus's demise—either because she had heard that Fausta had accused Crispus of rape, or because she had never liked her, or both—Helena went to Constantine and demanded Fausta's death.

"As if to soothe her feelings, Constantine tried to remedy the evil with a greater evil," wrote Zosimus, resulting in Constantine's immediate execution order for the wife who had been so loyal to him that she had informed on her own father sixteen years earlier, and who, according to Julian, had been a noble and devoted wife to Constantine. Aurelius Victor, who lived through this period, agrees that Constantine killed Fausta after Helena rebuked him for the death of Crispus.[142]

On past occasions, Constantine had ordered executions as a knee-jerk reaction to accusations, dreams, and sudden fears. It is possible that Fausta was already in the bathhouse when Constantine suddenly ordered her execution. Or perhaps he waited until she was there before going forward with what would have been a slow and tortured execution. He had the door locked and the fires stoked, with Fausta's removal only permitted once she was dead. Her remains would have been secretly cremated, and her death kept from her children and the public.

Constantine had intended to spend some weeks in Rome on this visit, but he cut short his stay after he sparked an uproar among the people of Rome: invited to lead a traditional religious procession in the city, he had unexpectedly refused to do so, creating public discontent. The occasion was probably the August 1 Festival of Spes, goddess of hope, and the linked festival dedicated to Victoria that took place the same day, with the procession going from the Temple of Spes in the Forum Holitorium, location of the vegetable market on the Field of Mars, to the Palatine Hill's two temples of Victoria.

Spes, it is to be remembered, was a goddess especially linked with Fausta on the coinage of Constantine, while Victoria had been a favored deity of Constantine for many years. It would certainly have come as a surprise to Romans if the emperor suddenly declined to honor the popular empress's goddess and the goddess of victory, the deity seen to have predicted Constantine's long reign and given him his many victories in battle. In fact, Constantine would still be associating himself with Victoria eight years after this, as demonstrated by his coins.

It is probable that, faced with public dissatisfaction and his mother's anger over Crispus's death, and conflicted over the cruel murder of Fausta, Constantine fled the city and set off back to Nicomedia. He would never again visit Rome. And he would never remarry. As he departed Rome, Constantine donated the House of Fausta to Sylvester I, Bishop of Rome, to become the official residence of all Bishops of Rome. Sylvester may have taken up residence without knowing the property was the site of the murder of the empress Fausta, but he certainly knew that her name had to be eradicated, for he promptly renamed the property the Domus Dei, or House of God. Non-Christian Romans would dub it the Domus Laterani, in reflection of previous owners of half the site. This name stuck, and for centuriesthe building has been known as the Lateran Palace.[143]

Constantine's executions did not stop there. As if again gripped by paranoia, he also ordered his eleven-year-old nephew Licinius II put to death. The boy's only crime was to have imperial blood flowing through his veins. The reaction of Constantine's sister Constantia, the boy's mother, can only be imagined. At the same time, the mother of the emperor, Helena, departed Rome and sailed to Palestine via Cyprus on what would prove to be a two-and-a-half-year odyssey in search of the Christian God in the Holy Land.

XXI

THE CHRISTIANIZING
OF CONSTANTINE

Following his return to the East, Constantine threw himself into military campaigns against the Goths, allying with 300,000 Sarmatians whom he settled in Roman territory, and, during a 332 campaign, taking the son of a Gothic king hostage.

Meanwhile, even from afar, his mother Helena exerted a powerful influence over him. At the city of Aelia Capitolina, formerly the site of Jerusalem, Helena was shown Golgotha, the place where Jesus Christ had, according to Christian tradition, been crucified. Since the second century, a Temple of Venus built by the emperor Hadrian had occupied the site. Helena wrote to Constantine demanding its removal, and as a result he ordered the destruction of the temple, and, later, the erection in its place of a Christian basilica, the Church of the Holy Sepulcher. Constantine's letters reveal that he would play an active part in the drawn-out design and sumptuous décor of the church, which would finally be completed and dedicated around 336.

According to Eusebius of Caesarea, "judging that such a temple was unfit for the light of heaven," Venus being a goddess Eusebius called a "foul demon"[144], Constantine also ordered the total destruction of another Temple of Venus, one that stood on Mount Lebanon in Phoenicia. The destruction of several temples of Venus may be coincidental, or it may have been related to the fact that Constantine's now-murdered and damned wife Fausta had been associated with Venus.[146]

According to Christian tradition, once the rubble of the Temple of Venus had been cleared at Aelia Capitolina, a Christian deacon told Helena that if she dug down deep enough at the site, she would find the remains of the cross on which Christ had been executed. The digging ordered by Helena was said to have unearthed the remains of three wooden crosses, one of which, Helena was assured by local Christians, was the cross that had borne Christ three hundred years before. To determine the "True Cross," a sick Christian woman was brought to the site. After touching the first two crosses, her condition did not change, but on touching the third she recovered—proof, the emperor's mother was convinced, that this was the holy cross.

Helena would take the rotting remains of this True Cross back to Rome, together with two rusty nails and a piece of rope said to have been used in Christ's crucifixion, plus, even more incredibly, a human finger that the old empress was assured was the finger that the Apostle Thomas put in Christ's side following the Resurrection. According to Christian tradition, too, Helena would have one nail attached to Constantine's helmet and the other placed in his horse's bridle. She also had earth from Golgotha sent to Rome to cover the floor of her chapel at the Sessorium. The chapel later became known as the Basilica of the Holy Cross in Jerusalem, because it housed what were claimned to be several pieces of the so-called True Cross from Jerusalem.

During her lengthy stay in Palestine, Helena also acquired a tunic said to have been the one worn by Christ at his crucifixion—she sent this to the bishop of Trier. How, where, or by whom the tunic had been preserved for three hundred years has never been explained. When told that a stone stairway at Aelia Capitolina led to the Antonia Fortress praetorium from where Christ had been taken prior to his execution, Helena had the twenty-eight narrow marble steps dug up and relocated to Rome, where they were laid up the Caelian Hill to the Lateran Palace.

That stairway was later moved a short distance to where it remains to this day, known as the Scala Sancta, or Holy Stairs. For centuries, devout Christians climbed the stairs on their knees, apparently unaware that this was a pagan rite previously practiced on the steps to the Temple of Jupiter

Best and Greatest at Rome. However, as the legionaries of Titus totally destroyed the remains of the Antonia Fortress as part of their demolition of Jerusalem in A.D. 70, after putting down the First Jewish Revolt, and the Antonia stairway was believed to have been somewhat wider to allow the passage of troops and supplies, the Scala Sancta's authenticity is questionable and Helena is likely to have been misled about it.

Before Helena returned to Rome in 328, she also instituted the construction of the Church of Eleona (Helena) on the Mount of Olives, and she was also instrumental in the construction or decoration of several other churches in the Middle East. By 330, Helena was dead, passing away at the age of eighty with her son at her side, after which her remains were taken to Rome and interred at her Sessorium mausoleum. Both the Catholic and Orthodox churches would canonize Helena. Her niece Constantina, Constantine's eldest daughter, would later be laid beside her. Constantina would also be canonized—as St. Constance—although Marcellinus described her as "disturbingly violent," and Gibbon said she had "an insatiate thirst for human blood."[147]

Following his mother's death, Constantine relocated permanently to his new capital, Constantinople, which he officially dedicated on May 11, 330. Nine years earlier, on March 7, 321, he had issued a decree making Sunday the official day of rest throughout the Western Empire. Christians had already been treating Sunday as their Sabbath for centuries. As the emperor's decree made clear, his affiliation with Sol Invictus was at that time still strong. "All judges and city people and the craftsmen shall rest upon *the venerable day of the sun*," he decreed. The decree was not universal; Constantine spared country people from observing it so that they could "freely attend to the cultivation of their fields."[148] Christian writers viewed the Sunday worship decree as proof of Constantine's committed Christianity, but during this period he also decreed that traditional priests must regularly conduct sacrifices to obtain guiding omens.

Sunday observance in the army was initially restricted to Christians by Constantine. The number of Christians in the army at this time was only small, and in the decades to come the military would prove slow to broadly adopt Christianity. Roman soldiers were now permitted to attend Sunday religious observances if they chose to, and they were issued with a special prayer to be recited every Sunday. It began "We acknowledge you, the only God," and ended with a plea for God "to preserve to us, safe and triumphant, our emperor Constantine and his pious sons." Christian clerics, meanwhile, were excused from military service.[149]

Now, settling into his new capital, Constantine began to show more Christian leanings while still seeming to conflate Christ with Sol Invictus. He celebrated Easter by keeping candles, lamps, and torches burning in Constantinople's streets until dawn on the night of Good Friday, so that the sun seemed to light the city from one day to the next. Among the numerous new buildings he pushed forward with in Constantinople was a rotunda to serve as his mausoleum—which would subsequently be incorporated into the Church of the Holy Apostles when it was inaugurated thirty-three years after Constantine's death.

His extensions to the city's imperial palace included an audience hall with a cruciform shape in the ceiling decorated with precious stones. Eusebius, who took pains to give a Christian slant to Constantine's acts, told his readers that this cross-shape in the palace ceiling was evidence of the emperor's Christian piety. To adorn Constantinople, the emperor took statues of gods and heroes from the temples and forums of the empire. His only obviously Christian monument at Constantinople would be a fountain depicting Old Testament figure Daniel with lions.

He "lavished much wealth on the city," said Valesianus, to the extent that he "all but exhausted the imperial fortunes." As the years passed, rather than fight the Goths after his last victory against them in 332, he began to pay to keep them at bay. And to fund his lavish lifestyle and continued adornment of Constantinople, he resorted to looting temples throughout the empire of their gold, silver, brass and bronze statues, fittings, and offerings, to melt them down for currency. Most temples were permitted to remain open, although the emperor removed the brass doors of many, leaving the interiors exposed to wind, rain, and snow. His nephew Julian, remarking that Constantine became a spendthrift who developed an inordinate interest in pastries and hairdressing, likened him to a potted plant, blooming gloriously at first, only to fade away.

With the death of his mother, Constantine recalled his half-brothers Dalmatius and Julius to his court and gave them important posts in his administration. At Constantinople, Dalmatius became a consul and censor in 333, after which Constantine based him in Antioch to watch over the eastern borders. From Antioch, Dalmatius would swiftly put down a 334 insurrection on Cyprus. In 335, Constantine elevated his brother's son, another Dalmatius, to the rank of Caesar, with responsibility for Thrace, Achaea, and Macedonia. That same year, Constantine brought his eldest brother Julius to Constantinople after decades of exile, most recently at Corinth. Appointing him a Patricius, ranking him just below a Caesar, he also made Julius a consul for the year.

By the spring of 337, the sixty-five-year-old emperor, now pudgy after too many lavish banquets, as revealed by the coins of his late reign and the criticism of Eusebius of Caesarea, had decided that he should embark on a campaign of conquest against the powerful and threatening Persian Empire in the East. As a prelude to that campaign, Constantine married his nephew Hannibalianus, second son of Dalmatius, to his eldest daughter Constantina, and appointed Hannibalianus King of Pontus. Assembling his entourage at Constantinople, and with his army in Syria preparing for the campaign, in early May the emperor set off, sailing to Nicomedia from Constantinople on the first leg of the journey to Antioch, jumping-off point for the intended Persian invasion.

He appears to have been suffering from ill health leading up to this, and the decision to conduct the eastern campaign may have been prompted by a desire to do so while his health continued to stand up. But he had not gone far from Nicomedia on the next, overland leg of the journey when he fell seriously ill and was forced to turn around. He only reached a villa named Achyron on Nicomedia's outskirts. Unable to travel farther, he knew that he was dying. Sending for Bishop Eusebius of Nicomedia and promising to lead a better life once he was a Christian, he had Eusebius baptize him.

Shortly after, on May 22, 337, the initially reluctant emperor, often impetuous soldier, and sometimes paranoid and murderous ruler Constantine the Great died at Achyron. Non-Christians would no doubt observe that he had fulfilled the prophesy of Apollo and Victoria and reigned for thirty years and more.

In his will, Constantine, having united the empire under one sovereign in 324, undid all his efforts by again splitting the empire, dividing power five ways between his sons by Fausta and two sons of his brother Dalmatius. It was a formula for disaster. On September 9, four months after his death, his sons Constantine II, Constantius II, and Constans met in Pannonia, where a plot initiated by Constantius to eliminate their relatives was implemented. From Constantinople to Antioch, troops of their father assassinated their cousins and fellow rulers Dalmatius and Hannibalianus, their uncles Dalmatius and Julius, and Julius's eldest son. Julius's younger children, five-year-old Julian and his brother Gallus, were spared due to their youth.

The Constantine brothers, who had all been raised Christian, then divided the empire among themselves. Twenty-one-year-old Constantine, the eldest, took Gaul, Spain, and Britain. Constantius took the East, while fifteen-year-old Constans took Italy, Africa, Illyricum, Thrace, and Macedonia. Constantine, who was guardian to Constans, soon complained that, as the eldest, he deserved more, so Constans surrendered Africa to him. That was not enough to satisfy Constantine, and less than three years later he marched into Italy to take it for himself. Troops sent by Constans from the Balkans ambushed Constantine near Aquileia, killing him, after which nineteen-year-old Constans added his dead brother's western territories to his own.

Ten years later, in 350, Constans was killed in Gaul by his general Magnentius, who declared himself Augustus of the West. Constantius II marched from the East to deal with the usurper; and in 353, after being defeated in two battles in Gaul, Magnentius committed suicide. Constantius II, now the sole remaining son of Constantine and sole Roman emperor, appointed his cousin Gallus his Caesar, only to have him executed in 355, elevating the twenty-four-year-old Julian to Caesar. Julian was a victorious general, a talented writer, and a charismatic and inspiring leader, and in 360, at Paris, his Gallic legions proclaimed him their emperor. As Constantius marched from the East to deal with him, he fell ill, dying in Cilicia from a fever. Before he died, he endorsed Julian as his successor.

As emperor, Julian, who had disavowed his Christian upbringing at age twenty and grew a beard in rebellion against the fashion established by his uncle, set out to buck the system. He executed and exiled Christian subordinates of his cousin and predecessor Constantius, appointed well-read, non-Christian officials such as the historians Aurelius Victor, a provincial governor under Julian, and Eutropius, Julian's correspondence secretary, and set out to restore Rome's old values and traditions, which he believed were being eroded by Christianity.

While tolerating Christianity, Julian limited the rights of Christians and strove to steer Romans back to the old gods. Julian's reign, and influence, did not last long, however. While leading a successful campaign against the Persians in Mesopotamia in 363, he was killed by a dart in mysterious circumstances, probably thrown by one of his own men, possibly a disenchanted Christian.

Julian was succeeded as emperor by his Christian general Jovian, who reversed Julian's measures. The Christianizing of the Roman Empire commenced under Constantine was now unstoppable, and future Roman and Byzantine emperors would follow the Christian faith, even if one or two would tolerate non-Christian officials.

XXII

CONSTANTINE WAS
THE BRIDGE

THE CHRISTIAN AUTHOR LACTANTIUS wrote that Constantine was the "most amiable" of men. According to Bishop Eusebius of Caesarea, Constantine was "the gentlest, mildest, and kindest man there ever was." Constantine's nephew Julian, writing to Constantius II while his Caesar, described his uncle as "far more humane and in very many other respects superior to others." Aurelius Victor described Constantine as a "scoffer," while the Byzantine author Cedrenus said that he was cheerful by nature and even prone to bouts of hilarity.[150]

The facts of Constantine's life tell a very different story, of a sometimes unpredictable, paranoid, and violent man; and despite efforts by Lactantius and Eusebius to paint Constantine as a long-time Christian by the time of his death, with the claim that he had put off his baptism until on his deathbed to ensure he was absolved of all sin, Constantine had led a very un-Christian life.

Ignoring his own 316 decree requiring the execution of those who killed fathers, sons, or other near relatives, Constantine had put to death his father-in-law and his eldest son and Caesar, and also executed, or was responsible for the deaths of: his wife, the empress Fausta; his sister Anastasia; three brothers-in-law—Maxentius, Licinius, and Bassianus; two sisters-in-law; an infant grandson; and several young nephews. He also executed two men who had attained the purple under Licinius and surrendered when promised their lives by Constantine. Most of these killings had been sudden and capricious, and without any demonstrated remorse. None of the Tetrarchs, including the vicious Galerius, Licinius and Daia, came close to Constantine's murderous record.

Clearly, Constantine struggled with his faith throughout adult life, being torn between loyalty to his father's favored deity, Sol Invictus, and his mother's adoration of Christ. Under the influence of his domineering mother, he became more inquisitive about Christianity in his last years, until he decided—almost as an insurance, it seems—to be baptized just before he died. It is true that he looted temples of statues of the old gods, yet it was a motive other than Christian zeal that drove him. After the melting down of statues only temporarily boosted the treasury he had emptied with his extravagances, he imposed taxes so severe that men reputedly resorted to prostituting their daughters.[151]

While Constantine was sympathetic to Christianity from early in his reign, later, when he had the power to do so, he made no attempt to make Christianity the state religion or to abolish the old Roman cults. Neither did his sons. Christianity would not officially become the state religion until the reign of the Eastern emperor Theodosius I, who decreed the measure in February 380, and ordered punishment for the practice of pagan rites.

Constantine was not the first Roman emperor to end the persecution of Christians—Maxentius and Galerius both beat him to it. Maxentius was also the first Roman emperor to return confiscated Christian property. Neither was Constantine the first emperor to embrace Christianity—Philip the Arab preceded him by a century.

What Constantine did do was set the Roman world on a course toward Christianity that, apart from the blip of Julian's brief reign, proved inexorable. In effect, Constantine acted as the bridge between the gods of old and the Christian God. Even so, the change to Christianity was far from easy, or overnight, even after Theodosius's 380 decree. When the emperor Gratian removed a statue of the goddess Victoria from one of her Palatine temples in 382, Romans rioted. A decade earlier, the emperor Valentinian I had still venerated Victoria, depicting himself on coins with Constantine's Labarum standard in one hand and Victoria on a globe in the other, with the goddess offering him a victory wreath.

Near the end of the fourth century, the much-awarded poet Claudian attracted admiring crowds as he recited poems lauding the classical gods from the steps of the Temple of Apollo on the Palatine, without fear of retribution. Many Romans still clung to their gods, and their traditions, and no imperial decree could make them turn to the Catholic Church. The Christianizing of reluctant Romans would take considerable time and the gradual replacement of old Roman traditions with look-alike Christian equivalents.

Christianity retained the trappings of the old cults including altars, burning incense, and religious processions and feasts, while many Roman religious festivals were so entrenched in Roman culture that they continued long after Constantine. The only way the Church could eradicate these pagan festivals was to overwhelm them with a calendar clogged with feasts dedicated to Christian saints.

In this way, a popular Roman festival, the *Lemuria*, a festival of the dead, would be replaced by All Saints' Day, also known as All Souls' Day, and, in Mexico, the Day of the Dead. The Lupercalia of February 15, ancient Rome's longest-lasting religious festival, was still being celebrated up until 496, when a scornful Pope Gelasius I instituted the February 14 feast of St. Valentine—Valentine's Day, although, one of the Lupercalia's rites was more about married women's hopes of pregnancy than the modern concept of "romance" that we associate with Valentine's Day. This entailed a high-spirited foot race around the Palatine Hill following a formal feast. Watched by a vast crowd, the runners, naked young noblemen ran carrying small leather straps with which they tried to hit evasive spectators. But married women would stand and hold out their hands to be struck in the superstitious belief that it would ensure they would fall pregnant and give their husband an heir, or, if they were already with child, it would bring an easy and complication-free delivery.

Prior to Constantine, Christ's birth had been celebrated on January 6, but by 336, a year before Constantine's death, Christmas was being marked on December 25—the day of the annual Festival of Sol Invictus. There is no record of Constantine ordering this change, but, considering his long affiliation with Sol Invictus, he may well have influenced it. With the passing of the years and the phasing out of December's popular old Festival of Saturn, the Saturnalia, Christmas absorbed the Saturnalia's pagan gift-giving tradition.

Many Roman temples in the West, such as Rome's gold-roofed Temple of Victoria on the Palatine, were destroyed by looting Visigoths in the fifth century. Others were gradually pulled down by the Church, with their materials used for new churches. Some temples survived as Christian churches, Rome's Pantheon being a classic example—its niches, previously home to the statues of Roman gods and emperors, were filled with the statues of Christian saints.

In the same way, shrines to household deities in homes were replaced by Christian shrines, statues, pictures of the Madonna, and representations of Christ on the cross. All of which were in blatant contravention of Christianity's Second Commandment, which outlaws the worship of graven images. Meanwhile, the golden eagle, symbol of Jupiter, the supreme Roman god, found its way into Anglican/Episcopal churches as a lectern. Even pagan myths were adopted and adapted by Christianity—Apollo killing a dragon with a lance to free a prophetess becoming St. George killing a Cappadocian dragon with a lance to save a princess, for example.

One significant problem the Church had to overcome was the fact that Rome's old religion had a number of female gods, with Cybele, the Magna Mater or Great Mother, among the most popular with women. So the Virgin Mary, the Benedicta Mater or Blessed Mother, became Cybele's replacement, right down to the annual parade where Cybele's statue was carried on a bier from her temple to a carriage that then carried her through the streets surrounded by worshippers. Christian parades where the statue of the Virgin Mary is carried through city streets are still part of the Catholic Church's Semana Sancta, or Holy Week, in Spain, Portugal, and much of Latin America during the week before Easter—combining theHoly Week of Cybele in March and the carrying of the statue of Cybele to the Circus Maximus on April 10.

Even the image of La Pieta, often reproduced in art and most famously seen in Michelangelo's fifteenth-century statue in St. Peter's Basilica at Rome, where the Virgin Mary holds Jesus Christ, was based on the ancient Roman statue Pietas Romana, or Roma's Devotions, where the goddess Roma held a child representing the Roman people—an image that was, as it happens, shown on coins commemorating Constantine's stepmother Theodora.

Similarly, the statues of the Virgin Mary that we see today on Italian street corners and crossroads replaced the statues of Roman gods such as

Cybele, in her guise as protector of cities, that had previously occupied such locations. Meanwhile, as more and more saints gained their own cult followings, St. Christopher replaced Mercury as the patron of travelers, St. Eligius replaced Minerva as the patron of craftsmen, St. Raymond replaced Juno as the patron of childbirth, and so it went, god by god, saint by saint.

Under Christianity, weddings would retain their pagan symbolism via the wedding ring, bridal veil, wedding cake, bridal floral corsage, bridesmaids, and wedding feast, along with the custom of the father giving away the bride and the groom carrying the bride over the threshold. The pagan Roman children's *Lustratio* naming ceremony, during which the newborn was supposedly cleansed of harmful spirits acquired at birth, was neatly replaced by childhood Christian baptism and the concept of original sin. Similarly, the *Liberalia* coming-of-age ceremony was replaced by the Christian Church's confirmation ceremony.

The blessing of fleets, and the releasing of birds at funerals, both go back to the old gods, showing how Christianity adopted countless pagan symbols, superstitions, and customs to ease the change from polytheism to monotheism. Yet, in effect, the Catholic and Orthodox churches, with their worship of saints, became paganism by another name and with another supreme deity and many minor deities.

Between Mary and the numerous other female saints, the Catholic Church was able to replace the goddesses of Rome, although it was never able to replicate the fact that the old religion permitted female priests and included festivals dedicated solely to female worshippers. In comparison, Christianity, like Judaism and Islam, has long been a male-dominated, misogynistic faith, one that led to a loss of female rights compared to pagan Roman times. Which, considering the fact that the spread of Christianity during Constantine's era was driven by noblewomen, many of them Constantine's relatives, is somewhat ironic.

Christianity has lasted longer than the Roman Empire. Yet, in the opinion of Edward Gibbon, Constantine, in leading Rome down the path to Christianity, weakened, and led to the fall of, the Western Empire. Rome would be sacked by the Visigoths in 410, seventy-three years after Constantine's death, and the last emperor of the West, sixteen-year-old Romulus Augustus, abdicated in 476. Still Christianity lived on in Europe. And in the East, the Constantinople-based Byzantine Empire—a title coined by the sixteenth-century German historian Hieronymus Wolf, even though it could more accurately be called the Constantinian Empire—would persist under Christianity for another thousand years, with Byzantines speaking Latin and calling themselves Romans, before falling to Muslim conquerors. And so began the next age of the mass conversion of populaces from one faith to another.

The Eastern Orthodox Church made Constantine a saint. The Catholic Church of the West did not, perhaps recognizing that Constantine was an unconscious conduit of religious history, not a deliberate soldier for Christ. The philosopher Seneca once chided the emperor Nero for trying to forestall the inevitable by killing all who might be his successor. In the same way, the spread of Christianity, whose inclusive community worship, sense of belonging, and promise of an afterlife proved much more attractive than the solitary form of worship and odious sacrifice of animals involved in appeasing the old gods, was inevitable and unstoppable.

The decree of Theodosius that made Christianity the state religion would have come whether there had been a Constantine or not. Even if Constantine had lost the Battle of the Milvian Bridge, the rise of Christianity would merely have been delayed, not forestalled. For, although they were not given credit for it by Eusebius or Lactantius, Maxentius and Licinius were already pragmatically steering their subjects toward the Christian path. However, Constantine did win the battle, and he should be given the credit, or the blame, for what followed.

NOTES

I. The Eve of Battle

1. The panegyric of 313, in Rodgers and Nixon's *In Praise of Later Roman Emperors,* states that Constantine marched on Italy with fewer than 40,000 men. Gibbon, in *The Decline and Fall of the Roman Empire*, endorsed that figure.
2. Zosimus, *New History.*
3. Van Dam, "Constantine's First Visit to Rome with Diocletian in 303."
4. The reaching of the Tiber on October 26 is recorded in Eusebius's *The Life of Constantine.*
5. Vegetius, *The Military Institutions of the Romans,* wrote that by the fourth century, lazy Roman generals no longer built fortified marching camps. However, Constantine is likely to have fortified a camp that was within easy striking distance of large opposing forces at Rome.
6. Eusebius, *Life of Constantine.*
7. Ibid.; Lactantius, *On the Deaths of the Persecutors.*
8. Eusebius, *Life of Constantine.* Some theologians, such as Bryan Liffin in "Eusebius on Constantine," feel the Labarum was not created until some years later, but the fact the Labarum appeared on Constantine's coins within months of the Battle of the Milvian Bridge seems to confirm its creation in 312.
9. Eusebius, *Life of Constantine.*
10. Vegetius.
11. The *Notitia Dignitatum* illustrates the Roman army's shield designs of the late fourth century.
12. Eusebius, *Life of Constantine.*

II. The Rise of Father and Son

13. Josephus, *Jewish War*.
14. Carausius's units can be identified by coins he minted for them. Carausius's coins for the Praetorian Guard contingent depict Praetorian standard-bearers holding four standards, representing four cohorts.
15. Rodgers and Nixon, Panegyrics VI and VII.
16. Rodgers and Nixon, Pan. VII.
17. Petronius, *Satyricon*. For a detailed description of the *deposito barbae*, see Dando-Collins, *The Ides*, chapter XII.
18. Victor, *De Caesaribus*. Gregory of Tours, *History of the Franks*.
19. Constantius's 294 Batavian campaign was another, less likely, candidate for the time of Crocus's capture. I have discounted this because this would have meant that a sixteen-year-old Constantine married Minervina in March 295 (if she indeed bore him a child in 295), making the year of Constantine's own birth 279. This would accordingly mean that Constantine's military career did not begin until 299, which was much too late for his known movements prior to 299.
20. Rodgers and Nixon, Pan. XI.
21. Barnes, *Constantine: Dynasty, Religion and Power*.

III. Soldier in White

22. Rodgers and Nixon, Pan. VII.
23. Ray et al., "A Ration Warrant for an Adiutor Memoria."
24. Rodgers and Nixon, Pan. VI.
25. Ibid.
26. Eusebius, *Life of Constantine*.

IV. The Young War Hero

27. Rodgers and Nixon, Pan. VI.
28. Holder, *The Roman Army in Britain*.
29. *Notitia Dignitatum*.
30. Rodgers and Nixon, Pan. VII.
31. Eusebius's *Life of Constantine* put Constantine in an army here nine years after this, in A.D. 305, for this episode with the Sarmatian, but the timeline of events in Constantine's life in 305 make it almost impossible for this to have occurred that year. It belongs more properly in the 296 campaign with Diocletian.

V. THE GREAT PERSECUTION

32. Marucchi, "Archaeology of the Cross and Crucifix."
33. Galerius's words are from his 311 Edict of Toleration, reprinted in Lactantius.
34. Ibid.
35. Gibbon.
36. Lactantius.
37. Gibbon.
38. Lactantius, as above. Eusebius, *The Church History.*
39. Burckhardt, *The Age of Constantine the Great.*
40. Hopkins and Beard, *The Colosseum.*
41. Foxe, *Foxe's Book of Martyrs.*
42. Watts de Peyster, *The History of Carausius.*
43. Letter appended to Eusebius's *Life of Constantine.*
44. Rodgers and Nixon, Pan. VII.

VI. THE ROAD TO POWER BEGINS IN BRITAIN

45. Rodgers and Nixon, Pan. VII.
46. Dando-Collins, *Legions of Rome,* discusses the fate of the 9th Hispana.
47. John Reid, quoted in Pringle, "Ancient Slingshot was as Deadly as a .44 Magnum."
48. Rodgers and Nixon, Pan. VI.
49. Ibid.
50. Johnson, "Where Were Constantius I and Helena Buried?"

VII. ENTER MAXENTIUS

51. Artists included Giullo Romano and Lazzaro Baldi.
52. Julian.
53. Victor.
54. Zosimus.
55. Speidel, *Riding for Caesar.*
56. Gibbon.
57. Zosimus.
58. No source specifically links the four hundred thousand sesterces contributed by each of the thirteen senators to this donative. Some authors speculate that Maxentius used this money for his building program at Rome, but a military donative was by far the most likely use for these funds.
59. Johnson.
60. Eusebius, *Life of Constantine.*
61. Rodgers and Nixon, Pan. VI.

VIII. United We Stand

62. Julianus is quoted in Carcopino, *Daily Life in Ancient Rome*.
63. Julian.
64. Carcopino.
65. Rodgers and Nixon, Pan. VII.
66. Ibid., for entire speech.

IX. Maximian Betrays All

67. Rodgers and Nixon, Pan. VI.
68. Ibid.
69. A 310 coin issued by Alexander at Carthage carried the inscription IMP ALEXANDER P F AUG—Imperator Alexander, pious and faithful Augustus.
70. Inscription CIL XIV 2826.
71. Rodgers and Nixon, Pan. VII.
72. Lactantius.
73. Rodgers and Nixon, Pan. XII.
74. Ibid.
75. *Codex Justinianus*, 9, 17, I.
76. Rodgers and Nixon, Pan. VII. This author's italics.
77. Eusebius, *Life of Constantine*.
78. Rogers and Nixon, Pan. VII.
79. Ibid.
80. Ibid.
81. Grant, *The Emperor Constantine*; Barnes, *Constantine: Dynasty, Religion and Power*.
82. Eutropius, *Breviariun Historiae Romanae*; Zonaras, *Epitome Historiarum*.
83. Strauss, *Ten Caesars*.
84. Lactantius.

X. Preparing for Civil War

85. Barnes, *Constantine: Dynasty, Religion and Power*.
86. Starr, *Imperial Roman Navy*.

XI. Constantine Invades Italy

87. Lactantius.
88. Ammianus Marcellinus, *History*.
89. Mannex, *History, Topography, and Directory of Westmorland and Lonsdale*.

90. Barnes, *Constantine: Dynasty, Religion and Power.*
91. Eusebius, *Life of Constantine.*
92. In the view of some historians, including Barnes, Lactantius lived out the rest of his days in Nicomedia. Others think he returned to Trier, and Crispus's service, in 317, remaining there for the remainder of his life.
93. Eusebius, *Life of Constantine;* Zosimus.
94. Vegetius.
95. Speidel, *Ancient German Warriors.*
96. Dando-Collins, *Conquering Jerusalem.*
97. Gray, *The Walls of Verona.*

XII. Maxentius Prepares for Battle

98. Lactantius mentions this race day, although he misdated his account of the Battle of the Milvian Bridge and events leading up to it. Chariot racing was not a frequent event on the Roman calendar, only occurring on several set days through the year as the culmination of major religious festivals. The last race day on the calendar prior to October 28, day of the Battle of the Milvian Bridge, was October 12, when this event must have taken place in 312.
99. Eusebius, *Life of Constantine.*
100. Ibid.
101. Barnes, "Lactantius and Constantine." 102. Burckhardt.
103. Lactantius.
104. Ibid.
105. Herodotus, *The History.* Dando-Collins, *Cyrus the Great.*
106. The Domus Faustae and its refurbishment are detailed in McFadden, "A Constantinian Image Program in Rome Rediscovered." 107. Caligula's bridge is detailed in Dando-Collins, *Caligula: Mad Emperor of Rome.*
108. Vegetius.
109. Rodgers and Nixon, Pan. XII.
110. These standards were depicted on coins.

XIII. A Day to Sink or Swim

111. Josephus, *Jewish War.*
112. Eusebius, *Life of Constantine.*

XIV. Constantine the Victor

113. Rodgers and Nixon, Pan. XII.
114. Eusebius, *Life of Constantine.*

115. Rodgers and Nixon, Pan. XII.
116. Speidel, *Riding for Caesar*; Curran, *Pagan City and Christian Capital.*
117. Eusebius, *Church History.*
118. Carcopino.
119. Rodgers and Nixon, Pan. XII.

XV. And Then There Were Two

120. Eusebius, *Life of Constantine.*
121. Ibid.
122. Eusebius, *Church History.*

XVI. Consolidating Power

123. Rodgers and Nixon, Pan. XII.
124. Valesianus, *Excerpta Valesiana.*
125. Victor.
126. Letters appended to Eusebius's *Life of Constantine.*
127. Barnes, *Constantine and Eusebius.* Hanson, *The Search for the Christian. Doctrine of God.*
128. Gibbon.

XVII. Dealing with Licinius

129. Eusebius, *Life of Constantine.*
130. Ibid.
131. Ibid. Roman troops launching an attack only drew swords after first using their darts and spears, indicating that Eusebius's description of Constantine's actions here owes more to hyperbole than fact.
132. Valesianus.
133. Ibid.
134. Some historians place Bassus's Praetorian prefect appointment in 319, but Barnes, in *Constantine: Dynasty, Religion and Power*, felt it was 317 or 318. It made sense for Bassus to take the post in 317 at the time of Crispus's elevation to Caesar and commander in Gaul, to be at his side from the outset.

XVIII. The Final Showdown

135. Constantine was depicted wearing this cuirass on a coin of 322–323.
136. Constantine to the Catholic Church of Nicomedia, November–December 325. Attachment to Eusebius of Caesarea's *Life of Constantine.*

XIX. Taking Control of the Eastern Church

137. Tacitus, *Histories.*
138. Eusebius, *Life of Constantine.*
139. Aristotle, "The Heavens."

XX. Killing His Wife and Son

140. Woods, "On the Death of the Empress Fausta."141. Ibid.
142. Zosimus; Victor.
143. According to Church historians today, the House of Fausta was dedicated by Bishop Sylvester in 324, when he consecrated the new Christian basilica next door, but the dramatic events of 326 make the 324 dating two years too early.

XXI. Christianizing Constantine

144. Eusebius, *Life of Constantine.*
145. Some historians claim Hadrian's Jerusalem temple was dedicated to Aphrodite, Greek predecessor of the Romans' Venus. The fact that Hadrian also built a massive temple dedicated to Venus on the north side of the Sacred Way at Rome seems clear evidence that his Jerusalem temple would also have been dedicated to Venus, not Aphrodite.
146. Ammianus Marcellinus; Gibbon.147. Eusebius, *Life of Constantine.*
148. Ibid.

XXII. Constantine Was the Bridge

149. Lactantius; Eusebius, *Life of Constantine*; Julian; Victor; Fowden, "The Last Days of Constantine."150. Zosimus.

BIBLIOGRAPHY

BOOKS

Ammianus Marcellinus, *The Surviving Books of the History of Marcellinus* (J. C. Rolfe, transl.). Cambridge, Mass., Harvard University Press, 1939.

Anonymous, *Excerpta Valesiana* (J. C. Rolfe, transl.). Cambridge, MA, Harvard University Press, 1939.

Anonymous, *Notitia Dignitatum*. Cambridge, Cambridge University Press, 2019.

Aristotle, *The Works of Aristotle*. Chicago, Encyclopedia Britannica, 1989.

Aurelius Victor, *Epitome De Caesaribus*. Scotts Valley, Cal., Createspace, 2014.

Barnes, T. D., *Constantine and Eusebius*. Cambridge, Mass., Harvard University Press, 2006.

Barnes, T. D., *Constantine: Dynasty, Religion and Power in the Late Roman Empire*. Hoboken, NJ, John Wiley & Sons, 2013.

Baynes, N. A., *Constantine the Great and the Christian Church*. Oxford, Oxford University Press, 1972.

Birley, A. R., "The Commissioning of Equestrian Officers," in *Documenting the Roman Army,* (J. J. Wilkes, ed.). London, University of London Press, 2003.

Boorstin, D., *The Discoverers: A History of Man's Search to Know His World and Himself.* London, Penguin, 1986.

Burckhardt, J., *The Age of Constantine the Great* (M. Hadas, transl.). Berkeley, University of California Press, 1949.

Carcopino, J., *Daily Life in Ancient Rome* (E. O. Lorimer, transl.). Harmondsworth, Penguin, 1975.

Cave, W., *Primitive Christianity, Or, the Religion of the Ancient Christians in the First Ages of the Gospel.* London, John Hatchard & Son, 1834.

Curran, J., *Pagan City and Christian Capital.* Oxford, Clarendon Press, 2000.

Dando-Collins, S., *Caligula: The Mad Emperor of Rome.* Nashville, Turner, 2019.

Dando-Collins, S., *Conquering Jerusalem: The A.D. 66–73 Roman Campaign to Crush the Jewish Revolt.* Nashville, Turner, 2021.

Dando-Collins, S., *Cyrus the Great; Conqueror, Liberator, Anointed One.* Nashville, Turner, 2020.

Dando-Collins, S., *Legions of Rome: The Definitive History of Every Imperial Roman Legion.* London, Quercus, 2010.

Dando-Collins, S., *The Great Fire of Rome: The Fall of the Emperor Nero and His City.* Cambridge, MA, Da Capo Press, 2010.

Dando-Collins, S., *The Ides: Caesar's Murder and the War for Rome.* Hoboken, NJ, John Wiley & Sons, 2010.

Eusebius, *Church History.* Grand Rapids, MI, Kregel, 2007.

Eusebius, *The Life of Constantine, Together with the Oration of Constantine to the Assembly of the Saints, and the Oration of Eusebius in Praise of Constantine* (E. C. Richardson, transl.). Hartford, Hartford Theological Seminary, 1890.

Eutropius, *The First and Second Books of Eutropius.* Whitefish, MT, Kessinger, 2019.

Fontenrose, J., *Didyma: Apollo's Oracle, Cult and Companions.* Berkeley, University of California Press, 1988.

Foxe, J., *Foxe's Book of Martyrs (The Actes and Monuments of the Martyrs).* Kensington, PA, Whitaker House, 1981.

Frend, W. H. C., *The Rise of Christianity*. Philadelphia, Fortress, 1984.

Geoffrey of Monmouth, *The History of the Kings of Britain*. London, Penguin, 1977.

Gibbon, E., *The Decline and Fall of the Roman Empire*. Chicago, Encyclopedia Britannica, 1989.

Grant, M., *Gladiators*. Harmondsworth, Penguin, 1971.

Grant, M., *Roman History from Coins*. New York, Barnes and Noble, 1995.

Grant, M., *The Emperor Constantine*. London, Weidenfield & Nicolson, 1993.

Gray, J. A., *The Walls of Verona*. Venice, International Fund for Monuments, 1954.

Gregory of Tours, *History of the Franks*. London, Penguin, 1974.

Hanson, R. P. C., *The Search for the Christian Doctrine of God: The Arian Controversy, 318–381*. London, Bloomsbury, 1988.

Harari, Y. V., *Sapiens: A Brief History of Mankind*. London, Harvill Secker, 2014.

Healy, P., "Lucius Caecilius Firmianus Lactantius," in *Catholic Encyclopedia*. New York, Robert Appleton, 1910.

Henry of Huntingdon, *The History of the English*. London, Longman, 1879.

Herodotus, *The History*. Chicago, Encyclopedia Britannica, 1989.

Holder, P. A., *The Roman Army in Britain*. London, Batsford, 1982.

Hopkins, K., and M. Beard, *The Colosseum*. Cambridge, MA, Harvard University Press, 2011.

Josephus, *The New Complete Works of Josephus* (W. Whiston, transl.). Grand Rapids, MI, Kregel, 1999.

Julian, *The Works of the Emperor Julian* (W. C. Wright, transl.). London, Heinemann, 1959.

Lactantius, *On the Deaths of the Persecutors* (W. Fletcher, transl.). Armidale, NSW, Northern Antiqities Press, 1998.

Mannex, P. J., *History, Topography and Directory of Westmorland and Londsdale North of the Sands in Lancashire*. London, Simkin Marshall, 1849.

Marucchi, O., "Archaelogy of the Cross and Crucifixion," in *Catholic Encyclopedia*. New York, Robert Appleton, 1908.

Petronius Arbiter, *The Satyricon* (W. C. Firebaugh, transl.). New York, Boni and Liveright, 1922.

Rodgers, B. S., and C. E. V. Nixon, *In Praise of Later Roman Emperors: The Panegyric Latini*. Berkeley, University of California Press, 1995.

Speidel, M. P., *Ancient German Warriors: Warrior Styles from Trajan's Column to Icelandic Sagas*. London, Routledge, 2004.

Speidel, M. P., *Riding for Caesar: The Roman Emperors' Horse Guards*. Cambridge, MA, Harvard University Press, 1994.

Starr, C. G., *The Roman Imperial Navy, 31 B.C.–A.D. 324*. Cambridge, Heffer & Sons, 1960.

Stephenson, P., *Constantine: Roman Emperor, Christian Victor*. New York, Overlook Press, 2010.

Strauss, B., *Ten Caesars: Roman Emperors from Augustus to Constantine*. New York, Simon & Schuster, 2019.

Suetonius, *Twelve Caesars* (R. Graves, transl.). London, Penguin, 1972.

Syme, R., *Ammianus and the Historia Augusta*. Oxford, Oxford University Press, 1968.

Tacitus, *The Annals* and *The Histories*. Chicago, Encyclopedia Britannica, 1954.

Vegetius, *The Military Institutions of the Romans* (J. Clark, transl.). Harrisburg, PA, Military Service Publishing, 1944.

Watts de Peyster, J., *The History of Carausius*. Whitefish, MT, Kessinger, 2009.

Weigall, A., *The Paganism in Our Christianity*. London, Hutchinson, 1928.

Zonaras, J., *Epitome Historiarum*. Delhi, Pranava, 2020.

Zosimus, *New History* (R. T. Ridley, transl.). Sydney, Australian Association of Byzantine Studies, 1982.

JOURNAL ARTICLES

T. D. Barnes, "Lactantius and Constantine," *The Journal of Roman Studies,* Vol. 63, 1973, Cambridge University Press, Cambridge.

R. Flower, "Visions of Constantine," *The Journal of Roman Studies,* Vol. 102, 2012, Cambridge University Press, Cambridge.

G. Fowden, "The Last Days of Constantine: Oppositional Versions and their Influence," *The Journal of Roman Studies,* Vol. 84, 1994, Cambridge University Press, Cambridge.

J. Johnson, "Where Were Constantine I and Helena Buried?" *Academia,* 1992, Brigham Young University Press, Provo, UT.

B. M. Liffin, "Eusebius on Constantine: Truth and Hagiography at the Milvian Bridge," *Journal of the Evangelical Theological Society,* 55/4, 2012, US.

E. Marlowe, "Framing the Sun: The Arch of Constantine and the Roman Cityscape," *Art Bulletin,* Vol. LXXXVIII, No. 2, June 2000, College Art Association, US.

S. McFadden, "A Constantinian Image Program in Rome Rediscovered: The Late Antique Megalographia from the So-Called Domus Faustae," *Memoirs of the American Academy in Rome,* Vol. 58, 2013, University of Michigan Press, Ann Arbor, MI.

L. Naphtali, and M. Reinhold, "Roman Empire: Selected Readings," *The Empire,* 1990, Columbia Univesity Press, New York.

H. Pringle, "Ancient Slingshot Was as Deadly as a .44 Magnum," *National Geographic,* May 24, 2017, Washington, DC.

J. Ray et al., "A Ration Warrant for an Adiutor Memoria," *Yale Classical Studies,* Vol. 28, 1985, Cambridge University Press, Cambridge.

R. Van Dam, "Constantine's First Visit to Rome with Diocletian in 303," *Journal of Late Antiquity,* Vol. 11, No. 1, Spring 2018, Johns Hopkins University Press, Baltimore.

D. Woods, "On the Death of the Empress Fausta," *Greece and Rome,* Vol. 45, No. 1, April 1998, Cambridge University Press, Cambridge.

INDEX

CPSIA information can be obtained
at www.ICGtesting.com
Printed in the USA
JSHW030922091021
19445JS00001B/1